THE PRINCIPLE of the TOTAL PICTURE

the first axiom in economic analysis

THE PRINCIPLE
of the
TOTAL PICTURE

The first axiom in economic analysis

---

by MARCEL SUCHESTOW

THE WILLIAM-FREDERICK PRESS

NEW YORK   1969

Manufactured in the United States of America
© Copyright   1969 by Marcel Suchestow

Library of Congress Catalog Card Number : 70-104076
Standard Book Number : 87164-104

William-Frederick Press
55 East 86th Street
New York, N.Y. 10028

Contents

Tables

THE PRINCIPLE of the TOTAL PICTURE

the first axiom in economic analysis

PREFACE

The monetary economy is the fundamental area of economics and therefore the money turnover is the most important element in economic development. The understanding of the mechanism of this turnover is essential for evaluation of almost all economic processes. However, the main problems of the monetary economy remain unsolved.

In this study we have examined all important phenomena in the monetary circuit on the basis of the Flow of Funds Accounts, as well as credit ranges of the Federal Reserve and all commercial banks. In these investigations we have applied strict accounting methods and could therefore arrive at exact and reliable results. We were in the position to disprove the existing doctrines and establish new theories concerning formation of demand deposits, credit creation, reserve positions, open-market operations. We have set up "the principle of the total picture," showing that in any investigation the overall situation ought to be taken into account. One must not pick out questions and examine them in isolation. If one loses sight of the total picture, one will usually arrive at a wrong conclusion.

In particular, accounting can prove the equality or inequality of some factors and their functional relationship, as in a mathematical or logical proof. We were thus able to set forth statements about inherent properties of the turnover of money and value. L. Robbins [170] explains that "economic laws have their limits," and "a human new volition interrupts the chain of causation." But in our presentation no limits are set on its validity because no human decision can change the interrelation.

We claim to furnish two parallel proofs of the actual development in the monetary system, operating with two different series of data (the statistics for 1967 and 1968 are available on request), and also to achieve results which can be interpreted only in one sense, to establish principles derived from known facts and proofs, to build up a knowledge proposed to be objective and neutral. We are absolutely certain of the validity of our findings, "in our subjective experience of conviction, in our subjective faith." (We are quoting Karl R. Popper [162], and also in the following we are influenced by Professor Popper's teachings [161, 163, 164].)

On the other hand, we qualify our assertions, saying that science can be only reasonably objective or objective up to some point, since our reasoning often implies value judgments, sometimes in ways we do not fully understand. The human mind is defective, especially when its functioning is not systematized. We have to check and to reexamine our results on any possible occasion.

1

A theory, for instance, could be anticipated and justified a posteriori by selective compilation of observation data. Also many apparently impressive verifications of a theory confirm only that a case could be interpreted in the light of this theory. This applies likewise to econometric models.

Professor Popper points out that the objectivity of scientific statements lies in the fact that they can be inter-subjectively tested. Any scientific system must be capable of being tested by experience. The criterion is therefore not the verifiability of the system but its testability and falsifiability. The method of testing involves deductive casual explanation after the theory has been formulated. If the theory is not refuted by experience, then it has passed its empirical test for the present, and it remains as acceptable in our selection of verified theories. In this manner, there are no ultimate statements in science and every such statement is tentative.

Inter-subjective testing implies thus mutual criticism and searching discussion. The attempt of an individual scholar to be objective is not sufficient - objectivity requires the cooperation of many scientists and connotes the social character of scientific methods. Scientific progress is promoted only by free competition of thought and ever more strict tests.

According to these views, it is necessary first to submit this study explicitly for professional discussion by academic, governmental, and corporate economists, rather than present to the general audience a comprehensive work intended to replace all traditional teachings in this domain. This study proposes to change our image of the whole economic development and therefore it should be preferable first to find some consensus on what is right and what is wrong in these fundamental questions. For this purpose, we have tried to present our argumentation as concisely as possible, and the second proof contains major abridgments.

Finally, we mention that we have prepared a further study of other areas in economics, since our present results are bound to involve important revisions in all other realms of economic knowledge. But in view of the above considerations, we regard the further investigations only as tentative for the time being.

M.S.

CHAPTER 1

The Flow of Funds Accounts

Section 1

We contend that it is now possible to undertake a comprehensive and thorough study of the banking and monetary circuit in
the United States thanks to the newly developed Flow of Funds Accounts on a quarterly basis.

In our opinion, the first domain which must be now explored
in economics is that of the monetary turnover. Divergencies in
this field must finally be clarified. (1) Without a thorough per-
ception of the monetary circuit no further progress in the capital
theory, in the theories of economic growth, as well as in all other areas of economics, is possible.

The proposed study aims first at a computation of increment in credit availability within a given period, especially in
each quarter since 1952, and at a computation of credit absorption
within these periods. On this basis, what shall be examined is
the impact of easy and tight money policy on the availability of
credit, and how changes in this policy have influenced the economic process in its cyclical variations in the past. (2) In view
of this:

(a) The increases (or decreases) in the availability of
credit have to be scrutinized in the light of the allegations that
in specified periods the monetary policy has resulted in substantial changes in volume of money and credit;

(b) A similar examination has to be conducted regarding
the changes in the reserve requirements of demand deposits which
have occurred several times since 1948. On such occasions, the
availability of credit is subject, as it is asserted, to large
fluctuations;

----

1. *M. Friedman and D. Meiselman [66] indicate that there
is "a striking division among students of economic affairs about
the role of money in determining the course of economic events.
One view is that the quantity of money matters little; the other
that it is the key factor in understanding, and even controlling
economic change. We badly need work on these problems that will
clarify the issues involved."*

2. *M. A. Copeland [40] recommends such a study "in connection with Federal Reserve and other policy questions" and observes that "this type of use is only just on the verge of beginning."*

*J. Kareken [116] notes: "Effective policy formation re-
quires an understanding of the path by which our economy adjusts
to a change in monetary variables."*

3

(c)   On the basis of investigations pointed out under (a) and (b), the efficiency of the policy of the Federal Reserve System can be evaluated. In this connection, periods of booms and recessions, as indicated by the GNP, have to be taken into account;

(d)   The described investigations will clarify the question as to whether credit creation is possible, to what degree it is possible, and whether it takes place in the periods commonly assumed;

(e)   What has to be scrutinized is how the absorption of credit in a given period develops in relation to the increase or decrease in availability of credit. In the difference which may result, the solution of the problem can be found as to whether the availability of credit is fully used or whether there exist idle balances and hoards, and to what extent, (3) and under which circumstances they "come out of hiding"; also, whether there exists active and inactive money.

Section 2

Our approach, however, in this study will be different in some respects from that applied in the few essays published so far on the basis of Flow of Funds Accounts. In these essays patterns of money flows through the capital market were investigated and compared in different periods. It was examined how these patterns fluctuate during cyclical variations, and in many cases it was found that their response was not significant. The conclusions were kept in general terms, and the studies indicated mainly how Flow of Funds figures can be used in interpreting recent cycles. Nevertheless, it is true that M. A. Copeland [40] has arrived at interesting results. (4) In his conclusions, however, he had to

---

3. *M. A. Copeland [40] writes: "We propose to inquire whether in any significant sense, there can be such a thing as hoarding, or rather such a thing as loanfund equivalent of hoarding, for the economy as a whole."*

4. *M. A. Copeland [40] points out: "The analysis...illustrates the proposition that the banking sector is a financial intermediary, not itself an important source of funds that finance aggregate demand. Businesses increased their cash balances and their other financial assets during both upswings and decreased them during the downswings. The Flow of Funds Accounts help to dispel various misconceptions in regard to the role of money and of other forms of credit in the income and money circuit. Among these misconceptions are such ideas as that...the banking sector is more than a mere financial intermediary, that by itself it can 'create' a substantial amount of 'money' that can be used to finance a substantial increase in aggregate demand.... There is a*

use such qualifications as "substantial," "presumably," "influencing," his study not being based on concrete figures; he uses only
"flows" and comparisons of "flows," i.e., conceptions which are
not tangible. (5)

     The only way to achieve exact and reliable results is to
apply accounting methods. Only in this case could one be certain
that every movement in question will be considered; nothing could
escape and the total picture would be preserved. Only in this way
could one avoid the fallacy - often encountered in economics - of
isolating one process in the development and thereby leaving out
the proper relationship.

     Fortunately, it is possible to use accounting methods

---

*view still entertained by quite a number of economists that an in-
crement in the currency and deposits liabilities of the banking
and monetary system creates a net addition to the total sources of
funds available to finance purchases of GNP and so, a net addition
to the aggregate demand. It seems unwise to assume such a possibility of manipulation or control of the quantity of currency outside banks plus demand deposits adjusted. We should, presumably,
speak of influencing rather than controlling this quantity, rec-
ognizing that it is through manipulation of quantities like Federal Reserve credit and member bank reserve requirements that influence on the quantity of currency outside banks plus demand deposits adjusted is exerted."*

     *5. J. C. Dawson [45] remarks: "Presumably, a standard
measure of ultimate borrowing would be some concept of funds raised
by nonfinancial sectors. Ultimate lending would be a measure of
funds advanced by nonfinancial sectors. Financial-institution sectors would lie between the two, absorbing a large share of the issues involved in ultimate borrowing, and simultaneously creating
debts to be absorbed by ultimate lending. The ultimate borrowing
and lending measures could be designed as to provide totals that
are significant in judging financial performance. They would bear
on how well the financial system meets the needs of borrowers and
savers. To preserve the one-directional flow...we are forced to
split up the various nonfinancial sectors. But there does not
seem to be any a priori ground for avoiding this procedure if it
sheds light on how the financial system operates."*

     *E. T. Wieler [215] writes: "I have examined the two six-
quarter periods - from December 31, 1951 to June 30, 1953 and from
June 30, 1956 to December 31, 1957 - to see if I could detect significant changes in the pattern of money flows through the capital
market during periods of severe monetary restraint." He concludes
that he did not "find significant changes."*

in connection with the Flow of Funds accounts. (6) For this purpose, we have to suppose that all individuals and all enterprises
in the economy keep records of their transactions and the data of
each sector in the Flow of Funds accounts are the totals of the
relative records. (7) The more often we take the computations,
the clearer the situation will become. For our calculations, the
quarterly Flow of Funds accounts are, however, quite sufficient.
Thus, they show for the relevant sectors: capital consumption,
net and gross domestic saving, as well as net and gross domestic
investment, and net financial investment. In this manner, we arrive at a regular, though abridged, statement of condition for
each sector at the end of a given period.

It is thus necessary to put oneself into the frame of mind
of an accountant and to apply in all those computations the principles of the theory of accounting. In this connection, it seems
that mastery of this subject is as important for an economist as
the knowledge of higher mathematics. Most erroneous conclusions
in the judgment of the money circuit can be traced back to an insufficient knowledge of the principles of accounting.

One must always bear in mind that on the money market, if
one pays in currency, or credits an account, something will be obtained in return - formerly it was gold, today it is mostly securities - and something has to be done with it. If, on the other
hand, securities are sold, other assets must form or liabilities
must decrease. All these processes, in one or the other direction,
must occur simultaneously, and each time they have opposite effects
within the money circuit.

Along with these movements all accounts will automatically
show formation and decay of values and preserve the total picture
at any moment of our examination. Subsequently, the further discussion will be nothing more than a detailed explanation based on
logical rules of computing and accounting.

In economic terms, the above method constitutes a strict
application of pure comparative statics. As the flows themselves
are unseizable and indefinable, we compare only the results at the
end of two accounting periods. However, since we use the accoun-

---

6. M. A. Copeland [39] indicates: "The social accounting
approach to the measurement of moneyflows implies that moneyflows
can be arranged and presented as a set of financial statements and
that we can expect these statements to balance."

7. E. Lindahl [129] notes that G. Myrdal wrote in 1927 in
a Swedish essay entitled The Pricing Problem and Change: "From
the viewpoint of the general determination of prices all human be-
ings are entrepreneurs."

tancy of all individuals as an entirety of the whole economy, all
occurring changes are comprised, differently from that in economics, and we are in the position to furnish full proof of the actual development in the monetary and banking system, also differently from what is possible in economics. (8)

---

8. M. A. Copeland [38] notes: "It seems fair to say that
accountants have not contributed much to social accounting thus
far. But their help is urgently needed."

At a hearing before the Joint Economic Committee of the
85th Congress, R. W. Goldsmith [81] recommended that balance sheets
for both economic segments and the national economy as a unit be
prepared, and that the presently separate reports (national income
and product, input-output, and flow of funds), together with the
federal budget and a national balance sheet, be integrated into a
single national accounting system. This type of program could be
the beginning of an ambitious expansion of national income analysis directed toward the creation of a more effective informational
apparatus to assist in national policy formation.

S. Kuznets [126] observes: "If 'economic accounting' is
used properly to denote a method of approach, the basic concepts
of accounting should be applied. These involve...an accounting
entity...related...ordinarily via the mechanism of the market." In
a reply to Kuznets, M. Gilbert, G. Jaszi, E. F. Denison, and C. F.
Schwartz [78] indicate that a system of economic accounting is "a
tremendous aid in revealing the structure of the economy and thereby contributes toward a better understanding of its functioning; a
powerful tool for the solution of many intricate problems; a peda-
gogical device for explaining...the relationship of the various
aggregates and their components; a great aid in defining the task
of statistical collection."

A. C. Littleton [131] remarks: "The chief function of statistical method is to clarify, compress and simplify, masses of
data so that their significance may be better understood. Accounting...does exhibit...a scientific approach to handling data....
Characterizations from science fit accounting theory and practice."

A. C. Littleton and V. K. Zimmerman [132]: "Accounting
principles never change. They may be discovered, forgotten and re-
discovered, but they are still the same (M. E. Peloubet). Accounting principles are shaped by common opinion and ideas which influence business thought and action (P. J. Graber). The development
of accounting thought follows a pattern basically not different
from that of the physical sciences (D. P. Hylton). National income
accounting may properly be considered a new branch of accounting
(J. P. Powelson). Economists...began to visualize the nation's
economic statistics as adaptable to a completely integrated system
of national accounting."

Moreover, the Flow of Funds Accounts since 1945 make possible comparisons of situations and conditions at different periods since World War II. Parallels can be drawn between the period of "pegging" and subsequent development, as well as between periods of slumps and booms. Also, in the same manner, the development in the case of deficit-spending may be investigated. Only movements and changes permit us to compare and to enlarge our knowledge in economic matters.

R. Masterssich [145] points out that in national accounting and international balance of payment accounting "technically the same accounting principles are used...as in business accounting. We have to consider both accountancy and economics as parts of a more comprehensive body, of 'economic science.' Accountancy and statistics are the inductive tools of economic research.... National accounting attempts only a comparatively rough approximation to reality, concentrates on averages and aggregates, and uses concepts derived from macroeconomics.... The next step would be the consolidation of all the individual savings and investment statements into the 'national savings and investment statement' with certain adjustments and regroupings of data to facilitate economic analysis.... A consolidation of all individual statements into the national statement with certain adjustments (e.g., elimination of interbusiness transactions) would be necessary. From a technical standpoint, the principles of business and of national accounting are the same. They are based on the same sets of equations, and portray the same underlying transactions, with the same rules of debit and credit."

O. Morgenstern [151] writes concerning economic and accounting theory: "Here we can only indicate the nature of the great task that faces economic science to bring about a better interaction of the two disciplines."

J. T. Wheeler [216] indicates: "Economists come to realize that accounting, like statistics, is an indispensable tool for research in economics. Much work remains to be done in bringing about...understanding of the many areas of common interest. Jevons was the first author to suggest its value for economic research. Marshall made frequent references to accounting. He appeared to have a good knowledge of the field.... We are on the threshold of a new area which promises to bring accounting into the field of economics as an indispensable tool rather than as a useful but seldom used appendage."

In a similar sense, A. Forstman [62], a sharp critic of the new theory of credit, demands that "its advocates should study more closely the foundation of the theory of monetary equilibrium."

The authorities often claim, for instance, that if their
intervention had not taken place, the situation would have taken a
much worse turn. (9) Such claims, without figures or any other
evidence, seem to be irrefutable at first, since they operate on a
conditional basis. Yet it is precisely comparisons and confronta-
tions which prove the incorrectness of these statements.

Section 3
On the basis of other statistics published so far by the
Federal Reserve, no changes in the range of disposable money nor
changes in the availability or absorption of credit could be computed. It is true that various general statements were made in
many official and nonofficial dispatches and declarations, yet numerical computations which would have put the individual economic
magnitudes into a mutual and meaningful relationship were lacking.
(10) One could assume that - in the opinion of the authorities -
taking current policy into account, such figures should not be published but in due course it should be possible to find out more
about them.
In the following statement the Federal Reserve itself admitted that on the basis of its statistics one could not arrive at
numerical results:
"Changes in the availability of credit, while not subjected
to statistical documentation, may be observed in a general way
from the terms and conditions which lenders require in granting
credit, from their passivity or aggressiveness in seeking out new
outlets for loan funds, and by the response that borrowers experi-

---

9. A. Hayes [97] states, for example: "While we may not
have succeeded fully in checking inflation, we seem to be achieving at least partial success."
The Federal Reserve Bank of New York [55]: "What was impressive, however, was that at a time of intense strain on resources, when general price increase of 10 or 15 per cent might
not have been at all unlikely, the average rose by roughly 3 to
4 per cent."
10. To choose one example at random: It was stated that
the Federal Reserve System has increased somewhat the volume of
reserves made available to its member banks and by these releases
increased loans and increased spending were made possible; it did
not release reserves in sufficient volume, however (W. W. Riefler
[166]). At once the questions pose themselves as to what precise
effect these released reserves had, why they were insufficient,
and how all this was computed.

ence to their applications for credit." (11) For this reason, probably, it is claimed that "the interpretation of central bank action, and the evaluation of its influence, has become, like many
other things in this modern day, a zone reserved largely for the
specialists." (12) However, it appears that in such computations,
based on one-sided, vague information, even specialists must fail.

All this is understandable as long as everything hovers
hopelessly, and we have no point d'appui to start the computation.
Intuition may be highly erroneus, and, in addition, the theory of
credit creation is apparently very suggestive. But this situation
cannot last forever. It would, indeed, be strange if the movements in the banking and monetary circuit could never be checked,
understood, and accounted for. If the mathematicians were able to
build up calculus and compute π to 2035 decimal places, and if it
could be figured out how astronauts may reach the moon, the money
turnover would be - ironically - the only domain of actual and, in
our opinion, greatest importance in which the human mind would
fail.

Section 4
In our computation we are interested only in the domestic
monetary circuit, so that all concepts explained below are to be
understood as referring to the turnover in the United States. The
following concepts and definitions will be used:
Credit range = claims and liabilities of a given sector.
Credit range of the whole economy = claim range (all claims
added) versus liability range (all liabilities added).
The computation will comprise nine sectors: (A) House-
holds, (C) Noncorporate Nonfinancial Business, (D) Corporate
Nonfinancial Business, (E) U. S. Government, (F) State and Local
Governments, (G) Monetary Authorities, (H) Commercial Banks,
(I) Nonbank Financial Institutions, (J) Rest of the World, ac-
cording to the Flow of Funds Accounts.
Compared with the arrangement of the Flow of Funds Accounts,
our "credit range" is equal to financial assets versus financial

---

11. *United States Monetary Policy: Recent Thinking and
Experience, Hearings, 6 and 7, December 1954 [207].*
W. McC. Martin, Jr., and A. Hayes [144] explain that in
such questions statistics can prove nothing and that "the situation was more a matter of feeling than statistics." Hayes added
that "most of the banks feel far from loaned up."
R. V. Roosa [181] notes that "meanwhile the Federal Reserve has had to rely primarily on experimental probing, to guage
the balance between the current forces of credit demand and the
current availability of new credit supply."
12. R. V. Roosa [179].

liabilities, excluding:

Currency, corporate stocks, gold and foreign exchange, deposits and direct investment abroad, foreign bonds, loans to Rest of the World, other financial assets (mainly nonconvertible foreign currencies and official foreign exchange position of Treasury) of U. S. Government, and miscellaneous financial assets (direct investments, unidentified assets, and miscellaneous deposits), official U. S. foreign exchange (official foreign currency holdings and net IMF position of U. S. IMF position consists of U. S. capital subscription less IMF holdings of special U. S. Government notes and deposits with Federal Reserve), and miscellaneous (direct investment abroad, foreign currency held by other than official U. S. foreign exchange, subscriptions to international organizations except IMF, and unidentified liabilities) of Rest of the World.

Corporate stocks are treated in the Flow of Funds Accounts on the one hand with the subscriber, as acquisition of financial assets, i.e., a part of financial investment, and on the other hand with the corporation as an equity market instrument, together with other financial liabilities. From our point of view, this seems to be unjustifiable for the following reasons:

The subscriber will in most cases keep the acquired stocks for many years and consider them as his investment in the industry, of a nonstrictly financial character. The circumstance that he is able to dispose of the stocks more easily than, for example, a house cannot be the basis of classification. The relatively few instances where the stocks are bought for speculation may be disregarded.

On the other hand, and a fortiori, the issued stocks do not constitute a normal obligation for the corporation. There is no requirement to repay the amount received. The financial liabilities of the corporation - sensu stricto - do not increase thereby.

For the economy as a whole, the nominal total investment in stocks is stable and rises every year by a small percentage, so that, for this reason, too, we shall regard the current investment in stocks as a nonfinancial capital expenditure. (13)

A further difference concerns demand deposits of the U. S. Government. According to the Federal Reserve Bulletin, (14) total borrowing is total net funds raised by nonfinancial sectors, less changes in Federal cash balances. This is correct as to currency,

---

13. In a recent letter to this author, the Flow of Funds and Savings Section of the Federal Reserve System agreed that it is probably more reasonable to view current investment in corporate stocks as a nonfinancial expenditure, for the reasons stated above.

14. November 1962, p. 1407 [58].

but not as to demand deposits of the U. S. Government which constitute the main part of the Federal cash balances. For these demand
deposits are used by commercial banks for granting credits or for
other financial investments, and thus increase the availability
and absorption of credit, as will be explained later in more detail. In our study, we will, therefore, not subtract demand deposits of the U. S. Government from net funds raised or from funds
supplied to credit markets, in contradistinction to the procedure
applied in the Flow of Funds Accounts.

Section 5
The claim range (all claims added) of the whole economy
within a given period will be *the availability of credit* within
this period. The increment in credit availability within a given
quarter will thus be the increase in claim range within this quarter. The increment in credit absorption within a given quarter
will be the increase in liability range (all liabilities added)
within this quarter.
We have to distinguish, however, between "gross" and "net"
availability of credit and between "gross" and "net" absorption of
credit, and similarly between "gross" and "net" credit range.
The "gross" availability of credit, i.e., all claims of
the whole economy added, will contain some duplicated items, because some amounts, passing through the intermediaries, will re-
peat themselves.
The calculation of the "net" availability of credit will
eliminate these duplicated items. The same applies to the "gross"
and "net" absorption of credit.
Our study will be based on "net" availability and "net"
absorption of credit. The Federal Reserve itself recommends a
similar computation and describes exactly how to arrive at it. (15)
Besides, in Federal Reserve *Bulletins*, "Funds supplied directly to
credit markets," i.e., the increment in credit availability, are
figured out.

---

15. Federal Reserve Bulletin*, November 1962, p. 1405 [58],
notes to Chart 1, p. 1407, and Table 2.*
*The Federal Reserve writes on this (ibid., p. 1396, foot-
note 2): "Total borrowing in the chart consists of net funds
raised in credit markets by all nonfinancial sectors - private,
Federal Government, and foreigners. It excludes trade credit,
noncorporate equities, and miscellaneous financial flows. While
no single measure of credit flows can be isolated as an undupli-
cated aggregate of primary borrowing in the economy, the total
shown here appears to be a useful proxy."*

We thus have the approval of the Federal Reserve for such
a computation. (16)

Section 6
The computation will consist of the following series:
(a) Increment in domestic availability of credit, including intermediaries (Table 1).
(b) Increment in domestic availability of credit after
distribution of balances in financial sectors among nonfinancial
sectors (Table 2).
(c) Increment in domestic absorption of credit (Table 3).
(d) Balances between increment in domestic availability
of credit and increment in domestic absorption of credit for each
sector, i.e., increment in net domestic financial investment (Table 4).
(e) Increment in net domestic saving, capital consumption,
and gross domestic saving (Tables 5, 6, 7).
(f) Increment in net domestic investment for each sector
(Table 8).
(g) Gross domestic investment and statistical discrepancy
between gross domestic saving and gross domestic investment (Tables
9, 10).
The series will comprise annual figures for the years 1945
through 1966, and quarterly unadjusted figures from 1952 on.
We will have to rely on quarterly unadjusted figures for
the following reasons:
The adjusted nonfinancial Flow of Funds Accounts reflect
almost exclusively the adjustments used in the income and product
accounts of the Department of Commerce, which are computed on a
purely seasonal basis. (17) Demand deposits and currency outside
banks are likewise adjusted for customary seasonal variations on a
monthly basis, but are applicable to the last Wednesday of the
month. (18) Seasonal adjustments of major financial accounts,
however, are calculated by an additive version of the Bureau of
Labor Statistics adjustment procedure. (19) According to this
procedure, the original series are partitioned into three compo-
nent parts - trend or cyclical, seasonal, and irregular - so that

16. Cf., also M. A. Copeland, A Study of Moneyflows in
the United States, National Bureau of Economic Research, 1952, pp.
166-67 [39].
17. Cf., Business Statistics, 1963, p. 201 [206].
18. H. C. Burton, Federal Reserve Bulletin, June 1941, and
March 1955 [12].
19. Federal Reserve Bulletin, November 1962 [58].

in this case cyclical movements are also taken into consideration. (20)

The seasonally adjusted financial accounts may be compared, therefore, only with one another. These series could not be compared with seasonally adjusted nonfinancial accounts, seasonally adjusted demand deposits and currency outside banks, or any seasonally adjusted series of income and product accounts of the Department of Commerce. Such juxtapositions would give us a distorted picture.

Moreover, observed seasonal variations are uncertain and weak and the data have the probably not uncommon error of 5 to 10 per cent. It is, of course, preferable to avoid this error in our comparisons. (21)

---

20. A Rothman, "Seasonal Factor Method" [182].

21. The author wishes to thank Stephen P. Taylor, chief of the Flow-of-Funds and Savings Section of the Board of Governors of the Federal Reserve System, Washington, D. C., for help in obtaining the necessary data, and Joe Brest and Lois Banks, of the Federal Reserve Bank of New York, for preparing these data in New York.

Table 1   15

Increment in Domestic Availability of Credit, Including Intermediaries

(figures in parentheses indicate relative series number of computer)
(in billion dollars)

1946	1947	1948	1949	1950	1951	1952	1953	1954	1955

(A) Households: Credit and Equity Market Instruments (154002505), less Corporate Stocks (153064005)

| -1.0 | 1.9 | 0.9 | 1.5 | -0.9 | 0.1 | 0.9 | 2.3 | -0.6 | 5.3 |

(C) Noncorporate Nonfinancial Business: Consumer Credit (113066005)

| 0.3 | 0.3 | 0.4 | 0.3 | 0.5 | 0.3 | 0.4 | 0.2 | 0.1 | 0.2 |

(D) Corporate Nonfinancial Business: U. S. Govt. Securities (103061005), Open Market Paper (103069005), and Consumer Credit (103066005)

| -5.1 | -0.5 | 1.4 | 2.6 | 3.7 | 1.7 | 0.4 | 2.0 | -2.2 | 5.0 |

(E) U. S. Government: Credit Market Instruments (314002505), less Loans to Foreigners (263169203)

| -0.3 | 0.4 | 0.5 | 0.8 | 1.1 | 1.5 | 1.2 | 0.3 | -0.1 | 1.5 |

(F) State and Local Governments: U. S. Government Securities (203061005), State and Local Oblig. (203062003) and Other (203069905)

| -0.4 | 1.1 | 0.9 | 0.9 | 1.5 | 1.5 | 2.0 | 2.4 | 2.9 | 1.9 |

(G) Monetary Authorities: Credit Market Instruments (714002105), less Due to U. S. Government (713123001)

| -0.2 | -0.4 | 0.7 | -4.3 | 2.0 | 3.4 | 1.0 | 1.8 | -1.1 | 0.0 |

(H) Commercial Banks: Total Loans and Investments (724005505), less Corporate and Foreign Bonds (723163003) and Bank Loans N.E.C. to Rest of the World (263168001)

| -10.2 | 1.8 | -2.5 | 6.0 | 6.5 | 5.8 | 10.1 | 4.5 | 9.8 | 4.7 |

(I) Nonbank Financial Institutions: Credit Market Instruments (Assets) (694002005), Security Credit (Assets) (683067005), and Investment Co. Shares (653164005), less Credit Market Instruments (Liabilities) (694102005), Security Credit (Liabilities) (663167100), and Corporate Stocks (693064005)

| 7.0 | 6.7 | 7.0 | 7.2 | 8.3 | 8.2 | 12.0 | 13.3 | 13.5 | 14.7 |

(J) Rest of the World: U. S. Govt. Securities (263061005) and Other Market Instruments (263069905), less Corporate Stocks (263064003)

| -0.7 | -0.7 | 0.3 | 0.4 | 1.3 | 0.0 | 1.1 | 0.6 | 0.4 | 0.9 |

Minus: Corporate and Foreign Bonds to Rest of the World (263163003) and Loans of Rest of the World (264140005),plus Loans to Foreigners (263169203) and Bank Loans N.E.C. to Rest of the World (263168001)

| 0.0 | 0.0 | -0.1 | 0.0 | -0.4 | -0.4 | -0.2 | -0.2 | -0.1 | 0.2 |
| -10.6 | 10.6 | 9.5 | 15.4 | 23.6 | 22.1 | 28.9 | 27.2 | 22.6 | 34.4 |

Minus: Net Increase in Banking System Liabilities (733120005), less Demand Deposits, Net (723163003)

| 0.7 | 1.0 | 0.0 | 0.8 | 0.3 | -0.4 | -1.4 | 0.1 | -0.1 | -0.2 |
| -9.9 | 11.6 | 9.5 | 16.2 | 23.9 | 21.7 | 27.5 | 27.3 | 22.5 | 34.2 |

Totals in computer (723120005 and 909010000):

| -10.0 | 11.7 | 9.8 | 16.3 | 24.1 | 21.7 | 27.6 | 27.4 | 22.4 | 34.3 |

Table 1 (continued)

<u>Increment in Domestic Availability of Credit, Including Intermediaries</u>

(text according to preceding page)

	1956	1957	1958	1959	1960	1961	1962	1963	1964	1965	1966
(A)	4.2	4.0	0.0	6.6	1.4	0.2	-0.2	4.2	4.1	5.6	11.0
(C)	0.3	0.1	0.0	0.2	0.3	0.2	0.4	0.4	0.4	0.4	0.4
(D)	-4.0	0.1	0.5	7.9	-4.6	-0.1	1.9	1.8	1.0	-0.3	3.0
(E)	1.1	2.1	1.1	3.8	1.7	2.1	2.6	1.5	2.1	2.9	6.6
(F)	2.0	1.9	1.6	3.1	3.3	3.1	3.6	3.5	3.7	7.3	6.2
(G)	0.1	-0.7	2.3	0.4	0.7	1.5	1.9	2.6	3.2	3.8	3.3
(H)	4.6	5.0	14.7	4.6	8.9	15.0	19.1	18.4	19.8	27.4	17.5
(I)	15.6	14.9	16.9	18.0	18.0	19.0	21.7	25.8	27.1	23.6	20.8
(J)	1.0	0.5	0.0	3.0	1.0	0.4	1.2	0.6	0.7	0.2	-1.1
Minus	-0.5	-0.9	-1.0	-0.4	-1.3	-1.1	-0.8	-1.6	-1.2	-1.1	-0.6
	24.4	27.0	36.1	47.2	29.4	40.3	51.4	57.2	60.9	69.8	67.1
Minus	-0.1	0.0	-0.2	-0.6	0.2	-0.8	-0.8	-1.9	-2.6	-2.1	-2.3
	24.3	27.0	35.9	46.6	29.6	39.5	50.6	55.3	58.3	67.7	64.8

Totals in computer (723120005 and 909010000):

24.2	26.8	35.8	46.6	29.7	39.5	50.4	55.1	58.2	67.7	64.8

	1952				1953				1954			
	I	II	III	IV	I	II	III	IV	I	II	III	IV
(A)	0.8	-0.7	1.1	-0.4	0.9	2.1	-0.1	-0.6	0.2	0.1	-0.6	-0.4
(C)	-0.3	0.2	0.0	0.4	-0.3	0.2	0.0	0.3	-0.4	0.1	-0.1	0.4
(D)	-1.1	-0.7	0.6	1.4	-0.1	-1.7	2.0	1.8	-2.0	-3.5	1.6	1.9
(E)	0.1	0.3	0.3	0.5	-0.2	0.3	0.2	-0.1	-0.3	-0.2	0.2	0.3
(F)	0.6	0.4	0.6	0.3	0.4	0.7	0.9	0.4	0.9	0.9	0.5	0.5
(G)	-1.2	0.4	0.6	1.1	-0.8	1.0	0.0	1.5	-1.7	0.3	-0.5	0.8
(H)	-0.2	3.0	2.2	5.1	-3.2	-0.3	5.2	2.8	-3.2	3.7	3.4	5.9
(I)	3.6	2.5	3.1	3.0	3.7	3.3	3.0	3.4	3.5	3.1	3.3	3.7
(J)	0.2	0.3	0.6	0.1	0.1	0.2	0.4	0.0	0.2	-0.1	0.2	0.1
Minus	-0.1	-0.2	0.1	0.0	0.0	0.1	0.0	-0.1	-0.2	0.1	-0.1	0.0
	2.4	5.5	9.2	11.5	0.5	5.9	11.6	9.4	-3.0	4.5	7.9	13.2
Minus	0.6	-0.9	-0.3	-0.7	0.5	0.0	-0.8	0.4	0.7	-0.4	0.5	-1.0
	3.0	4.6	8.9	10.8	1.0	5.9	10.8	9.8	-2.3	4.1	8.4	12.2

Totals in computer:

2.8	4.8	9.3	10.7	1.1	6.2	10.5	9.6	-2.4	4.0	8.6	12.2

	1955				1956				1957			
	I	II	III	IV	I	II	III	IV	I	II	III	IV
(A)	2.0	1.0	2.0	0.4	3.2	0.6	0.7	-0.3	3.0	0.0	2.2	-1.2
(C)	-0.4	0.2	0.0	0.4	-0.4	0.2	0.0	0.4	-0.5	0.2	0.0	0.4
(D)	-0.3	-0.1	1.8	3.7	-2.8	-3.2	0.2	1.9	-0.9	-1.8	0.6	2.2
(E)	0.3	0.6	0.4	0.2	0.0	0.4	0.3	0.4	0.5	0.7	0.4	0.5
(F)	0.5	0.4	0.6	0.7	1.0	0.3	0.3	0.3	0.7	0.6	0.5	0.1
(G)	-1.6	0.4	0.1	1.1	-1.3	0.1	-0.1	1.4	-2.0	0.0	0.4	1.0
(H)	-3.4	2.6	1.3	4.3	-2.5	1.7	1.6	3.8	-1.2	0.9	3.0	2.4
(I)	4.1	3.3	4.3	3.1	4.2	3.6	4.7	3.1	4.3	3.6	3.9	3.2
(J)	0.2	0.2	0.4	0.2	0.5	0.0	0.4	0.2	0.0	-0.1	0.1	0.3
Minus	0.1	0.1	0.0	0.1	-0.1	-0.1	-0.1	-0.2	-0.3	-0.4	-0.1	-0.2
	1.5	8.7	10.9	14.2	1.8	3.6	8.0	11.0	3.6	3.7	11.0	8.7
Minus	1.2	-0.4	-0.4	-0.6	0.6	-0.6	0.3	-0.4	0.4	-0.5	0.9	-0.7
	2.7	8.3	10.5	13.6	2.4	3.0	8.3	10.6	4.0	3.2	11.9	8.0

Totals in computer:

2.5	8.0	10.3	13.4	2.3	2.8	8.2	11.0	4.0	3.1	11.7	8.1

Table 1 (continued)   17

Increment in Domestic Availability of Credit, Including Intermediaries

(text according to preceding pages)

	1958				1959				1960			
	I	II	III	IV	I	II	III	IV	I	II	III	IV
(A)	1.3	-2.0	0.2	0.6	2.6	1.2	1.9	0.8	4.1	-0.9	-0.1	-1.7
(C)	-0.6	0.2	0.0	0.4	-0.3	0.2	-0.1	0.4	-0.3	0.3	-0.1	0.4
(D)	-2.0	-2.4	0.9	4.0	1.0	1.4	2.6	2.9	-1.6	-1.2	-2.1	0.4
(E)	-0.1	0.3	0.3	0.7	0.7	1.5	1.0	0.7	-0.1	1.1	0.4	0.4
(F)	0.6	0.0	0.5	0.6	0.6	0.4	1.1	0.8	1.2	0.8	0.4	0.9
(G)	-0.6	1.9	-0.5	1.4	-0.9	0.7	0.3	0.3	-1.5	1.3	0.5	0.4
(H)	-0.5	8.3	0.3	6.5	-4.2	3.3	2.0	3.4	-6.7	3.8	4.5	7.2
(I)	4.3	3.5	4.9	4.2	5.2	4.4	5.0	3.5	5.5	3.7	4.8	3.7
(J)	-0.5	-0.6	0.7	0.3	0.3	0.9	1.2	0.7	0.6	-0.2	0.3	0.3
Minus	-0.3	-0.4	-0.1	-0.2	-0.2	0.0	-0.2	0.1	-0.4	-0.3	-0.4	-0.2
	1.6	8.8	7.2	18.5	4.8	14.0	14.8	13.6	0.8	8.4	8.2	11.8
Minus	1.0	-0.3	0.3	-1.2	0.7	-0.5	0.1	-0.8	0.9	-0.3	-0.4	-0.2
	2.6	8.5	7.5	17.3	5.5	13.5	14.9	12.8	1.7	8.1	7.8	11.6

Totals in computer:

2.7	8.3	7.5	17.3	5.5	13.5	14.9	12.7	2.0	8.1	7.9	11.6

	1961				1962				1963			
	I	II	III	IV	I	II	III	IV	I	II	III	IV
(A)	-0.3	-1.0	0.9	0.6	1.4	-1.1	0.3	-0.8	0.8	-0.2	1.7	1.8
(C)	-0.4	0.2	-0.1	0.5	-0.3	0.3	-0.1	0.5	-0.4	0.2	0.0	0.6
(D)	-1.6	0.4	-1.1	2.2	0.0	-0.1	-0.4	2.3	-0.2	0.7	-0.8	2.3
(E)	-0.1	0.8	0.6	0.8	0.3	1.1	0.6	0.7	-0.8	0.4	1.0	1.0
(F)	1.2	0.8	0.7	0.5	1.3	0.9	0.6	0.6	1.1	1.6	0.4	1.3
(G)	-0.7	0.5	0.5	1.0	0.3	0.4	0.3	0.9	-0.2	1.1	0.4	1.3
(H)	-4.0	5.7	6.6	6.7	-3.3	8.0	3.9	10.5	-2.6	8.3	3.1	9.6
(I)	5.3	4.1	5.1	4.6	6.2	4.2	6.0	5.5	7.6	5.3	7.3	5.5
(J)	0.0	-0.4	0.7	0.1	0.0	0.3	0.5	0.3	0.1	0.6	0.1	-0.2
Minus	-0.5	-0.3	-0.2	-0.2	-0.2	-0.2	0.0	-0.7	-0.5	-0.6	-0.2	-0.2
	-1.1	10.6	13.7	16.8	5.7	13.8	11.7	19.8	4.9	17.4	13.0	22.0
Minus	0.6	-0.5	-0.1	-0.7	0.3	-0.8	0.4	-0.7	-0.5	-0.7	0.1	-1.0
	-0.5	10.1	13.6	16.1	6.0	13.0	12.1	19.1	4.4	16.7	13.1	21.0

Totals in computer:

-0.4	10.3	13.7	15.9	6.2	13.0	12.3	19.0	4.3	16.8	12.9	21.0

	1964				1965				1966			
	I	II	III	IV	I	II	III	IV	I	II	III	IV
(A)	1.1	0.7	1.5	0.7	1.1	1.4	2.3	0.8	4.0	1.2	3.9	1.9
(C)	-0.4	0.3	-0.1	0.6	-0.4	0.3	-0.1	0.7	-0.5	0.2	0.0	0.7
(D)	0.1	-0.1	-0.8	1.7	-1.5	-1.3	-0.3	2.8	0.6	-1.0	0.3	3.1
(E)	-0.1	1.0	0.5	0.8	0.1	1.5	0.7	0.6	1.6	2.6	1.8	0.6
(F)	1.8	1.7	0.5	-0.1	3.2	2.4	0.5	1.3	2.5	1.8	1.0	0.8
(G)	0.1	0.9	0.6	1.6	0.5	1.5	0.3	1.6	-0.1	1.1	0.6	1.7
(H)	-3.9	8.4	4.3	11.0	-0.3	9.8	3.0	14.9	-3.1	12.5	-0.4	8.6
(I)	7.1	6.0	7.7	6.2	7.3	4.2	7.3	5.1	8.7	2.1	5.4	4.4
(J)	-0.3	0.0	0.7	0.5	-0.4	-0.1	0.2	0.5	-0.7	0.2	-0.2	-0.3
Minus	-0.3	-0.6	0.2	-0.6	-0.4	-0.3	-0.2	-0.2	-0.4	-0.1	0.1	-0.3
	5.2	18.3	15.1	22.4	9.2	19.4	13.7	28.1	12.6	20.6	12.5	21.2
Minus	0.5	-1.0	-0.2	-1.8	1.1	-0.6	-1.2	-1.3	0.5	-1.2	-0.7	-0.8
	5.7	17.3	14.9	20.6	10.3	18.8	12.5	26.8	13.1	19.4	11.8	20.4

Totals in computer:

5.9	17.2	14.6	20.6	10.2	18.7	12.5	26.5	13.1	19.4	11.8	20.4

Table 2

Increment in Domestic Availability of Credit After Distribution of Balances in Financial Sectors Among Nonfinancial Sectors

(figures in parentheses indicate relative series number of computer)
(in billion dollars)

	1946	1947	1948	1949	1950	1951	1952	1953	1954	1955

(A) Households: According to Talbe 1, plus Demand Deposits and Currency (153020001), Savings Accounts at Commercial Banks (153031101), Savings Accounts at Savings Institutions (153032505), and Insurance and Pension Reserves (583154005)

	1946	1947	1948	1949	1950	1951	1952	1953	1954	1955
	13.1	8.2	5.1	6.2	8.7	12.5	16.2	17.3	16.2	21.2

(C) Noncorporate Nonfinancial Business: According to Table 1, plus Demand Deposits and Currency (113020003)

	0.8	0.6	-0.1	0.3	0.7	1.5	0.0	0.0	0.5	0.5

(D) Corporate Nonfinancial Business: According to Table 1, plus Demand Deposits and Currency (103020001) and Time Deposits (103031103)

	-4.0	1.7	1.6	3.7	5.2	3.5	1.2	2.1	0.1	5.9

(E) U. S. Government: According to Table 1, plus Demand Deposits and Currency (313020001)

	-23.0	-0.2	1.7	1.1	0.9	1.6	3.0	-1.2	-0.4	1.7

(F) State and Local Governments: According to Table 1, plus Demand Deposits and Currency (203020001) and Time Deposits (203031001)

	0.5	1.9	1.6	1.3	2.0	2.0	2.5	3.1	3.1	1.6

(G) Monetary Authorities: According to Table 1

	-0.2	-0.4	0.7	-4.3	2.0	3.4	1.0	1.8	-1.1	0.0

(H) Commercial Banks: According to Table 1, less distribution (153020001, 153031101, 113020003, 103020001, 103031103, 313020001, 203020001, 203031001, 693020005, 463031003, 263020000 and 263031003), as computed in (909020000)

	1.5	-1.4	-2.8	6.0	1.4	-2.7	2.2	1.5	2.3	0.9

(I) Nonbank Financial Institutions: According to Table 1, plus Demand Deposits and Currency (693020005) and Time Deposits (463031003), less distribution (153032505 and 583154005), as computed in (909010000)

	1.3	1.2	1.2	0.9	1.3	1.1	1.5	1.8	1.0	1.6

(J) Rest of the World: According to Table 1, plus U. S. Demand Deposits and Currency (263020000) and Time Deposits (263031003)

	-0.7	-0.9	0.6	0.1	1.7	-0.4	1.5	0.8	1.1	0.7

Minus: According to Table 1

	0.0	0.0	-0.1	0.0	-0.4	-0.4	-0.2	-0.2	-0.1	0.2
	-10.7	10.7	9.5	15.3	23.5	22.1	28.9	27.0	22.7	34.3

Minus: According to Table 1

	0.7	1.0	0.0	0.8	0.3	-0.4	-1.4	0.1	-0.1	-0.2
	-10.0	11.7	9.5	16.1	23.8	21.7	27.5	27.1	22.6	34.1

Table 2 (continued)   19

Increment in Domestic Availability of Credit After Distribution of Balances
in Financial Sectors Among Nonfinancial Sectors

(text according to preceding page)

	1956	1957	1958	1959	1960	1961	1962	1963	1964	1965	1966
(A)	21.6	22.1	23.3	28.1	21.0	27.0	36.2	42.7	46.5	51.8	44.9
(C)	0.4	0.8	1.6	-1.1	-0.2	0.2	0.4	0.4	0.4	0.4	0.4
(D)	-3.8	0.1	2.9	6.5	-3.8	3.4	3.3	3.8	1.6	1.4	3.0
(E)	0.9	2.2	1.4	4.5	2.7	2.2	3.6	1.2	2.7	1.5	6.5
(F)	1.6	2.4	2.3	2.8	3.6	4.3	5.5	7.1	6.1	9.8	8.3
(G)	0.1	-0.7	2.3	0.4	0.7	1.5	1.9	2.6	3.2	3.8	3.3
(H)	1.4	-0.8	1.0	3.1	4.5	1.0	-1.3	-1.3	-1.7	1.4	0.8
(I)	1.5	1.1	1.3	1.3	0.8	0.3	0.7	0.7	0.7	0.2	1.1
(J)	1.1	0.7	0.9	2.1	1.4	1.4	1.9	1.7	2.6	0.6	-0.6
Minus	-0.5	-0.9	-1.0	-0.4	-1.3	-1.1	-0.8	-1.6	-1.2	-1.1	-0.6
	24.3	27.0	36.0	47.3	29.4	40.2	51.4	57.3	60.9	69.8	67.1
Minus	-0.1	0.0	-0.2	-0.6	0.2	-0.8	-0.8	-1.9	-2.6	-2.1	-2.3
	24.2	27.0	35.8	46.7	29.6	39.4	50.6	55.4	58.3	67.7	64.8

	1 9 5 2				1 9 5 3				1 9 5 4			
	I	II	III	IV	I	II	III	IV	I	II	III	IV
(A)	1.2	2.4	5.8	6.5	4.0	4.2	3.9	5.2	1.8	3.6	5.2	5.5
(C)	-0.3	0.1	-0.2	0.3	-0.3	0.2	0.0	0.3	-0.3	0.3	0.1	0.5
(D)	-2.5	0.7	1.2	1.7	-3.2	0.5	2.3	2.5	-5.1	-1.6	3.1	3.6
(E)	2.7	0.3	0.4	-0.5	0.6	-1.9	3.0	-2.9	1.6	0.3	-1.8	-0.3
(F)	0.8	0.6	0.6	0.4	0.4	1.0	0.6	1.1	1.5	0.7	0.0	0.8
(G)	-1.2	0.4	0.6	1.1	-0.8	1.0	0.0	1.5	-1.7	0.3	-0.5	0.8
(H)	0.6	0.7	-0.6	1.6	-0.5	0.5	0.7	0.8	-1.2	0.6	1.3	1.6
(I)	0.9	0.1	0.5	0.2	0.4	0.2	0.6	0.8	0.2	-0.1	0.5	0.6
(J)	0.2	0.5	0.8	0.1	0.0	0.2	0.5	0.3	0.5	0.2	0.2	0.1
Minus	-0.1	-0.2	0.1	0.0	0.0	0.1	0.0	-0.1	-0.2	0.1	-0.1	0.0
	2.3	5.6	9.2	11.4	0.6	6.0	11.6	9.5	-2.9	4.4	8.0	13.2
Minus	0.6	-0.9	-0.3	-0.7	0.5	0.0	-0.8	0.4	0.7	-0.4	0.5	-1.0
	2.9	4.7	8.9	10.7	1.1	6.0	10.8	9.9	-2.2	4.0	8.5	12.2

	1 9 5 5				1 9 5 6				1 9 5 7			
	I	II	III	IV	I	II	III	IV	I	II	III	IV
(A)	4.9	4.2	6.9	5.4	6.2	4.2	5.2	5.7	5.9	5.4	5.2	5.7
(C)	-0.3	0.3	0.1	0.5	-0.3	0.3	0.1	0.5	-0.3	0.4	0.2	0.6
(D)	-2.0	0.9	2.4	4.8	-6.1	-2.1	0.6	3.9	-3.6	-1.2	1.4	3.5
(E)	0.3	2.5	-0.4	-0.6	2.4	-0.2	0.1	-1.5	3.5	-1.1	1.9	-2.3
(F)	0.6	0.4	0.0	1.0	1.3	0.3	-0.6	0.5	1.0	0.8	0.2	0.3
(G)	-1.6	0.4	0.1	1.1	-1.3	0.1	-0.1	1.4	-2.0	0.0	0.4	1.0
(H)	-0.7	-0.2	0.2	1.8	-1.0	0.6	1.0	0.6	-0.9	-0.4	1.0	-0.4
(I)	0.4	-0.1	1.4	0.0	0.4	-0.1	1.5	-0.2	0.5	-0.1	0.8	0.0
(J)	0.0	0.3	0.5	0.1	0.4	0.3	0.3	0.3	-0.3	0.3	0.1	0.4
Minus	0.1	0.1	0.0	0.1	-0.1	-0.1	-0.1	-0.2	-0.3	-0.4	-0.1	-0.2
	1.7	8.8	11.2	14.2	1.9	3.3	8.0	11.0	3.5	3.7	11.1	8.6
Minus	1.2	-0.4	-0.4	-0.6	0.6	-0.6	0.3	-0.4	0.4	-0.5	0.9	-0.7
	2.9	8.4	10.8	13.6	2.5	2.7	8.3	10.6	3.9	3.2	12.0	7.9

Table 2 (continued)

Increment in Domestic Availability of Credit After Distribution of Balances in Financial Sectors Among Nonfinancial Sectors

(text according to preceding pages)

	1958				1959				1960			
	I	II	III	IV	I	II	III	IV	I	II	III	IV
(A)	5.3	2.3	7.9	7.9	6.4	6.9	6.6	8.2	5.4	2.7	6.9	5.8
(C)	-0.3	0.6	0.4	0.6	-0.4	-0.1	-0.4	0.2	-0.4	0.2	-0.1	0.4
(D)	-4.5	-0.6	1.8	6.0	-2.2	2.5	1.9	4.3	-4.7	-0.3	-1.4	2.7
(E)	1.6	4.0	-4.8	0.7	0.2	2.5	2.5	-0.5	-0.5	4.0	0.6	-1.3
(F)	1.2	1.0	-0.2	0.5	0.5	0.4	1.0	0.6	1.2	0.7	0.7	1.0
(G)	-0.6	1.9	-0.5	1.4	-0.9	0.7	0.3	0.3	-1.5	1.3	0.5	0.4
(H)	-1.4	0.4	0.9	1.2	0.3	0.8	1.2	0.8	0.8	0.3	0.0	3.2
(I)	0.3	-0.3	1.4	-0.2	1.0	-0.1	1.2	-0.6	0.9	-0.5	0.8	-0.7
(J)	0.1	-0.3	0.3	0.7	0.2	0.7	0.8	0.4	0.1	0.2	0.5	0.6
Minus	-0.3	-0.4	-0.1	-0.2	-0.2	0.0	-0.2	0.1	-0.4	-0.3	-0.4	-0.2
	1.4	8.6	7.1	18.6	4.9	14.3	14.9	13.8	0.9	8.3	8.1	11.9
Minus	1.0	-0.3	0.3	-1.2	0.7	-0.5	0.1	-0.8	0.9	-0.3	-0.4	-0.2
	2.4	8.3	7.4	17.4	5.6	13.8	15.0	13.0	1.8	8.0	7.7	11.7

	1961				1962				1963			
	I	II	III	IV	I	II	III	IV	I	II	III	IV
(A)	5.2	3.8	8.0	9.9	8.8	6.4	10.4	10.7	9.0	7.8	12.4	13.3
(C)	-0.4	0.2	-0.1	0.5	-0.3	0.3	-0.1	0.5	-0.4	0.2	0.0	0.6
(D)	-3.5	2.3	-0.4	5.0	-3.3	0.7	-0.3	6.2	-4.1	2.1	-0.2	6.1
(E)	-1.9	2.6	2.9	-1.4	0.6	4.6	-0.5	-1.1	-0.4	4.4	-1.4	-1.4
(F)	1.2	1.3	0.6	1.3	1.3	1.8	0.1	2.1	1.5	2.5	-0.2	3.3
(G)	-0.7	0.5	0.5	1.0	0.3	0.4	0.3	0.9	-0.2	1.1	0.4	1.3
(H)	-1.4	1.4	0.1	1.0	-3.0	0.9	0.2	0.5	-1.1	0.1	0.1	-0.4
(I)	0.8	-0.8	1.2	-1.0	1.2	-1.6	1.4	-0.2	0.7	-1.2	1.9	-0.8
(J)	0.1	-0.4	1.1	0.6	0.3	0.3	0.1	1.0	0.2	0.9	0.2	0.2
Minus	-0.5	-0.3	-0.2	-0.2	-0.2	-0.2	0.0	-0.7	-0.5	-0.6	-0.2	-0.2
	1.1	10.6	13.7	16.7	5.7	13.6	11.6	19.9	4.7	17.3	13.0	22.0
Minus	-0.6	-0.5	-0.1	-0.7	0.3	-0.8	0.4	-0.7	-0.5	-0.7	0.1	-1.0
	-0.5	10.1	13.6	16.0	6.0	12.8	12.0	19.2	4.2	16.6	13.1	21.0

	1964				1965				1966			
	I	II	III	IV	I	II	III	IV	I	II	III	IV
(A)	9.7	9.6	12.0	15.2	10.9	9.7	14.4	16.7	10.6	7.3	11.5	15.4
(C)	-0.4	0.3	-0.1	0.6	-0.4	0.3	-0.1	0.7	-0.5	0.2	0.0	0.7
(D)	-3.8	1.8	-0.1	3.6	-4.2	-0.1	-0.6	6.2	-2.8	0.7	0.0	5.1
(E)	1.4	3.6	-0.2	-1.9	2.1	4.7	-3.6	-1.6	1.4	9.3	-1.4	-2.9
(F)	1.3	1.7	0.7	2.6	1.8	3.5	0.9	3.7	3.0	2.4	0.1	2.6
(G)	0.1	0.9	0.6	1.6	0.5	1.5	0.3	1.6	-0.1	1.1	0.6	1.7
(H)	-3.3	1.7	-0.7	0.6	-1.9	1.8	-0.4	1.9	-0.2	0.5	0.3	0.5
(I)	0.6	-1.0	1.5	-0.6	1.0	-2.0	2.3	-1.0	2.3	-1.6	1.8	-1.5
(J)	0.2	0.3	1.3	1.1	-0.3	0.2	0.6	0.2	-0.7	0.8	-0.5	-0.1
Minus	-0.3	-0.6	0.2	-0.6	-0.4	-0.3	-0.2	-0.2	-0.4	-0.1	0.1	-0.3
	5.5	18.3	15.2	22.2	9.1	19.3	13.6	28.2	12.6	20.6	12.5	21.2
Minus	0.5	-1.0	-0.2	-1.8	1.1	-0.6	-1.2	-1.3	0.5	-1.2	-0.7	-0.8
	6.0	17.3	15.0	20.4	10.2	18.7	12.4	26.9	13.1	19.4	11.8	20.4

Table 3   21

Increment in Domestic Absorption of Credit

(figures in parentheses indicate relative series number of computer)
(in billion dollars)

	1946	1947	1948	1949	1950	1951	1952	1953	1954	1955

(A) Households: Credit Market Instruments (154102005) and Security Credit (153167205)
| 3.9 | 7.4 | 8.1 | 7.9 | 12.8 | 8.5 | 12.7 | 13.0 | 12.1 | 20.5 |

(C) Noncorporate Nonfinancial Business: Credit Market Instruments (164102005)
| 3.1 | 2.8 | 0.8 | 1.1 | 4.2 | 3.6 | 1.7 | 0.3 | 1.9 | 3.6 |

(D) Corporate Nonfinancial Business: Credit and Equity Market Instruments (104102005), less Corporate Stock (103164003)
| 4.6 | 6.1 | 5.6 | 2.3 | 6.2 | 8.5 | 6.8 | 3.3 | 3.1 | 7.0 |

(E) U. S. Government: U. S. Government Securities (313161005) and Other Loans (313169305)
| -23.4 | -7.1 | -5.7 | 2.4 | -0.7 | -0.3 | 4.8 | 6.9 | 2.1 | 0.0 |

(F) State and Local Governments: Credit Market Borrowing (204102005)
| 0.4 | 0.9 | 1.2 | 1.5 | 1.4 | 1.2 | 3.0 | 3.4 | 4.1 | 3.4 |
| -11.4 | 10.1 | 10.0 | 15.2 | 23.9 | 21.5 | 29.0 | 26.9 | 23.3 | 34.5 |

Minus: Net Increase in Banking System Liabilities (733120005), less Demand Deposits, Net (723163003)
| 0.7 | 1.0 | 0.0 | 0.8 | 0.3 | -0.4 | -1.4 | 0.1 | -0.1 | -0.2 |
| -10.7 | 11.1 | 10.0 | 16.0 | 24.2 | 21.1 | 27.6 | 27.0 | 23.2 | 34.3 |

Totals in computer (909030000)
| -10.6 | 11.2 | 10.0 | 16.1 | 24.3 | 21.2 | 27.6 | 26.9 | 23.2 | 34.2 |

	1956	1957	1958	1959	1960	1961	1962	1963	1964	1965	1966

(A) Households: (text as above)
| 16.0 | 12.6 | 12.6 | 21.7 | 18.0 | 16.7 | 20.4 | 26.1 | 27.1 | 28.7 | 21.4 |

(C) Noncorporate Nonfinancial Business: (text as above)
| 2.4 | 2.1 | 3.3 | 4.6 | 3.1 | 4.3 | 7.0 | 8.5 | 8.7 | 10.3 | 10.1 |

(D) Corporate Nonfinancial Business: (text as above)
| 8.8 | 8.6 | 6.3 | 7.7 | 6.4 | 6.6 | 10.6 | 10.6 | 12.1 | 19.9 | 22.3 |

(E) U. S. Government: (text as above)
| -5.7 | -0.9 | 8.9 | 8.9 | -1.9 | 7.6 | 7.8 | 5.0 | 6.7 | 3.6 | 6.3 |

(F) State and Local Governments: (text as above)
| 3.1 | 4.6 | 5.5 | 4.7 | 3.8 | 5.2 | 5.6 | 7.0 | 6.2 | 7.7 | 6.8 |
| 24.6 | 27.0 | 36.6 | 47.6 | 29.4 | 40.4 | 51.4 | 57.2 | 60.8 | 70.2 | 66.9 |

Minus: (text as above)
| -0.1 | 0.0 | -0.2 | -0.6 | 0.2 | -0.8 | -0.8 | -1.9 | -2.6 | -2.1 | -2.3 |
| 24.5 | 27.0 | 36.4 | 47.0 | 29.6 | 39.6 | 50.6 | 55.3 | 58.2 | 68.1 | 64.6 |

Totals in computer (909030000)
| 24.6 | 26.9 | 36.4 | 46.9 | 29.6 | 39.6 | 50.4 | 55.2 | 58.3 | 68.2 | 64.6 |

Table 3 (continued)

Increment in Domestic Absorption of Credit

(text according to preceding page)

	1952				1953				1954			
	I	II	III	IV	I	II	III	IV	I	II	III	IV
(A)	1.3	3.6	3.1	4.6	2.5	3.9	2.5	4.0	0.2	2.9	3.1	5.8
(C)	0.4	0.7	0.5	0.1	0.1	0.6	0.4	-0.8	0.3	0.9	0.5	0.2
(D)	1.9	1.0	1.9	2.2	0.7	0.9	1.2	0.5	0.3	0.5	1.6	0.7
(E)	-2.2	-0.4	3.3	4.1	-3.3	-0.1	6.7	3.7	-4.4	-0.9	1.9	5.6
(F)	0.7	0.8	1.1	0.4	0.6	0.7	1.1	1.0	1.1	1.2	0.9	1.0
	2.1	5.7	9.9	11.4	0.6	6.0	11.9	8.4	-2.5	4.6	8.0	13.3
Minus	0.6	-0.9	-0.3	-0.7	0.5	0.0	-0.8	0.4	0.7	-0.4	0.5	-1.0
	2.7	4.8	9.6	10.7	1.1	6.0	11.1	8.8	-1.8	4.2	8.5	12.3
Totals in computer (909030000)												
	2.6	4.9	9.5	10.6	1.0	6.0	11.1	8.9	-1.9	4.2	8.5	12.3

	1955				1956				1957			
	I	II	III	IV	I	II	III	IV	I	II	III	IV
(A)	3.3	5.8	5.3	6.0	2.8	4.4	3.6	5.3	1.2	4.4	3.0	3.8
(C)	0.7	1.5	1.0	0.5	0.5	1.3	0.7	-0.1	0.5	0.9	0.6	0.1
(D)	0.8	1.8	1.8	2.6	1.8	2.6	2.2	2.3	2.0	2.8	1.7	2.0
(E)	-4.2	-1.5	2.0	3.8	-4.5	-5.5	1.0	3.4	-1.4	-5.7	4.2	2.0
(F)	1.0	0.4	0.9	1.0	1.4	0.6	0.5	0.6	1.3	1.0	1.3	1.0
	1.6	8.0	11.0	13.9	2.0	3.4	8.0	11.5	3.6	3.4	10.8	8.9
Minus	1.2	-0.4	-0.6		0.6	-0.6	0.3	-0.4	0.4	-0.5	0.9	-0.7
	2.8	7.6	10.6	13.3	2.6	2.8	8.3	11.1	4.0	2.9	11.7	8.2
Totals in computer (909030000)												
	2.7	7.6	10.6	13.3	2.6	2.7	8.3	11.0	4.1	3.0	11.6	8.2

	1958				1959				1960			
	I	II	III	IV	I	II	III	IV	I	II	III	IV
(A)	0.3	3.6	2.7	6.0	3.0	6.5	5.6	6.6	2.4	5.9	4.0	5.6
(C)	0.2	0.9	0.9	1.2	0.8	2.4	0.9	0.6	0.7	1.3	0.4	0.7
(D)	1.3	0.7	1.5	2.8	0.8	2.5	2.1	2.3	1.3	1.8	0.8	2.5
(E)	-1.9	2.1	0.9	7.7	-0.5	1.2	4.7	3.4	-4.3	-1.5	1.4	2.4
(F)	1.9	1.5	1.3	0.7	1.2	1.3	1.7	0.4	1.0	0.8	1.6	0.4
	1.8	8.8	7.3	18.4	5.3	13.9	15.0	13.3	1.1	8.3	8.2	11.6
Minus	1.0	-0.3	0.3	-1.2	0.7	-0.5	0.1	-0.8	0.9	-0.3	-0.4	-0.2
	2.8	8.5	7.6	17.2	6.0	13.4	15.1	12.5	2.0	8.0	7.8	11.4
Totals in computer (909030000)												
	2.9	8.5	7.6	17.4	6.0	13.5	15.0	12.4	2.3	8.0	7.8	11.5

Table 3 (continued)

Increment in Domestic Absorption of Credit

(text according to preceding pages)

	1961				1962				1963			
	I	II	III	IV	I	II	III	IV	I	II	III	IV
(A)	0.8	5.4	3.1	7.4	1.5	5.9	4.7	8.2	2.5	8.2	6.2	9.1
(C)	0.5	1.5	1.4	0.9	0.8	2.7	1.8	1.6	1.0	3.3	1.8	2.4
(D)	-0.5	2.3	1.8	3.0	0.7	3.6	2.8	3.5	0.8	3.1	2.1	4.6
(E)	-2.8	0.4	5.7	4.3	0.5	0.5	1.0	5.8	-0.6	0.4	0.9	4.3
(F)	1.4	0.9	1.7	1.2	2.1	1.5	1.1	0.9	1.4	2.3	1.9	1.4
	-0.6	10.5	13.7	16.8	5.6	14.2	11.4	20.0	5.1	17.3	12.9	21.8
Minus	0.6	-0.5	-0.1	-0.7	0.3	-0.8	0.4	-0.7	-0.5	-0.7	0.1	-1.0
	0.0	10.0	13.6	16.1	5.9	13.4	11.8	19.3	4.6	16.6	13.0	20.8
Totals in computer (909030000)												
	-0.1	10.0	13.6	16.0	5.9	13.4	11.8	19.3	4.6	16.6	13.1	20.9

	1964				1965				1966			
	I	II	III	IV	I	II	III	IV	I	II	III	IV
(A)	3.4	8.9	5.5	9.4	3.1	9.0	6.0	10.7	2.3	8.0	3.7	7.4
(C)	1.3	3.8	1.8	1.8	2.1	3.8	2.2	2.2	3.1	4.3	1.2	1.6
(D)	-0.2	4.2	2.6	5.6	2.8	5.9	4.4	6.9	4.3	8.2	4.5	5.3
(E)	-0.1	-0.6	3.0	4.4	-0.2	-2.2	-0.2	6.3	1.4	-2.1	1.7	5.3
(F)	1.0	2.1	1.9	1.2	1.5	2.7	1.8	1.7	1.3	2.5	1.6	1.5
	5.4	18.4	14.8	22.4	9.3	19.2	14.2	27.8	12.4	20.9	12.7	21.1
Minus	0.5	-1.0	-0.2	-1.8	1.1	-0.6	-1.2	-1.3	0.5	-1.2	-0.7	-0.8
	5.9	17.4	14.6	20.6	10.4	18.6	13.0	26.5	12.9	19.7	12.0	20.3
Totals in computer (909030000)												
	5.8	17.2	14.6	20.6	10.4	18.5	12.9	26.4	12.9	19.7	12.0	20.3

Table 4

Increment in Net Domestic Financial Investment

(= Balance between Increment in Domestic Availability of Credit,
Without Intermediaries, and Increment in Domestic Absorption of Credit
for each Sector, i.e., totals in Table 2, less totals in Table 3)

(in billion dollars)

	1946	1947	1948	1949	1950	1951	1952	1953	1954	1955
(A) Households:	9.2	0.8	-3.0	-1.7	-4.1	4.0	3.5	4.3	4.1	0.7
(C) Noncorporate Nonfinancial Business:	-2.3	-2.2	-0.9	-0.8	-3.5	-2.1	-1.7	-0.3	-1.4	-3.1
(D) Corporate Nonfinancial Business:	-8.6	-4.4	-4.0	1.4	-1.0	-5.0	-5.6	-1.2	-3.0	-1.1
(E) U. S. Government:	0.4	6.9	7.4	-1.3	1.6	1.9	-1.8	-8.1	-2.5	1.7
(F) State and Local Governments:	0.1	1.0	0.4	-0.2	0.6	0.8	-0.5	-0.3	-1.0	-1.8
(G) Monetary Authorities:	-0.2	-0.4	0.7	-4.3	2.0	3.4	1.0	1.8	-1.1	0.0
(H) Commercial Banks:	1.5	-1.4	-2.8	6.0	1.4	-2.7	2.2	1.5	2.3	0.9
(I) Nonbank Financial Institutions:	1.3	1.2	1.2	0.9	1.3	1.1	1.5	1.8	1.0	1.6
(J) Rest of the World:	-0.7	-0.9	0.6	0.1	1.7	-0.4	1.5	0.8	1.1	0.7
Minus: According to Table 2	0.0	0.0	-0.1	0.0	-0.4	-0.4	-0.2	-0.2	-0.1	0.2
Turnover:	12.5	9.9	10.3	8.4	8.6	11.2	9.7	10.2	8.5	5.8
	-11.8	-9.3	-10.8	-8.3	-9.0	-10.6	-9.8	-10.1	-9.1	-6.0
Discrepancy:	0.7	0.6	-0.5	0.1	-0.4	0.6	-0.1	0.1	-0.6	-0.2

Table 4 (continued)   25

Increment in Net Domestic Financial Investment

(text according to the preceding page)

	1956	1957	1958	1959	1960	1961	1962	1963	1964	1965	1966
(A)	5.6	9.5	10.7	6.4	3.0	10.3	15.8	16.6	19.4	23.1	23.5
(C)	-2.0	-1.3	-1.7	-5.7	-3.3	-4.1	-6.6	-8.1	-8.3	-9.9	-9.7
(D)	-12.6	-8.5	-3.4	-1.2	-10.2	-3.2	-7.3	-6.8	-10.5	-18.5	-19.3
(E)	6.6	3.1	-7.5	-4.4	4.6	-5.4	-4.2	-3.8	-4.0	-2.1	0.2
(F)	-1.5	-2.2	-3.2	-1.9	-0.2	-0.9	-0.1	0.1	-0.1	2.1	1.5
(G)	0.1	-0.7	2.3	0.4	0.7	1.5	1.9	2.6	3.2	3.8	3.3
(H)	1.4	-0.8	1.0	3.1	4.5	1.0	-1.3	-1.3	-1.7	1.4	0.8
(I)	1.5	1.1	1.3	1.3	0.8	0.3	0.7	0.7	0.7	0.2	1.1
(J)	1.1	0.7	0.9	2.1	1.4	1.4	1.9	1.7	2.6	0.6	-0.6
Minus	-0.5	-0.9	-1.0	-0.4	-1.3	-1.1	-0.8	-1.6	-1.2	-1.1	-0.6
Turnover	16.3	14.4	16.2	13.3	15.0	14.5	20.3	21.7	25.9	31.2	30.4
	-16.6	-14.4	-16.8	-13.6	-15.0	-14.7	-20.3	-21.6	-25.8	-31.6	-30.2
Discrepancy	-0.3	0.0	-0.6	-0.3	0.0	-0.2	0.0	0.1	0.1	-0.4	0.2

	1 9 5 2				1 9 5 3				1 9 5 4			
	I	II	III	IV	I	II	III	IV	I	II	III	IV
(A)	-0.1	-1.2	2.7	1.9	1.5	0.3	1.4	1.2	1.6	0.7	2.1	-0.3
(C)	-0.7	-0.6	-0.7	0.2	-0.4	-0.4	-0.4	1.1	-0.6	-0.6	-0.4	0.3
(D)	-4.4	-0.3	-0.7	-0.5	-3.9	-0.4	1.1	2.0	-5.4	-2.1	1.5	2.9
(E)	4.9	0.7	-2.9	-4.6	3.9	-1.8	-3.7	-6.6	6.0	1.2	-3.7	-5.9
(F)	0.1	-0.2	-0.5	0.0	-0.2	0.3	-0.5	0.1	0.4	-0.5	-0.9	-0.2
(G)	-1.2	0.4	0.6	1.1	-0.8	1.0	0.0	1.5	-1.7	0.3	-0.5	0.8
(H)	0.6	0.7	-0.6	1.6	-0.5	0.5	0.7	0.8	-1.2	0.6	1.3	1.6
(I)	0.9	0.1	0.5	0.2	0.4	0.2	0.6	0.8	0.2	-0.1	0.5	0.6
(J)	0.2	0.5	0.8	0.1	0.0	0.2	0.5	0.3	0.5	0.2	0.2	0.1
Minus	-0.1	-0.2	0.1	0.0	0.0	0.1	0.0	-0.1	-0.1	0.1	-0.1	0.0
Turnover	6.7	2.4	4.7	5.1	5.8	2.6	4.3	7.8	8.7	3.1	5.6	6.3
	-6.5	-2.5	-5.4	-5.1	-5.8	-2.6	-4.6	-6.7	-9.1	-3.3	-5.6	-6.4
Discrepancy	0.2	-0.1	-0.7	0.0	0.0	0.0	-0.3	1.1	-0.4	-0.2	0.0	-0.1

	1 9 5 5				1 9 5 6				1 9 5 7			
	I	II	III	IV	I	II	III	IV	I	II	III	IV
(A)	1.6	-1.6	1.6	-0.6	3.4	-0.2	1.6	0.4	4.7	1.0	2.2	1.9
(C)	-1.0	-1.2	-0.9	0.0	-0.8	-1.0	-0.6	0.6	-0.8	-0.5	-0.4	0.5
(D)	-2.8	-0.9	0.6	2.2	-7.9	-4.7	-1.6	1.6	-5.6	-4.0	-0.3	1.5
(E)	4.5	4.0	-2.4	-4.4	6.9	5.3	-0.9	-4.9	4.9	4.6	-2.3	-4.3
(F)	-0.4	0.0	-0.9	0.0	-0.1	-0.3	-1.1	-0.1	-0.3	-0.2	-1.1	-0.7
(G)	-1.6	0.4	0.1	1.1	0.1	0.1	-0.1	1.4	-2.0	0.0	0.4	1.0
(H)	-0.7	-0.2	0.2	1.8	-1.0	0.6	1.0	0.6	-0.9	-0.4	1.0	-0.4
(I)	0.4	-0.1	1.4	0.0	0.4	-0.1	1.5	-0.2	0.5	-0.1	0.8	0.0
(J)	0.0	0.3	0.5	0.1	0.4	0.3	0.3	0.3	-0.3	0.3	0.1	0.4
Minus	0.1	0.1	0.0	0.1	-0.1	-0.1	-0.1	-0.2	-0.3	-0.4	-0.1	-0.2
Turnover	6.6	4.8	4.4	5.3	11.1	6.3	4.4	4.9	10.1	5.9	4.5	5.3
	-6.5	-4.0	-4.2	-5.0	-11.2	-6.4	-4.4	-5.4	-10.2	-5.6	-4.2	-5.6
Discrepancy	0.1	0.8	0.2	0.3	-0.1	-0.1	0.0	-0.5	-0.1	0.3	0.3	-0.3

Table 4 (continued)

<u>Increment in Net Domestic Financial Investment</u>

(text according to the preceding pages)

	1958 I	II	III	IV	1959 I	II	III	IV	1960 I	II	III	IV
(A)	5.0	-1.3	5.2	1.9	3.4	0.4	1.0	1.6	3.0	-3.2	2.9	0.2
(C)	-0.5	-0.3	-0.5	-0.6	-1.2	-2.5	-1.3	-0.4	-1.1	-1.1	-0.5	-0.3
(D)	-5.8	-1.3	0.3	3.2	-3.0	0.0	-0.2	2.0	-6.0	-2.1	-2.2	0.2
(E)	3.5	1.9	-5.7	-7.0	0.7	1.3	-2.2	-3.9	3.8	5.5	-0.8	-3.7
(F)	-0.7	-0.5	-1.5	-0.2	-0.7	-0.9	-0.7	0.2	0.2	-0.1	-0.9	0.6
(G)	-0.6	1.9	-0.5	1.4	-0.9	0.7	0.3	0.3	-1.5	1.3	0.5	0.4
(H)	-1.4	0.4	0.9	1.2	0.3	0.8	1.2	0.8	0.8	0.3	0.0	3.2
(I)	0.3	-0.3	1.4	-0.2	1.0	-0.1	1.2	-0.6	0.9	-0.5	0.8	-0.7
(J)	0.1	-0.3	0.3	0.7	0.2	0.7	0.8	0.4	0.1	0.2	0.5	0.6
Minus	-0.3	-0.4	-0.1	-0.2	-0.2	0.0	-0.2	0.1	-0.4	-0.3	-0.4	-0.2
Turnover	8.9	4.2	8.1	8.4	5.6	3.9	4.5	5.4	8.8	7.3	4.7	5.2
	-9.3	-4.4	-8.3	-8.2	-6.0	-3.5	-4.6	-4.9	-9.0	-7.3	-4.8	-4.9
Discrepancy	-0.4	-0.2	-0.2	0.2	-0.4	0.4	-0.1	0.5	-0.2	0.0	-0.1	0.3

	1961 I	II	III	IV	1962 I	II	III	IV	1963 I	II	III	IV
(A)	4.4	-1.6	4.9	2.5	7.3	0.5	5.7	2.5	6.5	-0.4	6.2	4.2
(C)	-0.9	-1.3	-1.5	-0.4	-1.1	-2.4	-1.9	-1.1	-1.4	-3.1	-1.8	-1.8
(D)	-3.0	0.0	-2.2	2.0	-4.0	-2.9	-3.1	2.7	-4.9	-1.0	-2.3	1.5
(E)	0.9	2.2	-2.8	-5.7	0.1	4.1	-1.5	-6.9	0.2	4.0	-2.3	-5.7
(F)	-0.2	0.4	-1.1	0.1	-0.8	0.3	-1.0	1.2	0.1	0.2	-2.1	1.9
(G)	-0.7	0.5	0.5	1.0	0.3	0.4	0.3	0.9	-0.2	1.1	0.4	1.3
(H)	-1.4	1.4	0.1	1.0	-3.0	0.9	0.2	0.5	-1.1	0.1	0.1	-0.4
(I)	0.8	-0.8	1.2	-1.0	1.2	-1.6	1.4	-0.2	0.7	-1.2	1.9	-0.8
(J)	0.1	-0.4	1.1	0.6	0.3	0.3	0.1	1.0	0.2	0.9	0.2	0.2
Minus	-0.5	-0.3	-0.2	-0.2	-0.2	-0.2	0.0	-0.7	-0.5	-0.6	-0.2	-0.2
Turnover	6.2	4.5	7.8	7.2	9.2	6.5	7.7	8.8	7.7	6.3	8.8	9.1
	-6.7	-4.4	-7.8	-7.3	-9.1	-7.1	-7.5	-8.9	-8.1	-6.3	-8.7	-8.9
Discrepancy	-0.5	0.1	0.0	-0.1	0.1	-0.6	0.2	-0.1	-0.4	0.0	0.1	0.2

	1964 I	II	III	IV	1965 I	II	III	IV	1966 I	II	III	IV
(A)	6.3	0.7	6.5	5.8	7.8	0.7	8.4	6.0	8.3	-0.7	7.8	8.0
(C)	-1.7	-3.5	-1.9	-1.2	-2.5	-3.5	-2.3	-1.5	-3.6	-4.1	-1.2	-0.9
(D)	-3.6	-2.4	-2.7	-2.0	-7.0	-6.0	-5.0	-0.7	-7.1	-7.5	-4.5	-0.2
(E)	1.5	4.2	-3.2	-6.3	2.3	6.9	-3.4	-7.9	0.0	11.4	-3.1	-8.2
(F)	0.3	-0.4	-1.2	1.4	0.3	0.8	-0.9	2.0	1.7	-0.1	-1.5	1.1
(G)	0.1	0.9	0.6	1.6	0.5	1.5	0.3	1.6	-0.1	1.1	0.6	1.7
(H)	-3.3	1.7	-0.7	0.6	-1.9	1.3	-0.4	1.9	-0.2	0.5	0.3	0.5
(I)	0.6	-1.0	1.5	-0.6	1.0	-2.0	2.3	-1.0	2.3	-1.6	1.8	-1.5
(J)	0.2	0.3	1.3	1.1	-0.3	0.2	0.6	0.2	-0.7	0.8	-0.5	-0.1
Minus	-0.3	-0.6	0.2	-0.6	-0.4	-0.3	-0.2	-0.2	-0.4	-0.1	0.1	-0.3
Turnover	9.0	7.8	10.1	10.5	11.9	11.9	11.6	11.7	12.3	13.8	10.6	11.3
	-8.9	-7.9	-9.7	-10.7	-12.1	-11.8	-12.2	-11.3	-12.1	-14.1	-10.8	-11.2
Discrepancy	0.1	-0.1	0.4	-0.2	-0.2	0.1	-0.6	0.4	0.2	-0.3	-0.2	0.1

Table 5   27

Increment in Net Domestic Saving

(figures in parentheses indicate relative series number of computer)
(in billion dollars)

	1946	1947	1948	1949	1950	1951	1952	1953	1954	1955
(A) Households: (156006105)	22.9	16.7	22.1	18.2	25.1	24.6	23.8	26.3	22.7	27.7
(D) Corporate Nonfinancial Business: (106006005)	3.3	6.9	11.8	11.3	9.3	9.9	10.0	8.3	8.7	12.2
(E) U. S. Government: Net saving = gross saving (316000105)	2.0	11.9	7.4	-3.6	8.0	5.4	-4.8	-7.6	-6.0	3.5
(F) State and Local Governments: Net saving = gross saving (206000105)	1.6	0.7	-0.3	-1.3	-1.9	-1.2	-0.9	-0.8	-2.2	-2.5
(G) Monetary Authorities: (716006001)	0.1	0.0	0.1	0.0	0.0	0.0	0.0	0.0	0.0	0.0
(H) Commercial Banks: (726006005)	0.0	0.0	0.0	0.0	0.0	0.0	0.7	0.8	0.7	1.1
(I) Nonbank Financial Institutions: (696006005)	0.0	0.0	0.0	0.0	0.0	0.0	1.1	1.3	1.3	1.2
	29.9	36.2	41.1	24.6	40.5	38.7	29.9	28.3	25.2	43.2

	1956	1957	1958	1959	1960	1961	1962	1963	1964	1965	1966
(A) Households: (156006105)	29.4	28.1	26.0	28.4	25.7	28.0	32.4	33.5	42.6	45.4	54.3
(D) Corporate Nonfinancial Business: (106006005)	10.5	10.3	8.1	12.1	10.2	10.1	12.6	13.3	17.0	20.4	22.7
(E) U. S. Government: Net saving = gross saving (316000105)	4.6	1.6	-11.2	-2.2	2.5	-4.8	-4.9	-1.0	-5.1	-0.6	-0.6
(F) State and Local Governments: Net saving = gross saving (206000105)	-2.3	-2.9	-4.0	-2.7	-1.9	-2.9	-1.4	-1.8	-2.1	-2.5	-2.7
(G) Monetary Authorities: (716006001)	0.1	0.1	0.1	-0.2	0.0	0.1	0.1	0.1	-0.5	0.2	0.0
(H) Commercial Banks: (726006005)	1.3	1.2	0.8	1.6	1.3	1.0	1.2	1.4	1.5	1.8	2.0
(I) Nonbank Financial Institutions: (696006005)	1.0	0.9	1.1	1.0	1.4	1.6	1.8	1.0	1.0	0.9	1.3
	44.6	39.3	20.9	38.0	39.2	33.1	41.8	46.5	54.4	65.6	77.0

Table 5 (continued)

Increment in Net Domestic Saving

(text according to preceding page)

	1952				1953				1954			
	I	II	III	IV	I	II	III	IV	I	II	III	IV
(A)	2.9	7.0	8.0	5.8	3.3	8.8	7.7	6.5	3.3	8.0	6.7	4.7
(D)	2.5	2.8	2.3	2.4	2.5	2.5	2.0	1.3	1.9	2.5	2.2	2.2
(E)	3.8	-2.4	-2.8	-3.4	2.6	-3.7	-1.1	-5.4	1.6	-4.0	-0.9	-2.7
(F)	-0.3	-0.6	-1.1	1.0	-0.4	-0.1	-1.2	1.0	-0.4	-0.7	-1.8	0.7
(G)	0.0	0.0	0.0	0.0	0.0	0.0	0.0	0.0	0.0	0.0	0.0	0.0
(H)	0.2	0.2	0.2	0.2	0.2	0.2	0.2	0.2	0.2	0.2	0.2	0.1
(I)	0.3	0.3	0.3	0.2	0.3	0.3	0.3	0.4	0.4	0.4	0.4	0.3
	9.4	7.3	6.9	6.2	8.5	8.0	7.9	4.0	7.0	6.4	6.8	5.3

	1955				1956				1957			
	I	II	III	IV	I	II	III	IV	I	II	III	IV
(A)	5.5	6.3	9.2	6.7	6.8	6.8	9.2	6.6	7.9	6.3	8.8	5.1
(D)	2.8	3.8	3.0	2.6	2.5	2.9	2.7	2.3	2.5	3.0	2.6	2.1
(E)	1.6	1.9	0.8	-0.8	2.9	2.3	0.8	-1.5	2.2	2.1	0.1	-2.8
(F)	-0.7	-0.9	-1.7	0.9	-0.6	-0.8	-1.8	0.9	-0.6	-0.9	-2.1	0.7
(G)	0.0	0.0	0.0	0.0	0.0	0.0	0.0	0.0	0.0	0.0	0.0	0.0
(H)	0.2	0.3	0.3	0.2	0.3	0.3	0.3	0.3	0.3	0.3	0.3	0.3
(I)	0.3	0.3	0.3	0.2	0.3	0.3	0.3	0.1	0.2	0.3	0.3	0.1
	9.7	11.7	11.9	9.8	12.2	11.8	11.5	8.7	12.5	11.1	10.0	5.5

	1958				1959				1960			
	I	II	III	IV	I	II	III	IV	I	II	III	IV
(A)	7.1	5.1	8.3	5.5	7.9	7.2	8.4	4.9	8.2	4.7	8.5	4.3
(D)	1.1	1.9	2.4	2.7	2.6	3.9	3.0	2.7	2.5	3.0	2.6	2.1
(E)	-1.4	-1.6	-3.1	-5.0	-0.6	2.2	-0.7	-3.1	1.9	4.2	-0.5	-3.1
(F)	-1.0	-1.3	-2.6	0.8	-1.1	-1.4	-1.7	1.4	-0.7	-0.7	-2.0	1.5
(G)	0.0	0.0	0.0	0.0	0.0	0.0	-0.1	-0.1	0.0	0.0	0.0	0.0
(H)	0.2	0.2	0.2	0.2	0.3	0.4	0.5	0.4	0.3	0.4	0.3	0.3
(I)	0.2	0.3	0.3	0.2	0.3	0.3	0.3	0.1	0.3	0.4	0.4	0.2
	6.2	4.6	5.5	4.4	9.4	12.6	9.7	6.3	12.5	12.0	9.3	5.3

	1961				1962				1963			
	I	II	III	IV	I	II	III	IV	I	II	III	IV
(A)	7.6	5.1	9.0	6.3	9.5	5.4	10.6	6.8	9.2	5.7	10.5	8.1
(D)	1.5	2.9	2.7	3.1	2.7	3.5	3.2	3.2	2.8	3.7	3.6	3.2
(E)	-1.6	1.5	-1.0	-3.6	-1.2	2.7	-1.2	-5.2	-0.3	4.3	-1.4	-3.6
(F)	-1.1	-0.8	-2.3	1.3	-0.6	0.0	-2.3	1.5	-0.7	-0.1	-2.5	1.5
(G)	0.0	0.0	0.0	0.0	0.0	0.0	0.0	0.0	0.0	0.0	0.0	0.0
(H)	0.3	0.3	0.3	0.2	0.2	0.4	0.3	0.3	0.3	0.4	0.4	0.3
(I)	0.4	0.5	0.5	0.2	0.4	0.5	0.5	0.3	0.3	0.4	0.3	0.0
	7.1	9.5	9.2	7.5	11.0	12.5	11.1	6.9	11.6	14.4	10.9	9.5

	1964				1965				1966			
	I	II	III	IV	I	II	III	IV	I	II	III	IV
(A)	10.8	8.5	13.4	9.9	12.6	8.0	14.6	10.2	15.4	9.0	16.9	12.9
(D)	3.7	4.9	4.5	3.9	4.5	5.5	5.2	5.2	5.1	6.2	5.6	5.8
(E)	-0.9	1.7	-1.2	-4.6	1.0	5.8	-2.2	-5.3	0.6	6.1	-3.0	-4.4
(F)	-0.6	-0.6	-2.5	1.6	-0.9	-0.8	-3.0	2.2	-0.4	0.2	-3.3	0.9
(G)	-0.1	-0.1	-0.1	-0.1	0.0	0.0	0.0	0.1	0.0	0.0	0.0	0.0
(H)	0.3	0.4	0.4	0.4	0.4	0.5	0.5	0.4	0.4	0.5	0.5	0.6
(I)	0.3	0.3	0.3	0.0	0.2	0.3	0.3	0.1	0.2	0.6	0.6	-0.1
	13.5	15.1	14.8	11.1	17.8	19.3	15.4	12.9	21.3	22.6	17.3	15.7

Table 6

Capital Consumption

(figures in parentheses indicate relative series number of computer)
(in billion dollars)

	1946	1947	1948	1949	1950	1951	1952	1953	1954	1955
(A)	Households: (156300005)									
	11.5	14.6	17.4	19.6	22.5	26.8	28.6	30.0	31.5	33.8
(C)	Noncorporate Nonfinancial Business: (166000105)									
	3.8	4.8	5.8	6.7	7.4	8.4	8.9	9.3	9.6	10.1
(D)	Corporate Nonfinancial Business: (106300005)									
	4.6	5.7	6.8	7.8	8.6	10.0	11.2	12.9	14.6	17.0
(H)	Commercial Banks: Gross Saving (726000105), less Net Saving (726006005)									
	0.6	0.6	0.6	0.7	0.7	0.8	0.1	0.1	0.1	0.1
(I)	Nonbank Financial Institutions: Gross Saving (696000105), less Net Saving (696006005)									
	0.6	0.5	1.0	1.2	1.0	1.1	0.1	0.2	0.2	0.2
	21.1	26.2	31.6	36.0	40.2	47.1	48.9	52.5	56.0	61.2

	1956	1957	1958	1959	1960	1961	1962	1963	1964	1965	1966
(A)	Households: (156300005)										
	37.4	40.8	42.6	44.5	46.3	47.8	49.7	52.4	55.8	59.3	64.3
(C)	Noncorporate Nonfinancial Business: (166000105)										
	10.8	11.5	11.7	12.3	12.5	12.6	13.2	13.5	14.0	14.4	15.9
(D)	Corporate Nonfinancial Business: (106300005)										
	18.4	20.3	21.4	22.9	24.2	25.4	29.2	31.0	32.9	34.9	38.4
(H)	Commercial Banks: Gross Saving (726000105), less Net Saving (726006005)										
	0.2	0.2	0.3	0.3	0.3	0.3	0.3	0.3	0.4	0.4	0.6
(I)	Nonbank Financial Institutions: Gross Saving (696000105), less Net Saving (696006005)										
	0.2	0.2	0.2	0.2	0.3	0.3	0.4	0.4	0.4	0.5	0.6
	67.0	73.0	76.2	80.2	83.6	86.4	92.8	97.6	103.5	109.5	119.8

Table 6 (continued)

Capital Consumption

(text according to preceding page)

	1952				1953				1954			
	I	II	III	IV	I	II	III	IV	I	II	III	IV
(A)	7.0	7.1	7.2	7.3	7.4	7.5	7.6	7.7	7.7	7.8	7.9	8.1
(C)	2.6	2.1	1.6	2.6	1.8	2.0	1.9	3.6	2.0	2.3	2.4	2.9
(D)	2.7	2.8	2.8	2.9	3.0	3.1	3.3	3.4	3.5	3.6	3.7	3.8
(H)	0.0	0.0	0.0	0.0	0.0	0.0	0.0	0.0	0.0	0.0	0.0	0.1
(I)	0.0	0.0	0.0	0.1	0.0	0.1	0.1	0.0	0.0	0.0	0.0	0.0
	12.3	12.0	11.6	12.9	12.2	12.7	12.9	14.7	13.2	13.7	14.0	14.9

	1955				1956				1957			
	I	II	III	IV	I	II	III	IV	I	II	III	IV
(A)	8.2	8.3	8.5	8.8	9.0	9.3	9.5	9.7	9.9	10.1	10.3	10.4
(C)	2.9	1.9	2.0	3.4	1.6	3.1	1.7	4.3	2.0	1.9	2.9	4.7
(D)	4.0	4.2	4.3	4.5	4.6	4.6	4.6	4.7	4.8	5.0	5.2	5.3
(H)	0.1	0.0	0.0	0.1	0.0	0.1	0.1	0.0	0.0	0.1	0.1	0.0
(I)	0.1	0.1	0.1	0.1	0.0	0.1	0.0	0.1	0.0	0.0	0.0	0.1
	15.3	14.5	14.9	16.9	15.2	17.2	15.9	18.8	16.7	17.1	18.5	20.5

	1958				1959				1960			
	I	II	III	IV	I	II	III	IV	I	II	III	IV
(A)	10.5	10.6	10.7	10.8	10.9	11.1	11.2	11.3	11.4	11.5	11.6	11.7
(C)	2.9	2.6	2.0	4.3	2.9	2.3	1.8	5.2	3.1	3.3	2.1	4.0
(D)	5.3	5.3	5.4	5.5	5.5	5.7	5.7	5.9	6.1	6.0	6.0	6.0
(H)	0.1	0.1	0.1	0.1	0.1	0.1	0.0	0.1	0.1	0.1	0.1	0.1
(I)	0.1	0.1	0.1	0.0	0.1	0.0	0.0	0.1	0.1	0.1	0.1	0.1
	18.9	18.7	18.3	20.7	19.5	19.2	18.7	22.6	20.8	21.0	19.9	21.9

	1961				1962				1963			
	I	II	III	IV	I	II	III	IV	I	II	III	IV
(A)	11.8	11.9	12.0	12.1	12.2	12.3	12.5	12.7	12.8	13.0	13.2	13.4
(C)	2.8	2.5	1.8	5.5	2.2	1.9	2.3	6.7	3.1	2.6	2.7	5.0
(D)	6.2	6.3	6.4	6.5	7.2	7.2	7.3	7.4	7 5	7.7	7.8	7.9
(H)	0.0	0.1	0.1	0.1	0.1	0.1	0.1	0.1	0.1	0.1	0.1	0.1
(I)	0.1	0.0	0.1	0.1	0.1	0.1	0.1	0.1	0.1	0.1	0.1	0.1
	20.9	20.8	20.4	24.3	21.8	21.6	22.3	27.0	23.6	23.5	23.9	26.5

	1964				1965				1966			
	I	II	III	IV	I	II	III	IV	I	II	III	IV
(A)	13.6	13.8	14.1	14.3	14.5	14.7	14.9	15.2	15.6	15.9	16.2	16.6
(C)	2.9	3.0	1.9	6.1	1.7	2.5	3.1	7.0	5.1	0.1	2.0	8.7
(D)	8.1	8.2	8.3	8.4	8.6	8.7	8.8	8.9	9.3	9.5	9.7	9.9
(H)	0.1	0.1	0.1	0.1	0.1	0.1	0.1	0.1	0.2	0.1	0.2	0.1
(I)	0.1	0.1	0.1	0.1	0.2	0.1	0.1	0.1	0.2	0.1	0.1	0.2
	24.8	25.2	24.5	29.0	25.1	26.1	27.0	31.3	30.4	25.7	28.2	35.5

Table 7   31

Gross Domestic Saving

(= Increment in Net Domestic Saving, plus Capital Consumption,
i.e., Table 5 plus Table 6)
(in billion dollars)

	1946	1947	1948	1949	1950	1951	1952	1953	1954	1955
(A)	Households:									
	34.4	31.3	39.5	37.8	47.6	51.4	52.4	56.3	54.2	61.5
(C)	Noncorporate Nonfinancial Business:									
	3.8	4.8	5.8	6.7	7.4	8.4	8.9	9.3	9.6	10.1
(D)	Corporate Nonfinancial Business:									
	7.9	12.6	18.6	19.1	17.9	19.9	21.2	21.2	23.3	29.2
(E)	U. S. Government:									
	2.0	11.9	7.4	-3.6	8.0	5.4	-4.8	-7.6	-6.0	3.5
(F)	State and Local Governments:									
	1.6	0.7	-0.3	-1.3	-1.9	-1.2	-0.9	-0.8	-2.2	-2.5
(G)	Monetary Authorities:									
	0.1	0.0	0.1	0.0	0.0	0.0	0.0	0.0	0.0	0.0
(H)	Commercial Banks:									
	0.6	0.6	0.6	0.7	0.7	0.8	0.8	0.9	0.8	1.2
(I)	Nonbank Financial Institutions:									
	0.6	0.5	1.0	1.2	1.0	1.1	1.2	1.5	1.5	1.4
	51.0	62.4	72.7	60.6	80.7	85.8	78.8	80.8	81.2	104.4

Totals in computer (909040000):

50.9	62.3	72.6	60.6	80.8	85.7	78.8	80.8	81.3	104.4

	1956	1957	1958	1959	1960	1961	1962	1963	1964	1965	1966
(A)	Households:										
	66.8	68.9	68.6	72.9	72.0	75.8	82.1	85.9	98.4	104.7	118.6
(C)	Noncorporate Nonfinancial Investment:										
	10.8	11.5	11.7	12.3	12.5	12.6	13.2	13.5	14.0	14.4	15.9
(D)	Corporate Nonfinancial Business:										
	28.9	30.6	29.5	35.0	34.4	35.5	41.8	44.3	49.9	55.3	61.1
(E)	U. S. Government:										
	4.6	1.6	-11.2	-2.2	2.5	-4.8	-4.9	-1.0	-5.1	-0.6	-0.6
(F)	State and Local Governments:										
	-2.3	-2.9	-4.0	-2.7	-1.9	-2.9	-1.4	-1.8	-2.1	-2.5	-2.7
(G)	Monetary Authorities:										
	0.1	0.1	0.1	-0.2	0.0	0.1	0.1	0.1	-0.5	0.2	0.0
(H)	Commercial Banks:										
	1.5	1.4	1.1	1.9	1.6	1.3	1.5	1.7	1.9	2.2	2.6
(I)	Nonbank Financial Institutions:										
	1.2	1.1	1.3	1.2	1.7	1.9	2.2	1.4	1.4	1.4	1.9
	111.6	112.3	97.1	118.2	122.8	119.5	134.6	144.1	157.9	175.1	196.8

Totals in computer (909040000):

111.6	112.0	97.1	118.1	122.9	119.7	134.5	144.1	158.0	175.1	196.8

Table 7 (continued)

Gross Domestic Saving

(text according to preceding page)

	1952				1953				1954			
	I	II	III	IV	I	II	III	IV	I	II	III	IV
(A)	9.9	14.1	15.2	13.1	10.7	16.3	15.3	14.2	11.0	15.8	14.6	12.8
(C)	2.6	2.1	1.6	2.6	1.8	2.0	1.9	3.6	2.0	2.3	2.4	2.9
(D)	5.2	5.6	5.1	5.3	5.5	5.6	5.3	4.7	5.4	6.1	5.9	6.0
(E)	3.8	-2.4	-2.8	-3.4	2.6	-3.7	-1.1	-5.4	1.6	-4.0	-0.9	-2.7
(F)	-0.3	-0.6	-1.1	1.0	-0.4	-0.1	-1.2	1.0	-0.4	-0.7	-1.8	0.7
(G)	0.0	0.0	0.0	0.0	0.0	0.0	0.0	0.0	0.0	0.0	0.0	0.0
(H)	0.2	0.2	0.2	0.2	0.2	0.2	0.2	0.2	0.2	0.2	0.2	0.2
(I)	0.3	0.3	0.3	0.3	0.3	0.4	0.4	0.4	0.4	0.4	0.4	0.3
	21.7	19.3	18.5	19.1	20.7	20.7	20.8	18.7	20.2	20.1	20.8	20.2
Totals in computer												
	21.8	19.4	18.6	19.0	20.7	20.7	20.8	18.6	20.2	20.1	20.8	20.2

	1955				1956				1957			
	I	II	III	IV	I	II	III	IV	I	II	III	IV
(A)	13.7	14.6	17.7	15.5	15.8	16.1	18.7	16.3	17.8	16.4	19.1	15.5
(C)	2.9	1.9	2.0	3.4	1.6	3.1	1.7	4.3	2.0	1.9	2.9	4.7
(D)	6.8	8.0	7.3	7.1	7.1	7.5	7.3	7.0	7.3	8.0	7.8	7.4
(E)	1.6	1.9	0.8	-0.8	2.9	2.3	0.8	-1.5	2.2	2.1	0.1	-2.8
(F)	-0.7	-0.9	-1.7	0.9	-0.6	-0.8	-1.8	0.9	-0.6	-0.9	-2.1	0.7
(G)	0.0	0.0	0.0	0.0	0.0	0.0	0.0	0.0	0.0	0.0	0.0	0.0
(H)	0.3	0.3	0.3	0.3	0.3	0.4	0.4	0.3	0.3	0.4	0.4	0.3
(I)	0.4	0.4	0.4	0.3	0.3	0.4	0.3	0.2	0.3	0.3	0.3	0.2
	25.0	26.2	26.8	26.7	27.4	29.0	27.4	27.5	29.2	28.2	28.5	26.0
Totals in computer												
	24.8	26.2	26.8	26.6	27.6	29.0	27.5	27.5	29.3	28.2	28.5	26.0

	1958				1959				1960			
	I	II	III	IV	I	II	III	IV	I	II	III	IV
(A)	17.6	15.7	19.0	16.3	18.8	18.3	19.6	16.2	19.6	16.2	20.1	16.0
(C)	2.9	2.6	2.0	4.3	2.9	2.3	1.8	5.2	3.1	3.3	2.1	4.0
(D)	6.4	7.2	7.8	8.2	8.1	9.6	8.7	8.6	8.6	9.0	8.6	8.1
(E)	-1.4	-1.6	-3.1	-5.0	-0.6	2.2	-0.7	-3.1	1.9	4.2	-0.5	-3.1
(F)	-1.0	-1.3	-2.6	0.8	-1.1	-1.4	-1.7	1.4	-0.7	-0.7	-2.0	1.5
(G)	0.0	0.0	0.0	0.0	0.0	0.0	0.1	0.1	0.0	0.0	0.0	0.0
(H)	0.3	0.3	0.3	0.3	0.4	0.5	0.5	0.5	0.4	0.5	0.4	0.4
(I)	0.3	0.4	0.4	0.2	0.4	0.3	0.3	0.2	0.4	0.5	0.5	0.3
	25.1	23.3	23.8	25.1	28.9	31.8	28.4	28.9	33.3	33.0	29.2	27.2
Totals in computer												
	25.0	23.2	23.7	25.1	28.9	31.7	28.6	29.0	33.2	33.2	29.4	27.1

Table 7 (continued)   33

Gross Domestic Saving

(text according to preceding pages)

	1 9 6 1				1 9 6 2				1 9 6 3			
	I	II	III	IV	I	II	III	IV	I	II	III	IV
(A)	19.4	17.0	21.0	18.4	21.7	17.7	23.1	19.5	22.0	18.7	23.7	21.5
(C)	2.8	2.5	1.8	5.5	2.2	1.9	2.3	6.7	3.1	2.6	2.7	5.0
(D)	7.7	9.2	9.1	9.6	9.9	10.7	10.5	10.6	10.3	11.4	11.4	11.1
(E)	-1.6	1.5	-1.0	-3.6	-1.2	2.7	-1.2	-5.2	-0.3	4.3	-1.4	-3.6
(F)	-1.1	-0.8	-2.3	1.3	-0.6	0.0	-2.3	1.5	-0.7	-0.1	-2.5	1.5
(G)	0.0	0.0	0.0	0.0	0.0	0.0	0.0	0.0	0.0	0.0	0.0	0.0
(H)	0.3	0.4	0.4	0.3	0.3	0.5	0.4	0.4	0.4	0.5	0.5	0.4
(I)	0.5	0.5	0.6	0.3	0.5	0.6	0.6	0.4	0.4	0.5	0.4	0.1
	28.0	30.3	29.6	31.8	32.8	34.1	33.4	33.9	35.2	37.9	34.8	36.0
Totals in computer												
	28.0	30.4	29.6	31.7	32.9	34.2	33.4	34.0	35.3	37.9	34.7	36.2

	1 9 6 4				1 9 6 5				1 9 6 6			
	I	II	III	IV	I	II	III	IV	I	II	III	IV
(A)	24.4	22.3	27.5	24.2	27.1	22.7	29.5	25.4	31.0	24.9	33.1	29.5
(C)	2.9	3.0	1.9	6.1	1.7	2.5	3.1	7.0	5.1	0.1	2.0	8.7
(D)	11.8	13.1	12.8	12.3	13.1	14.2	14.0	14.1	14.4	15.7	15.3	15.7
(E)	-0.9	1.7	-1.2	-4.6	1.0	5.8	-2.2	-5.3	0.6	6.1	-3.0	-4.4
(F)	-0.6	-0.6	-2.5	1.6	-0.9	-0.8	-3.0	2.2	-0.4	0.2	-3.3	0.9
(G)	-0.1	-0.1	-0.1	-0.1	0.0	0.0	0.0	0.1	0.0	0.0	0.0	0.0
(H)	0.4	0.5	0.5	0.5	0.5	0.6	0.6	0.5	0.6	0.6	0.7	0.7
(I)	0.4	0.4	0.4	0.1	0.4	0.4	0.4	0.2	0.4	0.7	0.7	0.1
	38.3	40.3	39.3	40.1	42.9	45.4	42.4	44.2	51.7	48.3	45.5	51.2
Totals in computer												
	38.3	40.3	39.4	40.0	42.9	45.4	42.5	44.3	51.7	48.3	45.5	51.2

Table 8

Increment in Net Domestic Investment

(= Increment in Net Domestic Saving, less Increment in Net Domestic Financial
Investment, for each Sector, i.e., Table 5 less Table 4)

(in billion dollars)

	1946	1947	1948	1949	1950	1951	1952	1953	1954	1955
(A) Households:	13.7	15.9	25.1	19.9	29.2	20.6	20.3	22.0	18.6	27.0
(C) Noncorporate Nonfinancial Business:	2.3	2.2	0.9	0.8	3.5	2.1	1.7	0.3	1.4	3.1
(D) Corporate Nonfinancial Business:	11.9	11.3	15.8	9.9	10.3	14.9	15.6	9.5	11.7	13.3
(E) U. S. Government:	1.6	5.0	0.0	-2.3	6.4	3.5	-3.0	0.5	-3.5	1.8
(F) State and Local Governments:	1.5	-0.3	-0.7	-1.1	-2.5	-2.0	-0.4	-0.5	-1.2	-0.7
(G) Monetary Authorities:	0.3	0.4	-0.6	4.3	-2.0	-3.4	-1.0	-1.8	1.1	0.0
(H) Commercial Banks:	-1.5	1.4	2.8	-6.0	-1.4	2.7	-1.5	-0.7	-1.6	0.2
(I) Nonbank Financial Institutions:	-1.3	-1.2	-1.2	-0.9	-1.3	-1.1	-0.4	-0.5	0.3	-0.4
(J) Rest of the World:	0.7	0.9	-0.6	-0.1	-1.7	0.4	-1.5	-0.8	-1.1	-0.7
Minus, according to Table 4:	0.0	0.0	0.1	0.0	0.4	0.4	0.2	0.2	0.1	-0.2
Totals:	29.2	35.6	41.6	24.5	40.9	38.1	30.0	28.2	25.8	43.4
Increment in Net Domestic Saving, according to Table 5:	29.9	36.2	41.1	24.6	40.5	38.7	29.9	28.3	25.2	43.2
Discrepancy, according to Table 4:	-0.7	-0.6	0.5	-0.1	0.4	-0.6	0.1	-0.1	0.6	0.2

Table 8 (continued)   35

Increment in Net Domestic Investment

(text according to preceding page)

	1956	1957	1958	1959	1960	1961	1962	1963	1964	1965	1966
(A)	23.8	18.6	15.3	22.0	22.7	17.7	16.6	16.9	23.2	22.3	30.8
(C)	2.0	1.3	1.7	5.7	3.3	4.1	6.6	8.1	8.3	9.9	9.7
(D)	23.1	18.8	11.5	13.3	20.4	13.3	19.9	20.1	27.5	38.9	42.0
(E)	-2.0	-1.5	-3.7	2.2	-2.1	0.6	-0.7	2.8	-1.1	1.5	-0.8
(F)	-0.8	-0.7	-0.8	-0.8	-1.7	-2.0	-1.3	-1.9	-2.0	-4.6	-4.2
(G)	0.0	0.8	-2.2	-0.6	-0.7	-1.4	-1.8	-2.5	-3.7	-3.6	-3.3
(H)	-0.1	2.0	-0.2	-1.5	-3.2	0.0	2.5	2.7	3.2	0.4	1.2
(I)	-0.5	-0.2	-0.2	-0.3	0.6	1.3	1.1	0.3	0.3	0.7	0.2
(J)	-1.1	-0.7	-0.9	-2.1	-1.4	-1.4	-1.9	-1.7	-2.6	-0.6	0.6
Minus	0.5	0.9	1.0	0.4	1.3	1.1	0.8	1.6	1.2	1.1	0.6
Totals	44.9	39.3	21.5	38.3	39.2	33.3	41.8	46.4	54.3	66.0	76.8

Increment in Net Domestic Saving

	1956	1957	1958	1959	1960	1961	1962	1963	1964	1965	1966
	44.6	39.3	20.9	38.0	39.2	33.1	41.8	46.5	54.4	65.6	77.0

Discrepancy

	1956	1957	1958	1959	1960	1961	1962	1963	1964	1965	1966
	0.3	0.0	0.6	0.3	0.0	0.2	0.0	-0.1	-0.1	0.4	-0.2

	1952				1953				1954			
	I	II	III	IV	I	II	III	IV	I	II	III	IV
(A)	3.0	8.2	5.3	3.9	1.8	8.5	6.3	5.3	1.7	7.3	4.6	5.0
(C)	0.7	0.6	0.7	-0.2	0.4	0.4	0.4	-1.1	0.6	0.6	0.4	-0.3
(D)	6.9	3.1	3.0	2.9	6.4	2.9	0.9	-0.7	7.3	4.6	0.7	-0.7
(E)	-1.1	-3.1	0.1	1.2	-1.3	-1.9	2.6	1.2	-4.4	-5.2	2.8	3.2
(F)	-0.4	-0.4	-0.6	1.0	-0.2	-0.4	-0.7	0.9	-0.8	-0.2	-0.9	0.9
(G)	1.2	-0.4	-0.6	-1.1	0.8	-1.0	0.0	-1.5	1.7	-0.3	0.5	-0.8
(H)	-0.4	-0.5	0.8	-1.4	0.7	-0.3	-0.5	-0.6	1.4	-0.4	-1.1	-1.5
(I)	-0.6	0.2	-0.2	0.0	-0.1	0.1	-0.3	-0.4	0.2	0.5	-0.1	-0.3
(J)	-0.2	-0.5	-0.8	-0.1	0.0	-0.2	-0.5	-0.3	-0.5	-0.2	-0.2	-0.1
Minus	0.1	0.2	-0.1	0.0	0.0	-0.1	0.0	0.1	0.2	-0.1	0.1	0.0
Totals	9.2	7.4	7.6	6.2	8.5	8.0	8.2	2.9	7.4	6.6	6.8	5.4

Increment in Net Domestic Saving:

	I	II	III	IV	I	II	III	IV	I	II	III	IV
	9.4	7.3	6.9	6.2	8.5	8.0	7.9	4.0	7.0	6.4	6.8	5.3

Discrepancy

	I	II	III	IV	I	II	III	IV	I	II	III	IV
	-0.2	0.1	0.7	0.0	0.0	0.0	0.3	-1.1	0.4	0.2	0.0	0.1

	1955				1956				1957			
	I	II	III	IV	I	II	III	IV	I	II	III	IV
(A)	3.9	7.9	7.6	7.3	3.4	7.0	7.6	6.2	3.2	5.3	6.6	3.2
(C)	1.0	1.2	0.9	0.0	0.8	1.0	0.6	-0.6	0.8	0.5	0.4	-0.5
(D)	5.6	4.7	2.4	0.4	10.4	7.6	4.3	0.7	8.1	7.0	2.9	0.6
(E)	-2.9	-2.1	3.2	3.6	-4.0	-3.0	1.7	3.4	-2.7	-2.5	2.4	1.5
(F)	-0.3	-0.9	-0.8	0.9	-0.5	-0.5	-0.7	1.0	-0.3	-0.7	-1.0	1.4
(G)	1.6	-0.4	-0.1	-1.1	1.3	-0.1	0.1	-1.4	2.0	0.0	-0.4	-1.0
(H)	0.9	0.5	0.1	-1.6	1.3	-0.3	-0.7	-0.3	1.2	0.7	-0.7	0.7
(I)	-0.1	0.4	-1.1	0.2	-0.1	0.4	-1.2	0.3	-0.3	0.4	-0.5	0.1
(J)	0.0	-0.3	-0.5	-0.1	-0.4	-0.3	-0.3	-0.3	0.3	-0.3	-0.1	-0.4
Minus	-0.1	-0.1	0.0	-0.1	0.1	0.1	0.1	0.2	0.3	0.4	0.1	0.2
Totals	9.6	10.9	11.7	9.5	12.3	11.9	11.5	9.2	12.6	10.8	9.7	5.8

Increment in Net Domestic Saving:

	I	II	III	IV	I	II	III	IV	I	II	III	IV
	9.7	11.7	11.9	9.8	12.2	11.8	11.5	8.7	12.5	11.1	10.0	5.5

Discrepancy

	I	II	III	IV	I	II	III	IV	I	II	III	IV
	-0.1	-0.8	-0.2	-0.3	0.1	0.1	0.0	0.5	0.1	-0.3	-0.3	0.3

Table 8 (continued)

Increment in Net Domestic Investment

(text according to preceding pages)

	1 9 5 8				1 9 5 9				1 9 6 0			
	I	II	III	IV	I	II	III	IV	I	II	III	IV
(A)	2.1	6.4	3.1	3.6	4.5	6.8	7.4	3.3	5.2	7.9	5.6	4.1
(C)	0.5	0.3	0.5	0.6	1.2	2.5	1.3	0.4	1.1	1.1	0.5	0.3
(D)	6.9	3.2	2.1	-0.5	5.6	3.9	3.2	0.7	8.5	5.1	4.8	1.9
(E)	-4.9	-3.5	2.6	2.0	-1.3	0.9	1.5	0.8	-1.9	-1.3	0.3	0.6
(F)	-0.3	-0.8	-1.1	1.0	-0.4	-0.5	-1.0	1.2	-0.9	-0.6	-1.1	0.9
(G)	0.6	-1.9	0.5	-1.4	0.9	-0.7	-0.4	-0.4	1.5	-1.3	-0.5	-0.4
(H)	1.6	-0.2	-0.7	-1.0	0.0	-0.4	-0.7	-0.4	-0.5	0.1	0.3	-2.9
(I)	-0.1	0.6	-1.1	0.4	-0.7	0.4	-0.9	0.7	-0.6	0.9	-0.4	0.9
(J)	-0.1	0.3	-0.3	-0.7	-0.2	-0.7	-0.8	-0.4	-0.1	-0.2	-0.5	-0.6
Minus	0.3	0.4	0.1	0.2	0.2	0.0	0.2	-0.1	0.4	0.3	0.4	0.2
Totals	6.6	4.8	5.7	4.2	9.8	12.2	9.8	5.8	12.7	12.0	9.4	5.0
Increment in Net Domestic Saving	6.2	4.6	5.5	4.4	9.4	12.6	9.7	6.3	12.5	12.0	9.3	5.3
Discrepancy	0.4	0.2	0.2	-0.2	0.4	-0.4	0.1	-0.5	0.2	0.0	0.1	-0.3

	1 9 6 1				1 9 6 2				1 9 6 3			
	I	II	III	IV	I	II	III	IV	I	II	III	IV
(A)	3.2	6.7	4.1	3.8	2.2	4.9	4.9	4.3	2.7	6.1	4.3	3.9
(C)	0.9	1.3	1.5	0.4	1.1	2.4	1.9	1.1	1.4	3.1	1.8	1.8
(D)	4.5	2.9	4.9	1.1	6.7	6.4	6.3	0.5	7.7	4.7	5.9	1.7
(E)	-2.5	-0.7	1.8	2.1	-1.3	-1.4	0.3	1.7	-0.5	0.3	0.9	2.1
(F)	-0.9	-1.2	-1.2	1.2	0.2	-0.3	-1.3	0.3	-0.8	-0.3	-0.4	-0.4
(G)	0.7	-0.5	-0.5	-1.0	-0.3	-0.4	-0.3	-0.9	0.2	-1.1	-0.4	-1.3
(H)	1.7	-1.1	0.2	-0.8	3.2	-0.5	0.1	-0.2	1.4	0.3	0.3	0.7
(I)	-0.4	1.3	-0.7	1.2	-0.8	2.1	-0.9	0.5	-0.4	1.6	-1.6	0.8
(J)	-0.1	0.4	-1.1	-0.6	-0.3	-0.3	-0.1	-1.0	-0.2	-0.9	-0.2	-0.2
Minus	0.5	0.3	0.2	0.2	0.2	0.2	0.0	0.7	0.5	0.6	0.2	0.2
Totals	7.6	9.4	9.2	7.6	10.9	13.1	10.9	7.0	12.0	14.4	10.8	9.3
Increment in Net Domestic Saving	7.1	9.5	9.2	7.5	11.0	12.5	11.1	6.9	11.6	14.4	10.9	9.5
Discrepancy	0.5	-0.1	0.0	0.1	-0.1	0.6	-0.2	0.1	0.4	0.0	-0.1	-0.2

	1 9 6 4				1 9 6 5				1 9 6 6			
	I	II	III	IV	I	II	III	IV	I	II	III	IV
(A)	4.5	7.8	6.9	4.1	4.8	7.3	6.2	4.2	7.1	9.7	9.1	4.9
(C)	1.7	3.5	1.9	1.2	2.5	3.5	2.3	1.5	3.6	4.1	1.2	0.9
(D)	7.3	7.3	7.2	5.9	11.5	11.5	10.2	5.9	12.2	13.7	10.1	6.0
(E)	-2.4	-2.5	2.0	1.7	-1.3	-1.1	1.2	2.6	0.6	-5.3	0.1	3.8
(F)	-0.9	-0.2	-1.3	0.2	-1.2	-1.6	-2.1	0.2	-2.1	0.3	-1.8	-0.2
(G)	-0.2	-1.0	-0.7	-1.7	-0.5	-1.5	-0.3	-1.5	0.1	-1.1	-0.6	-1.7
(H)	3.6	-1.3	1.1	-0.2	2.3	-1.3	0.9	-1.5	0.6	0.0	0.2	0.1
(I)	-0.3	1.3	-1.2	0.6	-0.8	2.3	-2.0	1.1	-2.1	2.2	-1.2	1.4
(J)	-0.2	-0.3	-1.3	-1.1	0.3	-0.2	-0.6	-0.2	0.7	-0.8	0.5	0.1
Minus	0.3	0.6	-0.2	0.6	0.4	0.3	0.2	0.2	0.4	0.1	-0.1	0.3
Totals	13.4	15.2	14.4	11.3	18.0	19.2	16.0	12.5	21.1	22.9	17.5	15.6
Increment in Net Domestic Saving	13.5	15.1	14.8	11.1	17.8	19.3	15.4	12.9	21.3	22.6	17.3	15.7
Discrepancy	-0.1	0.1	-0.4	0.2	0.2	-0.1	0.6	-0.4	-0.2	0.3	0.2	-0.1

Table 9　　　　　　　　　　　37

Gross Domestic Investment

(figures in parentheses indicate relative series number of computer)
(in billion dollars)

	1946	1947	1948	1949	1950	1951	1952	1953	1954	1955
(A) Households: (155090505)	36.8	35.0	40.7	39.8	51.3	58.1	54.4	59.4	57.3	66.1
(C) Noncorporate Nonfinancial Business: (165090005)	3.8	4.8	5.8	6.7	7.4	8.4	8.9	9.3	9.6	10.1
(D) Corporate Nonfinancial Business: (105090005)	12.6	16.1	17.6	14.7	19.8	17.1	17.2	18.0	21.1	26.2
(E) U. S. Government: (315000505)	1.1	13.9	8.9	-3.3	7.3	5.3	-5.2	-7.9	-5.5	3.9
(F) State and Local Governments: (205000005)	-0.4	0.5	-0.1	-0.9	0.0	0.2	-1.5	-1.3	-2.4	-2.8
(G) Monetary Authorities: Net Saving (716006001)	0.1	0.0	0.1	0.0	0.0	0.0	0.0	0.0	0.0	0.0
(H) Commercial Banks: Gross Saving (726000105), less Discrepancy (727005005)	0.6	0.5	0.3	0.5	0.6	0.5	0.5	0.6	0.8	0.7
(I) Nonbank Financial Institutions: Gross Saving (696000105), less Discrepancy (697005005)	0.3	0.6	1.1	0.9	1.3	0.8	1.3	1.8	1.7	1.6
	54.9	71.4	74.4	58.4	87.7	90.4	75.6	79.9	82.6	105.8

	1956	1957	1958	1959	1960	1961	1962	1963	1964	1965	1966
(A) Households: (155090505)	70.7	73.6	73.5	75.5	72.7	77.9	87.8	9.15	102.1	111.6	112.9
(C) Noncorporate Nonfinancial Business: (165090005)	10.8	11.5	11.7	12.3	12.5	12.6	13.2	13.5	14.0	14.4	15.9
(D) Corporate Nonfinancial Business: (105090005)	26.6	29.2	28.3	32.2	29.6	33.2	36.8	41.2	45.7	50.5	58.7
(E) U. S. Government: (315000505)	3.8	1.5	-10.7	-2.0	2.3	-5.0	-4.2	-1.1	-2.4	-2.0	-0.1
(F) State and Local Governments: (205000005)	-2.9	-4.0	-5.1	-3.8	-2.4	-3.3	-2.5	-2.6	-3.6	-2.0	-2.2
(G) Monetary Authorities: Net Saving (716006001)	0.1	0.1	0.1	-0.2	0.0	0.1	0.1	0.1	-0.5	0.2	0.0
(H) Commercial Banks: Gross Saving (726000106), less Discrepancy (727005005)	0.8	0.8	1.1	0.9	1.3	1.3	1.2	1.2	1.8	1.7	1.7
(I) Nonbank Financial Institutions: Gross Saving (696000105), less Discrepancy (697005005)	1.1	1.3	1.4	1.5	1.4	1.8	2.6	1.9	2.3	2.6	1.9
	111.0	114.0	100.3	116.4	117.4	118.6	135.0	145.7	159.4	177.0	188.8

38

Table 9 (continued)

Gross Domestic Investment

(text according to preceding page)

	1952				1953				1954			
	I	II	III	IV	I	II	III	IV	I	II	III	IV
(A)	11.3	11.5	14.8	16.8	14.2	14.2	15.1	15.9	13.9	13.6	14.5	15.2
(C)	2.6	2.1	1.6	2.6	1.8	2.0	1.9	3.6	2.0	2.3	2.4	2.9
(D)	3.6	5.2	4.2	4.1	4.3	5.3	5.0	3.4	4.0	6.2	5.5	5.4
(E)	2.9	-1.6	-2.2	-4.3	2.1	-3.4	-1.0	-5.6	1.5	-2.5	-1.3	-3.2
(F)	-0.2	-0.6	-0.6	-0.2	-0.4	0.2	-0.8	-0.3	-0.1	-0.9	-1.1	-0.3
(G)	0.0	0.0	0.0	0.0	0.0	0.0	0.0	0.0	0.0	0.0	0.0	0.0
(H)	0.1	0.2	0.1	0.2	0.0	0.2	0.2	0.0	0.2	0.3	0.1	0.3
(I)	0.4	0.0	0.5	0.3	0.3	0.3	0.4	0.8	0.2	0.5	0.3	0.7
	20.7	16.8	18.4	19.5	22.3	18.8	20.8	17.8	21.7	19.5	20.4	21.0

	1955				1956				1957			
	I	II	III	IV	I	II	III	IV	I	II	III	IV
(A)	15.8	14.5	18.2	17.6	18.7	15.0	17.9	19.0	20.1	17.0	17.0	19.5
(C)	2.9	1.9	2.0	3.4	1.6	3.1	1.7	4.3	2.0	1.9	2.9	4.7
(D)	5.3	7.8	6.9	6.1	6.0	7.4	6.2	6.9	6.3	8.0	7.7	7.2
(E)	1.9	2.3	0.7	-1.0	2.8	2.5	0.6	-2.1	2.6	1.9	0.3	-3.3
(F)	-0.9	-0.5	-1.2	-0.3	-0.7	-0.7	-1.3	-0.3	-0.8	-0.7	-1.4	-1.1
(G)	0.0	0.0	0.0	0.0	0.0	0.0	0.0	0.0	0.0	0.0	0.0	0.0
(H)	0.3	0.2	0.2	0.2	0.1	0.3	0.3	-0.1	0.2	0.3	0.3	0.1
(I)	0.3	0.3	0.6	0.5	0.0	0.3	0.5	0.3	0.1	0.2	0.5	0.4
	25.6	26.5	27.4	26.5	28.5	27.9	25.9	28.0	30.5	28.6	27.3	27.5

	1958				1959				1960			
	I	II	III	IV	I	II	III	IV	I	II	III	IV
(A)	19.7	14.1	20.5	19.3	19.4	17.6	17.7	20.8	19.7	14.9	19.1	19.1
(C)	2.9	2.6	2.0	4.3	2.9	2.3	1.8	5.2	3.1	3.3	2.1	4.0
(D)	5.3	7.0	7.6	8.5	6.8	9.1	8.6	7.6	7.3	6.3	9.0	7.0
(E)	-0.3	-1.5	-3.7	-5.2	-0.1	2.1	-0.5	-3.4	2.0	3.7	-0.2	-3.2
(F)	-1.4	-1.2	-2.0	-0.6	-1.1	-1.3	-1.1	-0.2	-0.5	-0.8	-1.3	0.1
(G)	0.0	0.0	0.0	0.0	0.0	0.0	-0.1	-0.1	0.0	0.0	0.0	0.0
(H)	0.4	0.3	0.4	0.1	0.1	0.3	0.3	0.1	0.3	0.4	0.3	0.3
(I)	0.0	0.2	0.4	0.8	0.3	0.6	0.3	0.4	-0.1	0.3	0.4	0.8
	26.6	21.5	25.2	27.2	28.3	30.7	27.0	30.4	31.8	28.1	29.4	28.1

	1961				1962				1963			
	I	II	III	IV	I	II	III	IV	I	II	III	IV
(A)	20.0	15.4	20.5	22.1	23.8	18.0	22.0	24.0	23.4	17.8	23.9	26.4
(C)	2.8	2.5	1.8	5.5	2.2	1.9	2.3	6.7	3.1	2.6	2.7	5.0
(D)	7.0	9.1	8.6	8.4	7.5	10.0	9.3	10.0	8.9	10.3	11.3	10.8
(E)	-1.2	0.1	0.2	-4.0	-1.5	3.3	-0.9	-5.2	-0.8	4.2	-0.8	-3.7
(F)	-0.9	-0.3	-1.6	-0.4	-1.3	-0.3	-1.5	0.6	-0.6	-0.5	-2.7	1.2
(G)	0.0	0.0	0.0	0.0	0.0	0.0	0.0	0.0	0.0	0.0	0.0	0.0
(H)	0.1	0.6	0.3	0.4	0.1	0.6	0.1	0.5	0.3	0.5	0.1	0.4
(I)	0.2	0.4	0.4	0.8	0.2	0.6	0.6	1.1	0.1	0.3	0.7	0.8
	28.0	27.8	30.2	32.8	31.0	34.1	31.9	37.7	34.4	35.2	35.2	40.9

	1964				1965				1966			
	I	II	III	IV	I	II	III	IV	I	II	III	IV
(A)	25.7	21.5	25.9	28.9	28.1	22.0	30.0	31.5	29.0	22.3	30 0	31.6
(C)	2.9	3.0	1.9	6.1	1.7	2.5	3.1	7.0	5.1	0.1	2.0	8.7
(D)	10.5	11.8	12.2	11.2	11.1	13.0	13.2	13.2	12.0	15.1	15.7	16.0
(E)	0.3	3.2	-1.8	-4.1	0.9	5.3	-2.3	-5.9	-0.3	7.1	-0.8	-6.1
(F)	-0.8	-1.2	-2.1	0.5	-0.8	-0.4	-2.0	1.1	0.8	-0.9	-2.3	0.2
(G)	-0.1	-0.1	-0.1	-0.1	0.0	0.0	0.0	0.1	0.0	0.0	0.0	0.0
(H)	0.2	0.9	0.1	0.6	0.2	0.9	0.1	0.5	0.2	0.8	0.2	0.5
(I)	0.1	0.3	0.7	1.0	0.5	0.4	0.7	1.0	0.1	0.4	0.7	0.7
	38.8	39.4	36.8	44.1	41.7	43.7	42.8	48.5	46.9	44.9	45.5	51.6

Table 10   39

<u>Discrepancy</u> <u>Between</u> <u>Gross</u> <u>Domestic</u> <u>Saving</u> <u>and</u> <u>Gross</u> <u>Domestic</u> <u>Investment</u>
<u>(according to computer)</u>

(figures in parentheses indicate relative series number of computer)
(in billion dollars)

	1946	1947	1948	1949	1950	1951	1952	1953	1954	1955	
(A)	Households: (157005005)										
	-2.4	-3.8	-1.2	-2.1	-3.7	-6.7	-2.0	-3.0	-3.0	-4.6	
(D)	Corporate Nonfinancial Business: (107005005)										
	-4.8	-3.5	1.0	4.4	-1.9	2.8	4.0	3.1	2.2	2.9	
(E)	U. S. Government: (317005005)										
	0.9	-2.1	-1.5	-0.2	0.7	0.0	0.4	0.3	-0.5	-0.4	
(F)	State and Local Governments: (207005005)										
	2.0	0.1	-0.3	-0.4	-1.9	-1.4	0.6	0.5	0.2	0.4	
(H)	Commercial Banks: (727005005)										
	0.0	0.1	0.3	0.2	0.1	0.3	0.3	0.3	0.0	0.5	
(I)	Nonbank Financial Institutions: (697005005)										
	0.3	-0.1	-0.1	0.3	-0.3	0.3	-0.1	-0.3	-0.2	-0.2	
	-4.0	-9.3	-1.8	2.2	-7.0	-4.7	3.2	0.9	-1.3	-1.4	

	1956	1957	1958	1959	1960	1961	1962	1963	1964	1965	1966
(A)	Households: (157005005)										
	-3.9	-4.7	-4.9	-2.6	-0.7	-2.1	-5.7	-5.6	-3.7	-6.9	5.7
(D)	Corporate Nonfinancial Business: (107005005)										
	2.3	1.3	1.2	2.8	4.8	2.4	5.0	3.1	4.2	4.8	2.3
(E)	U. S. Government: (317005005)										
	0.8	0.1	-0.4	-0.2	0.2	0.3	-0.6	0.1	-2.6	1.4	-0.5
(F)	State and Local Governments: (207005005)										
	0.6	1.1	1.1	1.1	0.5	0.4	1.1	0.8	1.5	-0.4	-0.5
(H)	Commercial Banks: (727005005)										
	0.7	0.6	0.0	1.0	0.3	0.0	0.3	0.5	0.1	0.5	0.9
(I)	Nonbank Financial Institutions: (697005005)										
	0.1	-0.2	-0.1	-0.3	0.3	0.1	-0.4	-0.5	-0.9	-1.2	0.0
	0.6	-1.8	-3.1	1.8	5.4	1.1	-0.3	-1.6	-1.4	-1.8	7.9

Table 10 (continued)

Discrepancy Between Gross Domestic Saving and Gross Domestic Investment
(according to computer)

(text according to preceding page)

	1 9 5 2				1 9 5 3				1 9 5 4			
	I	II	III	IV	I	II	III	IV	I	II	III	IV
(A)	-1.3	2.6	0.4	-3.7	-3.6	2.1	0.2	-1.8	-2.9	2.1	0.1	-2.4
(D)	1.6	0.3	0.9	1.1	1.1	0.4	0.3	1.3	1.3	-0.1	0.4	0.6
(E)	0.9	-0.8	-0.6	0.9	0.5	-0.4	0.0	0.2	0.1	-1.5	0.3	0.5
(F)	-0.1	0.0	-0.4	1.2	0.0	-0.3	-0.5	1.3	-0.3	0.2	-0.7	1.0
(H)	0.1	0.0	0.1	0.0	0.2	0.0	0.0	0.2	0.0	-0.1	0.1	-0.1
(I)	-0.1	0.3	-0.2	0.0	0.0	0.1	0.0	-0.4	0.2	-0.1	0.1	-0.4
	1.1	2.4	0.2	-0.5	-1.8	1.9	0.0	0.8	-1.6	0.5	0.3	-0.8

	1 9 5 5				1 9 5 6				1 9 5 7			
	I	II	III	IV	I	II	III	IV	I	II	III	IV
(A)	-2.1	0.1	-0.5	-2.1	-2.9	1.1	0.7	-2.8	-2.3	-0.6	2.1	-4.0
(D)	1.4	0.1	0.4	0.9	1.1	0.1	1.2	0.0	1.0	0.0	0.1	0.3
(E)	-0.4	-0.4	0.1	0.2	0.1	-0.1	0.3	0.6	-0.4	0.1	-0.1	0.5
(F)	0.1	-0.3	-0.6	1.2	0.1	-0.1	-0.5	1.2	0.2	-0.2	-0.7	1.8
(H)	0.0	0.1	0.1	0.1	0.2	0.1	0.1	0.4	0.1	0.1	0.1	0.2
(I)	0.1	0.1	-0.2	-0.2	0.3	0.1	-0.2	-0.1	0.1	0.1	-0.2	-0.2
	-0.9	-0.3	-0.7	0.1	-1.1	1.2	1.6	-0.7	-1.3	-0.5	1.3	-1.4

	1 9 5 8				1 9 5 9				1 9 6 0			
	I	II	III	IV	I	II	III	IV	I	II	III	IV
(A)	-2.0	1.6	-1.4	-3.0	-0.6	0.7	1.8	-4.6	-0.1	1.4	1.0	-3.1
(D)	1.1	0.2	0.1	-0.3	1.2	0.5	0.1	1.0	1.3	2.7	-0.4	1.2
(E)	-1.2	-0.1	0.6	0.2	-0.4	0.1	-0.2	0.3	-0.1	0.5	-0.2	0.1
(F)	0.3	0.0	-0.6	1.4	0.1	0.0	-0.6	1.7	-0.2	0.1	-0.7	1.3
(H)	-0.1	0.0	-0.1	0.2	0.3	0.2	0.2	0.4	0.1	0.1	0.1	0.1
(I)	0.3	0.2	0.0	-0.6	0.1	-0.3	0.0	-0.2	0.5	0.2	0.1	-0.5
	-1.6	1.9	-1.2	-2.1	0.7	1.2	1.3	-1.4	1.5	5.0	-0.1	-0.9

	1 9 6 1				1 9 6 2				1 9 6 3			
	I	II	III	IV	I	II	III	IV	I	II	III	IV
(A)	-0.6	1.6	0.5	-3.7	-2.1	-0.2	1.1	-4.6	-1.4	0.8	-0.2	-4.9
(D)	0.6	0.1	0.5	1.2	2.4	0.8	1.2	0.6	1.5	1.2	0.2	0.3
(E)	-0.4	1.5	-1.2	0.4	0.3	-0.6	-0.3	0.0	0.4	0.1	-0.6	0.2
(F)	-0.2	-0.5	-0.6	1.7	0.7	0.3	-0.8	0.9	0.0	0.4	0.2	0.3
(H)	0.2	-0.2	0.1	-0.1	0.2	-0.1	0.3	-0.1	0.1	0.0	0.4	0.0
(I)	0.3	0.1	0.2	-0.5	0.3	0.0	0.0	-0.7	0.3	0.2	-0.3	-0.7
	-0.1	2.6	-0.5	-1.0	1.8	0.2	1.5	-3.9	0.9	2.7	-0.3	-4.8

	1 9 6 4				1 9 6 5				1 9 6 6			
	I	II	III	IV	I	II	III	IV	I	II	III	IV
(A)	-1.3	0.8	1.6	-4.8	-1.0	0.7	-0.4	-6.2	2.0	2.7	3.1	-2.1
(D)	1.3	1.2	0.6	1.1	2.0	1.2	0.8	0.9	2.4	0.6	-0.4	-0.3
(E)	-1.1	-1.6	0.5	-0.5	0.1	0.5	0.2	0.6	1.0	-1.0	-2.2	1.8
(F)	0.2	0.6	-0.4	1.1	-0.1	-0.5	-1.0	1.2	-1.2	1.1	-1.0	0.7
(H)	0.2	-0.4	0.4	-0.1	0.3	-0.3	0.5	0.0	0.4	-0.2	0.5	0.2
(I)	0.3	0.1	-0.3	-0.9	-0.1	0.0	-0.3	-0.8	0.3	0.3	0.0	-0.6
	-0.4	0.7	2.4	-4.1	1.2	1.6	-0.2	-4.3	4.9	3.5	0.0	-0.3

CHAPTER 2

The Juxtaposition

To proceed in our investigation of the monetary and credit circuit
in the United States, we intend first to confront chronologically
the results of our computation of the annual and quarterly increment in availability and absorption of credit since 1946 with the
relevant statements of monetary authorities, economists, and commentators, as they understand and interpret the given events in
those periods. In this chapter we want only to indicate the ensu-
ing contradictions and differences, without entering into the
causes of the discrepancies. Then, in the subsequent chapters,
we will examine in detail the actual development in the monetary
markets on the basis of our evidence, explain the described discrepancies, and arrive finally at conclusive results.
        (a) The first period comprises the years until the Accord
between the Treasury and the Federal Reserve in March 1951, i.e.,
roughly from 1945 to 1950 inclusively.
        In official statements for this period it is claimed that
"pegging" operations cause high liquid conditions of banks and
"require the creation of more and more money." "The reserve funds
that were available almost automatically under the technique of
pegging operated to augment the availability of credit and thus to
increase the demand for commodities to a volume that was in excess
of what could be supplied," and this happened "at the expense of
monetary policies appropriate to the stability of the economy." (1)
        One spoke of "unfortunate consequences" of the Federal Re-
serve policy before the Accord. It was maintained that the forced
purchases of securities led directly to an expansion of the money
supply; an inflation developed; the government had "printed" money
billions by billions to finance its own deficits and to create an
aura of boom; the money supply grew tremendously. Changes in the
money supply had no longer "any relation to changes in the availability of man and material." (2)
        Finally, the opinion was expressed that after nearly twen-
ty years of a "kept" market, the Treasury and the Federal Reserve
succeeded in reestablishing free markets in government securities,
permitting a much freer administration of Federal Reserve policies;

---

        1. W. Thomas [203], United States Monetary Policy: Re-
cent Thinking and Experience, Hearings 6 and 7, December 1954
[207].
        2. G. F. Allen [5], The Guaranty Survey [83], G. Hauge
[94], Journal of Commerce, September 3, 1957, Wall Street Journal,
July 10, 1957, January 23, 1958.

the Accord gave the Federal Reserve greater flexibility, so that
it could restrain the expansion of bank credit; the Treasury was
very proud that it has "stopped telling the Federal Reserve what
they must do" and "given them freedom to carry out their policies...
free to make money 'tight' or 'easy.'" (3)

---

3.   E. M. Bernstein [16], W. R. Burgess [27, 28], G. M.
Humphrey [105].
        The Board of Governors of the Federal Reserve System [18]
stated in its Annual Reports for this period: "The Federal Reserve System will need to regain control over the volume of
credit. Commercial banks can readily obtain additional reserves by selling some of securities to the Reserve System. Certain measures of monetary regulation that can be adopted...would
not be sufficient to counteract strong tendencies toward inflationary or speculative credit expansion (1946). Funds to meet
current demand for credit...have been readily obtainable by banks
through selling some part of their greatly expanded holdings of
Government securities...thereby creating additional bank reserves
(1947). The Federal Reserve System is also much better equipped
than ever before to meet the credit needs of the economy in a period of downward readjustment. Through open market operations,
the System has virtually unlimited means of supplying the money
market with additional reserves, if the situation should call for
such action. Commercial banks alone hold more than 60 billion
dollars of marketable Government securities, which they can convert at will into reserves capable of supporting an enormous credit expansion. The anti-inflationary effect on bank reserves were
more than offset by purchases of Government securities by the Federal Reserve System in carrying out its market support policy.
Banks were also in a position to meet increases in reserve requirements be selling Government securities. As long as the Reserve System functioned as the residual buyer of the securities offered for
sale the initiative in the creation of bank credit rested with the
market, not with those charged with responsibility for national
monetary policy (1948). The Board of Governors shifted the empha-
sis of credit policy from restraint to ease. The Board reduced
reserve requirements early in May and again in August. Required
reserves were also released on June 30. A total of 3.8 billion
dollars of reserves was released to banks within four months.
During most of 1949 Federal Reserve policies were directed primarily toward assuring private borrowers that ample credit would
be available to facilitate readjustments in the economy (1949).
Inflationary pressures again became a challenge to credit and monetary policy. Federal Reserve policy was directed toward restricting, so far as possible, the availability of bank reserves

Our computation (Table 1) shows, however, that from 1947 through 1950 the increment in availability of credit rose much less than in the subsequent years. The annual average for these pre-Accord years amounted to 15.5 billion dollars, while for the next four years after the Accord it increased to 24.8 billion dollars. (4)

---

on which multiple credit expansion could be based (1950)."
    Further statements:
    E. S. Adams [3, 4]: "Prior to 1951...open market policy was rendered largely inoperative by the program of supporting government bond prices at par.... Rigid pegging of interest is generally recognized as being highly inflationary.... The only alternative would have been rampant inflation."
    L. V. Chandler [32]: "From 1942 to March 1951 any restrictive policy was prohibited."
    E. A. Goldenweiser [79]: "So long as this commitment to support the government security market remains in effect, the initiative in loosing or tightening credit conditions is not in the hands of the Federal Reserve but in the hands of the member banks, or the market."
    G. M. Humphrey [104]: "Prior to 1951, the Federal Reserve policy...created cruel inflationary conditions.... The Federal Reserve's abandonment of pegging of prices in the bond market has prevented an unlimited growth in credit.... The Reserve's proper withdrawal from the pegging of the government bond market...was the most effective single action in the battle against inflation."
    J. J. O'Leary [57]: "What a heavy cost the American people were required to pay for this interest-pegging operation! In supporting the Government securities market the Federal Reserve became an 'engine of inflation.'"
    W. McC. Martin, Jr. [138] pointed out that bond-pegging "provides additional funds for the banking system, permits the expansion of loans and investments and a comparable increase in the money supply - a process sometimes referred to as monetization of the public debt."
    M. Nadler [155]: "The policy of pegging long-term government bonds - in force up to March 1951 - deprived the Reserve authorities of their power to regulate the volume of bank reserves."
    C. R. Whittlesey [217]: "Because of maintaining a pattern of interest rates, it was not longer possible for the Federal Reserve to control the volume of member bank reserves."
    4. A. H. Hansen [91, 92] also disagrees with the statements of the Board of Governors concerning pegging: He wrote that "one gets the impression from the Board's submissions in these Hearings (December 1954) that in the pre-Accord days money

As to the movements in reserve requirements, we disregard the increases in this period, since the Board of Governors contends that the commercial banks were able to meet these increases by selling Government securities. But the reduction in reserve requirements in 1949 "released to banks a total of 3.8 billion dollars of reserves...on which multiple credit expansion could be based," as the Board indicates. The increment, however, in the availability of credit in 1949 was much lower than in all subsequent years (Table 1), although, for instance, in 1951 an increase in reserve requirements occurred.

This increment in availability of credit in 1949 was fully covered by funds supplied directly to the credit markets by all sectors. Every dollar furnished by these individual sectors can be counted up on the basis of our computation. The calculation shows, however, that the financial sectors supplied relatively small amounts - not only in 1949, but also in all subsequent years until 1965 (Table 2, under H and I). How, therefore, did credit creation take place in 1949, as well as in all other years in which the Federal Reserve has reduced reserve requirements or otherwise released reserves to its member banks? When accounting for all those years shows no traces whatsoever of increases in the availability (or absorption) of credit through credit creation how could credit creation occur?

(b) The second period constitutes the upswing until June 1953. (5) A. Murad [153] indicates that Chairman Martin of the

---

and bank credit ran wild," and he cites a statement of the Board that at that time "mounting sales of securities to the Federal Reserve made funds abundantly and cheaply available." He stresses that "the facts are, however, quite otherwise" and quotes data from 1946 to 1950, for instance, that Federal Reserve holdings of government securities were 5.1 billion dollars less in June 1950 than in December 1946. On the basis of the data cited, he states that at that time "a stability of money and credit" existed, and remarks concerning the official declarations that "there occurred no 'mounting' monetization of the debt, the debt was not 'monetized in volume,' the money supply did not increase," and that "it would be difficult to find statements more misleading." Cf., C.R. Whittlesey [217].

The money supply rose on the average in the four pre-Accord years by 1.5 billion dollars, and in the following four years by 4.5 billion dollars (Table 11, under 5).

5. The Board of Governors of the Federal Reserve System [18] reports for this period: "The year 1951 marked a transition from strong inflationary trends to relative stability at high levels of activity. The monetary and credit situation reflected the

Board of Governors "adduces the experience of the period from April
1952 to April 1953 as proof of the success of a restrictive monetary policy," but in these four quarters the increment in domestic
availability of credit rose more than in the subsequent four quarters while an easy monetary policy was in effect (Table 1).

The money supply rose in 1950 by 5.2 billion dollars, and
in 1951 and 1952 by 7.1 and 6.5 billion dollars (Table 11, under
5), in spite of an increase in reserve requirements in 1951. According to the prevailing theory of credit creation, this increase
in the money supply should have inflated the market by an additional 25 to 35 billion dollars in each of these years; however,
the increments in the availability of credit revolve only in the
scope of the credit supply from the individual sectors. This situation, i.e., no additional credit supply is relevant for all increases in reserve requirements and in the money supply in all
following years.

The development in the first half of 1953 constitutes a
famous issue in the monetary policy of the 1950's. It is claimed
that in those months the Federal Reserve policy contributed to the
subsequent recession. The increment in domestic availability of
credit during this time was, however, about equal to that of the
first two quarters of 1952, and much larger than that in the first
two quarters of 1954 (Table 1). (6)

---

interplay of market forces of demand and supply with a minimum of
Federal Reserve intervention in the money market. Effective in
January and early February, the Board raised reserve requirements
against demand deposits for member banks by two percentage points
and against time deposits by one percentage point, thereby increas-
ing the amount of reserve requirements about two billion dollars
or more than ten per cent. In summary, the Accord made it possi-
ble to restore the discount function as a complement to open mar-
ket operations in influencing the availability of credit at member
banks (1951). Federal Reserve credit policy in 1952 was designed
to limit bank credit expansion.... While additional restrictions
on credit seemed unnecessary at the time, relaxation of restraint
was not called for.... Limiting the availability of bank reserves...
had been pursued since October 1951.... Policy of modest re-
straint...(1952). Early in 1953, when increasingly heavy utiliza-
tion of productive resources presented an inflationary threat,
Federal Reserve policy was directed toward restraint of excessive
bank credit expansion...exercising restraint upon inflationary de-
velopments.... Open market operations were employed over the year
to establish first a situation of credit restraint...."

6. M. Friedman and A. Jacobson Schwartz [67] remark: "At
the outset of 1953 the monetary authorities became concerned about

(c) The third period lasts until the fall of 1954. (7)

---

*inflationary pressures and initiated a series of restrictive ac-
tions, which produced a drastic tightening of money markets and
the closest thing to a money market crisis since 1933."*

*The New York Times writes on July 24, 1956: "In the first
half of 1953 money was kept tight by the Federal Reserve.... All
the Administration economic leaders concede privately now that
they let things get too tight for a while. Basically, they mis-
judged how much their onslought in the credit field would frighten
the money markets."*

*P. A. Samuelson [183] observes on "the hard money episode
of the first five months of 1953," that "the verdict of history
will be that hard money was overdone in this period."*

*7. The Board of Governors of the Federal Reserve System
[18] reports: ".... Subsequently, as private credit demands re-
laxed and inflationary pressure abated, the Federal Reserve moved
to expand the supply of funds available for bank lending and to
ease the credit markets generally. By the year-end the Federal
Reserve was actively pursuing a policy of credit ease designed to
avoid deflationary tendencies. The System began early in May to
increase the availability of credit by enlarging the supply of reserve funds. These actions were promptly reflected in a decline
in member bank borrowing, easier conditions of credit availability,
a marked decline in interest rates, and an improved tone in credit
markets generally. The System in late summer and early autumn
again used open market operations to supply additional reserves to
the banking system and thus actively promoted credit ease. On
June 24, 1953, the Board announced a reduction in member bank reserve requirements on net demand deposits of two percentage points
for central reserve city banks and one percentage point for reserve
city and country banks. This step...released an estimated 1.2 billion dollars in reserves (1953). Developments in credit markets
and interest rates reflected in part the effects of Federal Reserve policy. The Federal Reserve until late 1954 followed a policy of actively promoting credit ease. By that time recovery was
sufficiently advanced to require modification of this aggressive
policy. Public policy measures which contributed to recovery included prompt actions by the Federal Reserve System to ease credit
conditions. The easy credit situation was also accompanied by increased availability of credit, reflected...in greater willingness
of lenders to make loans to credit worthy risks. In response to
greater availability of credit...lending activity expanded in some
areas and maintained relatively high levels in others. Late in
the year, as business expansion began to gather momentum, open-
market purchases were moderated and bank reserve positions were*

W. McC. Martin, Jr. [136, 137] commented: "When the economy had a downturn in 1953, the Reserve System acted promptly to
stimulate credit expansion, to help halt the decline and foster
the recovery that began in 1954 and carried through into 1955....
During that period, policy was directed toward assuring ready
availability of credit in the economy generally, and toward creating liquidity conditions favorable to revival and expansion.... In
1954, when production was falling away from capacity and unemployment was rising, the Federal Reserve System followed a policy of
combating deflation by facilitating an expansion of credit and an
increase in the money supply so that idle resources might be
brought back into use." Later, in 1957, he remarked, however,
that he thought the Federal Reserve System "got a little enthusi-
astic" about increasing the supply of money in the mild year's recession that ended in 1954. This helped to foment "a psychology
of expansion." (8)
        C. N. Shepardson [195] noted: "The response to the policy
of credit easing was so strong and insistent that we were soon confronted with rising prices and inflationary credit developments.
The Federal Reserve can and does contribute materially to the mod-
eration of business cycles through its power to influence the supply, cost and availability of credit."
        These statements are automatically followed by commentar-
ies and evaluations from private circles and from the financial
press. Thus, it is remarked that the Federal Reserve pumped large
sums of money into the market, and supplied the banks with all the
funds they needed and more; it turned to a policy of massive easy
money, and flooded the banks with credit; the money supply rose
rapidly; the Federal Reserve poured great aggregates of money into
the market and deluged it with funds. (9)

----

*subjected to some tightening. Changes in reserve requirements...
completed on August 1, 1954...included a reduction of one percentage point on time deposits at all member banks, a reduction of two
percentage points on net demand deposits at central reserve city
banks, and a reduction of one percentage point on net demand deposits at reserve city and country banks. The reduction in reserve
requirements...released about 1.6 billion dollars of reserve
funds.... Expansion in the economy had started to take place during the fall months, following a period of relative stability during the second and third quarter of 1954 (1954)."*
        8. The New York Times, August 15, 1957.
        *9. E. V. Bell [13], J. Bogen [19], J. T. Chippendale, Jr.
[35], The Guaranty Survey [84], P. Heffernan [99], W. Nadler [154].*
        *These presentations operate hardly at all with figures or
useful comparisons, so that only a few such examples can be cited.*

The actual development contradicts the statements above on every point. During these five quarters the increment in domestic availability of credit rose much less than in the corresponding preceding and subsequent periods (Table 1). It is reported that late in 1954 "some tightening" occurred, but only in the fourth quarter of 1954, the increment in the domestic availability of credit increased more than in all the preceding and many subsequent quarters. The same obtains for the supply in the fourth quarter of 1954. All this took place, although two reductions in reserve requirements were carried out during this time. Also, the money supply rose less than in the corresponding subsequent period (Table 11, under 5) in which no further reduction in reserve requirements occurred.

Moreover, no particular "willingness of lenders to make loans" occurred when the increment in the domestic availability of credit diminished. Further, no "idle balances" could "be brought back into use," since in the presented computation the entire domestic availability of credit was absorbed at all times by the economy.

It appears that during a recession the Federal Reserve is not in the position to increase the domestic availability of credit, regardless of its good intentions and its means applied for this purpose. Our analysis of the subsequent periods also confirms this state of affairs. The assertion, therefore, that "the Federal Reserve System is also much better equipped than ever before to meet the credit needs of the economy in a period of downward readjustment...assuring private borrowers that ample credit would be available," as quoted above under (a), is without foundation. (10)

Thus it is stated that during the recession a rapid increase in bank money and money supply took place; that the influence of Federal Reserve policy was reflected in the fact that total bank deposits and total bank investments actually increased during this period; that an estimated seventeen billion dollars of lending power was added to the commercial banking system; that only in 1954 did the newly created money amount to 10.2 billion dollars (E. S. Adams [3], N. J. Jacoby [109], R. Rodgers [175]).

10. N. V. Breckner [22] observes: "It is difficult to distinguish the behavior of the System during this period from that of the preceding year when inflationary pressures appeared dominant. Then for months from the end of 1953 into 1954...was the usual substantial seasonal decline in total reserves and no perceptible easing in free reserves. Such behavior would seem to bear greater similarity to the System's seasonal pattern than to an 'active' easy money open-market policy."

(d) The fourth period comprises three years, from the
fall of 1954 to the fall of 1957. (11)
     In private commentaries it was emphasized that in the pre-
vious period the Federal Reserve stepped in with some more inflation of the money supply; it acted too fast and went too far in
correcting the downturn and this compounded its problems in 1956
and 1957. The boost given housing and automobiles by that increase in the money supply led to a relaxation in credit terms.
(12)
     Notwithstanding the alleged interventiohs of the Federal
Reserve System, the increment in domestic availability of credit
rose during these years by more than that in all corresponding
preceding quarters, as well as, on the average, more than in the
subsequent recession, until autumn 1958 (Table 1). The same relation applies to the money supply in the preceding years; during
the subsequent recession the increment in the money supply was, on
the average, approximately equal, in spite of the fact that in the
first half of 1958 the System reduced thrice its reserve requirements (Table 11, under 5). (13)

---

11. The Board of Governors of the Federal Reserve System
[18] reports for these years: "As recovery turned into vigorous
expansion...Federal Reserve policy shifted from maintaining ease
in the money market to restraint of inflationary developments.
Measures were adopted to moderate the pace of credit expansion....
Increased credit demand exerted pressure on bank reserve positions,
borrowed funds became less readily available.... While policy had
become restrictive, it had resulted in some restraint of credit
expansion (1955). Federal Reserve policy continued to exert restraint.... The degree of restraint was altered from time to time
during the year in response to changes in economic climate....
Banks had become more sensitive to Federal Reserve policies and a
given level of member bank borrowings represented a greater degree
of restraint (1956). The policy of restraint - which continued
with varying intensity until the autumn of 1957 - was implemented
by a combination of open-market operations and discount rate
changes." From October to December the "purpose of action" of the
Board was "to increase the availability of bank reserves" and to
"eliminate any undue restraint on bank borrowing in view of the
decline in business activity and evidences of economic recession"
(1957).
     12. E. S. Adams [3], L. Fertig [61], R. Rodgers [176].
     13. C. C. Balderson [9] remarked in May 1957, contrary to
the statements of the Board: "The so-called tightness of credit
is often attributed to insufficient supply, whereas it has in fact
resulted chiefly from a pyramiding of demand. Actually, the sup-

(e) The fifth period comprehends the recession from the
fall of 1957 to the fall of 1958. (14)
       During this recession the situation developed precisely in
the same manner as during the recession 1953-54, described above
under (c). Also, in official and private commentaries and evaluations the same views were maintained, and the same judgment of the
situation was passed. (15)

---

*ply of money and credit is larger than a year ago, instead of be-
ing smaller as many imply when they use the phrase 'tight money.'"*
       *14.   The Board of Governors of the Federal Reserve System
[18] reports for 1958: "Federal Reserve policy began to move in a
counter-recession direction in late October of 1957. At that time,
the System began to shift its open-market operations toward supplying reserves more liberally to the banking system. From late
fall 1957 through April 1958, there were four reductions in Federal Reserve Bank discount rates, from 3 1/2 per cent to 1 3/4 per
cent. Through continuing open-market operations from late fall of
1957 to early summer of 1958, the Reserve System supplied the commercial banks with some two billion dollars of reserve funds.
Through three successive reserve requirements reductions in late
winter and early spring 1958, the System released for the use of
member banks about 1.5 billion dollars of their required reserves
.... Although the immediate impact of Federal Reserve policy was
on commercial banks, it clearly had broader effects upon the economy generally. For one thing, since commercial banks are direct
participants in some degree in all important credit markets, expansion in bank lending and investing activities intensified competition among all lenders for the acquisition of the available
supply of credit-worthy loans and securities. This widened access
of all potential borrowers to credit funds. Another effect of the
credit ease was a greater willingness on the part of banks and
other lenders to make new loans to business customers and to renew
outstanding credits. These observable effects of easier monetary
conditions which developed from efforts to combat inflation were,
of course, important and salutary. Activation of idle cash balances, which had occurred in other recent years, when interest
rates were rising, apparently did not continue in 1958.... Federal
Reserve policy actions...increase further the availability of bank
reserves in order to encourage bank credit and monetary expansion
conducive to resumed growth in economic activity."*
       *15.   B. B. Anderson [8] stated: "The Federal Reserve Sys-
tem has demonstrated a flexible willingness to utilize its power
and since October 1957...has taken a number of steps which have
resulted in substantially increasing the volume of money and credit."*

We have already stated under (d) that, on the average during this recession, in comparison with the preceding period, the
increment in the domestic availability of credit was smaller, and
the increment in the money supply approximately equal. Also, in
relation to the following year of an upturn, the increments in the

---

W. McC. Martin, Jr. [139, 141]: "Monetary policy...is
thus helping to set the stage for recovery in activity and employment." Commenting that the money supply is gradually turning upward, he added, "We feel it's quite an impressive response" to the
Federal Reserve System's credit easing actions.
A. L. Mills, Jr. [148]: "Federal Reserve System monetary
and credit policy can link the savings based credit granting activities of mutual savings banks, savings and loan associations,
and insurance companies to those of commercial banks so as to help
stimulate economic activity when, as now, it is a purpose of policy to do so...to regulate not only the volume of commercial bank
credit, but to influence the investment policies of the savings
credit-granting institutions to the end of fostering economic stability and growth."
M. S. Szymczak [202]: "Whether in time or demand form,
the growth of bank deposits is serving to increase the liquidity
of the economy and thus to provide the financial basis for renewed
economic growth. Thus monetary policy has contributed to an increase in the availability of borrowed funds.
In the financial press and in private statements it was re-
peated that the Reserve System had given the commercial banks a
massive injection of reserve funds, that the money supply was
growing rapidly and had expanded significantly and, further, that
it was the belief in most quarters that there would be favorable
measures taken to increase the money supply. It was emphasized
that the drastic reversal of Reserve credit policy was a factor
in ending the decline in business activity and that the Reserve
must be given a considerable share of the honors for the upturn
(J. T. Chippendale [35], J. C. Hall [89], M. Nadler [155], L.
Reierson [165], A. Sproul [197]).
Some voices, however, expressed a different opinion:
D. H. Bellemore [15] remarked in January 1958: "The reserve position of member banks during the last four months has become easier largely due to a decline in the demand for loans rather than by Federal Reserve action."
M. O. Johnson [113]: "The relief had not come from Federal Reserve operations but rather...beginning in October 1957, from
the weakening of credit demands associated with business efforts
to curtail inventory and cut expenditures on plant and equipment
programs."

domestic availability of credit and in the money supply were smaller (Table 1, and Table 11, under 5). This took place despite re-
peated reductions of reserve requirements and the supply of an additional two billion dollars of reserve funds to the commercial
banks through open market operations.

Furthermore, "the willingness on the part of banks and
other lenders to make new loans to business customers" is irrelevant, as in any case all funds are utilized in the economy, as
shown by our computation. For the same reason, no "activation of
idle balances" for the whole economy can happen, regardless of the
level of interest rates.

(f) The sixth period comprises the upturn from the fall
of 1958 until the first months of 1960. (16)

During this upturn, the development was again similar to
that during the upturn described under (d). The comparison with
the preceding period was already made under (e). As to the subsequent period, the increment in the domestic availability of credit
during this upturn was much larger than in either of the following
two years (Table 1). The increment in the money supply was, on
the average, about the same as in the two compared periods (Table
11, under 5), although in the second half of 1960 the Federal Re-

---

G. Shea [191]: "The easing of credit conditions not only
has started but is being allowed to take place rather rapidly.
This process is being speeded, of course, by...inventory cutting,
which recently has permitted repayment of business borrowing at
the banks."

16. The Board of Governors of the Federal Reserve System
[18] reports for 1959: "Federal Reserve actions initially influence only the availability of loan and investment funds at banks,
but changes in the availability of bank credit are reflected in
the general availability of loan funds in other credit markets....
This process limits the availability of credit from these other
sources except to the extent that saving increases or the public
tends to substitute other financial assets for cash. Many observers of financial processes assign great importance to changes in
credit availability in restricting or accelerating the volume of
current borrowing; indeed, some assign a more decisive role to
availability than to changes in interest costs. The Federal Reserve, in discussing and evaluating the market impact of its policy actions, has continuously stressed the importance of changes in
the availability of funds in affecting satisfaction of demands....
Principal Federal Reserve Policy actions, 1959: to...maintain restraint on credit expansion...to keep bank reserve positions under
pressure."

serve authorized member banks to count all their vault cash in
meeting their reserve requirements, and, as well, reduced reserve
requirements, thereby releasing about two billion dollars of reserves.

The contentions of the Federal Reserve concerning "the
market impact of its policy actions" on the general availability
of loan funds are gratuitous assertions as long as no computation
is undertaken as to the total availability of credit. Only a calculation of "the total picture," as presented here, permits an
evaluation of the real state of affairs.

(g) The seventh period extends from the first months of
1960 to mid-1963. (17)

In this period, the increment in domestic availability of
credit was, on the average, smaller than during the preceding up-

---

17. *The Board of Governors of the Federal Reserve System*
[18] reports: "The Federal Reserve policy of restraint on expan-
sion of bank credit and money, which carried over from 1959, was
progressively moderated over the first half of 1960. Thereafter,
as output declined, monetary policy became increasingly stimula-
tive...to encourage bank credit and monetary expansion...in a pe-
riod when economic activity was showing signs of recession, over-
all credit demands were contracting, and interest rates were de-
clining (1960). The Federal Reserve continued through 1961 to
follow a policy of supplying reserves to permit substantial bank
credit and monetary expansion. It did this to encourage recovery
from recession and to facilitate economic growth. Continuation of
monetary ease through 1961 meant that bank credit - and, in a less
direct way, other types of credit and capital - continued to be
readily available. Credit markets had ample funds to meet the en-
larged demand for credit (1961). Federal Reserve actions in 1962
continued to encourage bank credit and monetary expansion. The
System supplied reserves to commercial banks in appreciable volume,
and bank loans, investments, and deposits rose sharply. With bank
reserves readily available because of monetary policy actions and
with consumer financing saving in substantial volume, the supply
of funds available to potential borrowers was ample...and credit
was more readily available.... The Federal Reserve reduced reserve
requirements against time deposits from 5 to 4 per cent, effective
October 25 for reserve city banks and November 1 for other member
banks, thereby releasing about 780 million dollars of reserves
(1962). During 1963 the Federal Reserve...gradually lessened the
degree of credit and monetary ease. On the supply side there was
some lessening of credit availability as a result of monetary pol-
icy actions (1963)."

turn, and much smaller than in the subsequent two years (Table 11, under 5), despite a release of almost three billion dollars of reserves in the second half of 1960 - as mentioned under (f) - and in 1962.

(h) The eighth period comprises the upturn from mid-1963 until the end of 1966. (18)

The development during this period was discussed already under (g) (compare, however, the discussion in Chapter 5, Section 9).

---

18. *The Board of Governors of the Federal Reserve System [18] reports: The posture of United States monetary policy throughout much of 1964 was little changed from that adopted in mid-1963. In the midsummer of 1964, however, the Federal Open Market Committee began to supply reserves to the banking system a little less freely (1964). Principal Federal Reserve policy actions in 1965...to move toward firmer conditions in the money market...accommodating no more than moderate growth in bank reserves, bank credit and money. The Federal Reserve...exerted further pressure on the net reserve position of banks (1965). Principal Federal Reserve policy actions in 1966...February-early June... to affect gradual reduction in net reserve availability...August... to apply some additional restraint upon the expansion of bank credit to business and other borrowers...October-late November...to permit somewhat less firm conditions in the money market in view of the recent lack of growth in bank credit (1966)."*

W. McC. Martin, Jr. [143] points out: "Since December 1964, the free reserve position of member banks has changed from a moderate plus to a moderate minus - limiting the ability of banks to increase their credit creation."

CHAPTER 3

First Proof Based on Flow of Funds Accounts

Section 1

Our computation shows that during the last twenty years the increment in domestic availability of credit was in every instance equal to the increment in the domestic absorption of credit, except for statistical discrepancies (and, of course, for the small difference concerning Rest of the World). This result is most important and has a far-reaching impact on the evaluation of the actual development in all economic areas - although such a result should have been self-evident to anyone acquainted with the principles of accountancy.

The computation proves that:

(a) The total increment in the domestic availability of credit in a given period depends only on saving, minus nonfinancial investment in each sector.

(b) During the whole period covered by the study, no correlation existed between the fluctuation in domestic availability of credit and variations in reserve requirements or money supply.

(c) Monetary policy has no effect on credit availability, except insofar as everything that happens in the economy has some effect, however remote, on everything else. Monetary policy, however, facilitates technically and quasi-automatically the fluctuations in banking and money turnover, as it will be argued at a later point.

(d) The proposition that the Federal Reserve directs the money circuit would be equivalent to the proposition that the Federal Reserve determines saving and investment.

This state of affairs also renders unnecessary any favorable disposition on the part of lenders to grant credit, since the available funds will be absorbed in any event by the economy. The effects of the Federal Reserve policy on the willingness of lenders to make loans can therefore neither be observable nor "important and salutory."

An allegation in any field, when made haphazardly, will in the long run usually turn out to be correct or incorrect in about the same number of cases, and in economics in such instances it is often inferred that the evidence is inconclusive. It could therefore be supposed that the unfounded assertions of the Federal Reserve as to its measures and policy would in many cases be correct. It appears, however, that such assertions are almost one hundred per cent incorrect! The reason for this is that during every upturn the Federal Reserve believes it ought to restrain the expansion and has, therefore, been consistently declaring that, in consequence of its measures, the increment in the money supply and in the availability of credit was decreasing. "Tight" money resulted

55

when, because of the upswing, saving and investment in different sectors rose, and business used more demand deposits and currency to handle the larger turnover; "tight" money ensued not by virtue of less available funds, but because of the stronger demand for credit. During a downturn, the standpoint of the Federal Reserve and the development was exactly opposite.

Section 2
The computation comprising "the total picture" solves conclusively the problem of the turnover, and especially of idle balances. It is shown that every sector can hold the difference between saving and nonfinancial investment only in claims, including demand deposits, so that there is no room for idle balances.
It is not correct that the availability of credit is extended when "the public tends to substitute other financial assets" for demand deposits or cash, since demand deposits are included in the circuit, and the fluctuation in cash influences the statement of condition of the Federal Reserve, which is also a participant in the turnover (these questions will be discussed in further detail). Thus, no funds can be regarded as idle funds for the total economy.
Yet for an individual or for an enterprise, idle balances can exist in the sense, for instance, that different amounts are kept idle temporarily and do not bring in any interest for their owners. In such cases, then, one can speak of a more or less intensive use of money for private purposes. If, further, a businessman, for example, as a result of inexact planning, channels too much in demand deposits for his turnover, the velocity of this turnover will decrease, so that these monies will be used less actively for their owner. But all this does not concern the entire economy, and is irrelevant for it.

Section 3
During the whole period, changes in reserve requirements, "on which multiple credit expansion could be based," in no case had influence on the money supply or the availability of credit, subjected, as is asserted, to large fluctuations on such occasions. Such changes could be of importance only for the internal relationship between the Federal Reserve and commercial banks as to what proportion they could profit in from the total, demand deposits, free of interest charge. (1)

---

1. A. Murad [153] remarks: "The idea that variations in reserves can be used to regulate the volume of bank credit, is a myth, unsupported by experience."

Concerning "money supply," it is necessary to emphasize that this concept is imprecise and that, therefore, it will often be misleading (cf., reservations concerning the computation of money supply in Chapter 4, Section 4). Even if we included bills, etc., in some way in this concept, it would nevertheless remain vague, since so many undefined factors play a role, so that its usefulness for the calculation of other economic magnitudes and comparisons cannot be much improved. We are using this concept in our calculation only because the Federal Reserve, as well as many commentators, utilize it often in their statements and discussions.

We note below some observations suggested by the computation (according to Table 11):

(a) There is no correlation between the quarterly increment in the availability of credit and quarterly increment in the money supply. This is especially evident in the first quarter of each year.

(b) GNP also decreased in the first quarter of each year, similarly to the money supply.

(c) Furthermore, the domestic availability of credit increased in the third quarter of 1958, 1962, 1963, 1965, and 1966 by 7.5, 12.3, 12.9, 12.5, and 11.8 billion dollars, respectively, but the money supply decreased in the third quarter of 1958, 1965, and 1966 by 2.0, 1.3, and 5.2 billion dollars, and rose in the third quarter of 1962 and 1963 only by 0.2 and 0.1 billion dollars, respectively.

(d) The money supply remained unchanged in 1953, fell 0.7 billion dollars in 1957, and rose only 0.1 and 2.6 billion dollars in 1960 and 1966, whereas the domestic availability of credit increased in these years by 27.4, 26.8, 29.7, and 64.8 billion dollars, respectively.

It appears, thus, that only business decides how much it requires in demand deposits and currency for the current turnover, and the banking system acts accordingly. The Federal Reserve assists only in promoting a well-balanced economic development, and in those periods in which the money supply rose more rapidly, its increase was certainly necessary for sustaining technically the growth of the economy.

An attempt of the Federal Reserve to check a rise in demand deposits would create a situation in which the banks would encounter difficulties in increasing their deposits in the Federal Reserve and would thus be hesitant in accepting their own deposits. However, such a situation has not occurred in the past years, and has never been reported. The banks had no difficulties in obtaining sums credited by the Federal Reserve and in covering their reserve requirements, except when occasionally they involved themselves too heavily, from the viewpoint of their possibilities, in loans and investments. Never did a precarious situation develop in the market in this respect, and such a development would be difficult to imagine. (2)

As to credit creation, our remarks in Chapter 2, under (a) and (b), which point only at the relevant development, are sufficient evidence that no credit originates artificially (cf., also Chapter 4, Section 9). Neither the commercial banks nor the Federal Reserve are able to create (or cancel) additional credit, and in this way add money and funds to (or withold them from) the economy. The oft-repeated calculation of multipliers of credit creation in relation to reserves released in different periods must be baseless. (3)

It is also incorrect that "through open market operations, the System has virtually unlimited means of supplying the money market with additional reserves," since all assets and liabilities of the Federal Reserve, excess reserves included, have to be used in some way within the economy. One falls into error here because it is well enough to note that the positions of the contractors of the Federal Reserve are influenced by its interventions, but it is believed that at the same time its own position can remain unchanged. The alleged power of the Federal Reserve confuses us. The circumstance that the Federal Reserve disposes of so much gold and money should not blind us to the fact that the Federal Reserve is unable within the present or similar structure to create of destroy money arbitrarily. Although the statement of condition of the Federal Reserve amounts to about sixty billion dollars, every additional dollar of assets or liabilities must cause a counterposition which keeps its full counterbalance.

---

2. *J. M. Culbertson [41] writes: "Let us ask, 'When the Federal Reserve dramatically reverses policy and shifts from credit restraint to credit ease, just what sort of change in the money supply does this entail?' It is perhaps surprising to find that these reversals of monetary policy, produced with such soul-searching and received with such fulness of praise and blame, often can scarcely be discovered in the behavior of the money supply. Such short-run variations in money supply as we have had were mainly procyclical, a declined or a reduced rate of growth in the supply occurring during recession and an accelerated growth during recovery. This raises some interesting questions, does it not? Does the Federal Reserve, in effect, laboriously contrive to bring about changes in credit conditions that, with a stable monetary system, would happen of their own accord? There is, I think, much truth in this interpretation."*

3. *A renowned German economist noted in a letter to this author that the denial of credit creation by commercial banks leads to a thicket of unsolved problems, so that teachings fail as guide.*

Finally, our computation, in addition to a similar computation of A. H. Hansen (quoted in Chapter 2, footnote 4), shows that during bond-pegging, the domestic availability of credit rose much less than in the subsequent period. The Federal Reserve System neither lost nor "regained control over the volume of credit," for this control never existed. The fact that there was also interest-pegging had little meaning for the situation.

Section 4

In our compilation we have first figured out the increment in domestic availability of credit with intermediaries, i.e., together with all their full accounts. We have then distributed all the relevant items of these accounts among all nonfinancial sectors, according to the relative transactions of the intermediaries with these sectors. In this manner, we have arrived at a computation of the domestic availability, as well as the absorption of credit, excluding intermediaries. Since the nonfinancial sectors of the economy always have a choice between placing funds with financial institutions or investing them directly, we have assumed that they fully made the second choice. The small remaining amounts of the accounts of the intermediaries concerning their own direct transactions demonstrate how insignificant their role is in the final turnover between other sectors and therefore for the economic development, disregarding their function, important in itself, as pure mediators.

The net domestic saving of every sector is employed for capital expenditures and other domestic nonfinancial investment in this sector, and the entire remainder (or deficiency) of this saving is directed to (or taken from) net domestic investment in other sectors. The increment in domestic availability of credit in any period, for any sector, amounts to its own saving minus direct investment. (4)

All these movements are accounted for in our calculation. It shows net domestic saving for every sector, followed by net domestic financial investment, i.e., the balance between domestic availability and domestic absorption of credit for those sectors and, furthermore, net domestic nonfinancial investment for every sector.

---

4. L. S. Ritter [168] remarks: "A complete sector sources-and-uses-of-funds statement, including transactions on current and capital account...are...the basic backbone underlying the FOF accounts." This statement "is a hybrid accounting statement which combines that sector's balance sheets and income statement."

The division of investment among individual sectors depends
on some cyclical variations, and does not concern us here. The
question of how this division occurs cannot alter our conclusions.
Net domestic saving-investment was, for instance, in 1955 and 1956
almost equal, but the increment in domestic availability of credit
fell in 1956 by about 10 billion dollars. In 1958, this increment
increased by 9 billion dollars, when net domestic saving-investment decreased by more than 18 billion dollars. In 1959, 1960,
and 1961, changes in net domestic saving-investment were small,
but the increment in domestic availability of credit declined in
1960 by almost 17 billion dollars and increased in 1961 by about
10 billion dollars. This question is connected with the problem
of whether private indebtedness in the United States is too high
and whether this might entail a danger for the economy. If, however, as the computation shows, the indebtedness originates from
a specific economic development, and every debt can be joined only
with genuine saving, it seems that this danger is greatly exaggerated.

In addition, the calculation shows, for every sector, capital consumption, gross domestic saving and gross domestic investment, and their statistical discrepancy. But the acknowledged,
formal equality of saving and investment remains insufficient for
further reasoning in economics, as actual teachings demonstrate.
The relationship between these two magnitudes must be evaluated
much more thoroughly. The crux of the problem is, again, that no
funds can be used for investment which have not been saved else-
where previously, unless we entirely destroy the framework of our
monetary system and embark on a gallopping inflation. Consequently, in our system, saving must provide likewise for all the debts
of the government.

Section 5
In general, it can be stated that in a modern economy the
central bank is materially in no position to change its own credit
range or that of the whole banking system; it is unable to affect
significantly the monetary turnover, and cannot therefore conduct
an active monetary policy.
From the "accountant's attitude," which we recommended for
the evaluation of the above problems, follows, per force, the im-
potence of the Federal Reserve System. It can be seen, for instance, that with a given availability of credit, if out of the
total current savings time deposits in the commercial banks have
increased to a relatively greater extent, other resources of the
economy have to decrease correspondingly. This fact could not
change the total situation in the economy. In a similar manner,
one might choose figures for savings bonds, for investment in the
stock market, or for other elements from total savings, and draw
conclusions from them. Besides, the prevailing theory does not

claim that time deposits in the commercial banks or other saving
are formed by an easing of bank reserve positions, by credit creation, or by other measures of the System. By allegedly linking
the "activities of mutual savings banks and loan associations and
insurance companies to those of commercial banks," the Federal Reserve cannot achieve "broader effects upon the economy generally"
and open "new investment opportunities."

On the basis of our investigations, the view must be rejected that the Federal Reserve can cause tight or easy money.
The tightening or easing on the money market takes place without
any assistance from the Federal Reserve, so that there can be no
tight or easy policy. Only the conditions or the situation in the
market can be tight or easy, depending on the pressure of demand
for credit in the economy. We have taken into account periods of
booms and recessions, as indicated by GNP. Since demand and supply pressures in the individual credit markets fluctuate parallel
to booms and recessions, the main misunderstanding arises from the
fact that the tightening and easing of credit are due only to
those pressures, while the total availability of credit is not
affected and varies very smoothly.

It is, hence, inconsequential when during a recession "Federal Reserve policies were directed primarily toward asserting
private borrowers that ample...bank credit - and, in less direct
way, other types of credit and capital - would be readily available." Money is borrowed by business to increase its turnover and
profits, and when demand for products is declining and profit mar-
gins are narrowing, business will repay large quantities of loans
week by week, and the intensity of demand for new loans will fall
off. The Federal Reserve will bring about little change in these
conditions by measures it may or may not undertake.

Section 6
This state of affairs changes to a considerable degree our
image of the economic development of the past. For decades, we
have been committing a fatal error in assessing the forces which
determine the economic process. It appears that it is beyond the
capacity of the Federal Reserve System to direct and to speed up
the economic evolution (we disregard here the negative influence
of a government which may conduct an evidently disordered monetary
policy). Nobody but the people themselves determine the rate of
economic growth through their decisions to buy present goods and
services or to save and to invest for the future. All fluctuations of the trend in this process should be traced back only to
the "real" factors, i.e., to disturbances in the course of production and consumption. (5)

---

5. *J. M. Culbertson [41] observes: "This approach would*

The basic idea of these results is that the economic system of a free society like ours, once set in motion, functions by itself and cannot be controlled, according to our present knowledge, by any artificial human intervention. These conclusions contradict clearly the traditional point of view in these matters. All of us were brought up on the doctrine that the Federal Reserve System discretionally regulates the monetary turnover and is particularly in the position to prevent the threat of a possible inflation. This view turns out now to be wrong.

Moreover, since the monetary economy is one of the fundamental areas of economics, and all economic areas are closely interconnected, our conclusions are bound to involve important revisions in all other realms of economic knowledge.

Section 7

The presented computation constitutes a full proof of economic development, and the result can be interpreted only in one sense. The extreme limitation of the means and possibilities of the banking system is a fact tested in terms of accounting. In the footnote we cite a few quotations of well-known economists, to show how serious are the doubts in monetary matters on the basis of our present knowledge. (6) Without reliable evidence of fac-

---

reflect the view that the changes in credit conditions that characteristically accompany changes in economic conditions reflect mainly forces naturally generated by the economy. Perhaps, at least, we can say that too much attention has been lavished on the procedures, the mechanics, the drama of Federal Reserve control, and too little has been directed to the behavior of the basic variable that is being controlled."

6. J. K. Galbraith [71] writes concerning monetary policy: "There is a certain mystery about it. It is one of the few areas of our profession which has a seeming association with the mystical, even the supernatural."

W. McC. Martin, Jr. [136] indicates: "The only thing I have learned is how very little any of us know about money.... The credit and money of this country is at the grassroots.... At some point I know, from my experience, that economics becomes theology. It becomes a matter of faith. You cannot get away from that turning point in it."

P. A. Samuelson [184] observes that in the monetary economy "relationships...are universally thought to be of exceptional complexity. Thoughtful students of these problems generally feel that no one has the evidence to be confident with respect to any single view in this difficult area, and that the above position imputed, I hope not wrongly, to the Fed is but one of a number of

tual development, no progress in monetary economics is possible. (7)

In view of this, it is difficult to understand why the Federal Reserve has not investigated more closely the efficiency of its policy, or why it has not tested whether and how the money creation has developed in the course of years. The current attitude and policy of the Federal Reserve does not rest upon an error of judgment, but on cardinal material errors. However, the Federal Reserve generally ignores any critiques, as was the case, for instance, with the remarks of A. H. Hansen concerning pegging, quoted in Chapter 2, footnote 4, or the pertinent article by A. Murad [153] published in 1956. The statements of the Federal Reserve are phrased in such positive language that they do not seem to allow for any doubts about the tremendous power and great achievements of the System. The reader is led to believe that he is being spared the trouble of having to check the data and contentions.

It can be expected that on the basis of the presented proof the discussion of economic events must in the end be much more exact. If the economic development thus became more understandable, practical business could be better assured about the possible prospects of its plans and undertakings, with considerable advantage resulting for the whole economy.

Section 8

Finally, we have to consider the low reliability of much statistical data and doubtfulness of conclusions based on such statistics. Skepticism must, therefore, arise concerning our calculations. Data related to the availability and absorption of credit are mostly derived from banking and financial statistics, and their trustworthiness is relatively high. On the other hand,

---

possible hypotheses and perhaps not the most plausible single one at that.... Once an interesting myth gets into the economic literature it is hard to get it out again."

J. C. R. Dow [47] writes concerning monetary policy in Great Britain: "The volume of money is sometimes regarded with an almost superstitious awe.... There is, in truth, something mysterious about the creation of money.... It may, for instance, be noted how frequently United States sources had to be quoted for lack of evidence drawn from this country."

7. R. F. Voertman [211] asks, in a review of an article, "Notes on the Pattern of the United States Economic Growth" by S. Kuznets: "Could it be that one carefully constructed time series is more persistently instructive than a thousand brilliantly logical speculative models?"

statistics regarding saving, nonfinancial investment, and capital
consumption are much less dependable, and the relevant conclusions
are more doubtful. The fact that the calculation comprises data
and comparisons for many years enhances their usefulness.

        For our purposes, however, the equality of credit availa-
bility and credit absorption and of their increments in every moment is most important, because from this the whole theory of
monetary turnover can be deduced, and especially the impossibility
of credit creation and idle balances for the economy as a whole.
These facts, however, are not proved statistically, but on the
basis of accounting, as accounting can prove the functional equality or inequality of some factors, or, otherwise, their relationship. The statistical data may be distorted or outright false,
but the calculation will in any event show the equality of availability and absorption of credit.

Table 11   65

GNP, Gross and Net Domestic Saving-Investment, Domestic Availability
of Credit, and Demand Deposits and Currency

(figures in parentheses indicate relative series number in computer)

(in billion dollars)

1.

1946	1947	1948	1949	1950	1951	1952	1953	1954	1955

GNP, according to the U.S. Department of Commerce, Survey of Current Business
(unadjusted):

208.5	231.3	257.6	256.5	284.8	328.4	345.5	364.6	364.8	398.0

2. Gross Domestic Saving-Investment, according to Table 7; totals in computer
(909040000):

50.9	62.3	72.6	60.6	80.8	85.7	78.8	80.8	81.3	104.4

3. Increment in Net Domestic Saving-Investment, according to Table 5:

29.9	36.2	41.1	24.6	40.5	38.7	29.9	28.3	25.2	43.2

4. Increment in Domestic Availability of Credit, including Intermediaries, according to Table 1; totals in computer (723120005 and 909010000):

10.0	11.7	9.8	16.3	24.1	21.7	27.6	27.4	22.4	34.3

5. Demand Deposits and Currency, Net Increment in Banking System Liabilities
(733120005), according to Table 1:

-14.5	1.2	-0.5	0.0	5.2	7.1	6.5	0.0	4.5	2.3

1956	1957	1958	1959	1960	1961	1962	1963	1964	1965	1966

1. GNP, according to the U.S. Department of Commerce, Survey of Current Business
(unadjusted):

419.2	441.1	447.3	483.6	503.8	520.1	560.3	590.5	631.7	681.2	743.3

2. Gross Domestic Saving-Investment, according to Table 7; totals in computer
(909040000):

111.6	112.0	97.1	118.1	122.9	119.7	134.5	144.1	158.0	175.1	196.8

3. Increment in Net Domestic Saving-Investment, according to Table 5:

44.6	39.3	20.9	38.0	39.2	33.1	41.8	46.5	54.4	65.6	77.0

4. Increment in Domestic Availability of Credit, including Intermediaries according to Table 1; totals in computer (723120005 and 909010000):

24.2	26.8	35.8	46.6	29.7	39.5	50.4	55.1	58.2	67.7	64.8

5. Demand Deposits and Currency, Net Increment in Banking System Liabilities
(733120005), according to Table 1:

1.8	-0.7	5.8	1.4	0.1	5.6	4.5	5.6	7.4	7.2	2.6

Table 11 (continued)

GNP, Gross and Net Domestic Saving-Investment, Domestic Availability
of Credit, and Demand Deposits and Currency

(text according to preceding page)

	1952				1953				1954			
	I	II	III	IV	I	II	III	IV	I	II	III	IV
1.	82.0	83.3	85.7	94.4	87.4	91.3	90.3	95.6	86.5	89.7	90.0	98.6
2.	21.8	19.4	18.6	19.0	20.7	20.7	20.8	18.6	20.2	20.1	20.8	20.2
3.	9.4	7.3	6.9	6.2	8.5	8.0	7.9	4.0	7.0	6.4	6.8	5.3
4.	2.8	4.8	9.3	10.7	1.1	6.2	10.5	9.6	-2.4	4.0	8.6	12.2
5.	-2.8	2.7	2.1	4.4	-4.8	-1.4	3.8	2.4	-5.1	2.2	1.6	5.9

	1955				1956				1957			
	I	II	III	IV	I	II	III	IV	I	II	III	IV
1.	92.6	97.4	100.4	107.6	98.6	102.9	104.1	113.7	104.4	109.1	110.6	117.0
2.	24.8	26.2	26.8	26.6	27.6	29.0	27.5	27.5	29.3	28.2	28.5	26.0
3.	9.7	11.7	11.9	9.8	12.2	11.8	11.5	8.7	12.5	11.1	10.0	5.5
4.	2.5	8.0	10.3	13.4	2.3	2.8	8.2	11.0	4.0	3.1	11.7	8.1
5.	-4.9	1.6	1.3	4.2	-3.6	0.3	0.5	4.5	-4.3	-0.1	0.5	3.1

	1958				1959				1960			
	I	II	III	IV	I	II	III	IV	I	II	III	IV
1.	103.9	108.8	111.7	123.0	113.1	121.4	119.3	129.9	120.5	125.6	124.6	133.1
2.	25.0	23.2	23.7	25.1	28.9	31.7	28.6	29.0	33.2	33.2	29.4	27.1
3.	6.2	4.6	5.5	4.4	9.4	12.6	9.7	6.3	12.5	12.0	9.3	5.3
4.	2.7	8.3	7.5	17.3	5.5	13.5	14.9	12.7	2.0	8.1	7.9	11.6
5.	-4.4	5.6	-2.0	6.6	-6.0	2.0	1.4	4.0	-8.2	2.7	2.0	3.6

	1961				1962				1963			
	I	II	III	IV	I	II	III	IV	I	II	III	IV
1.	120.6	128.2	129.1	142.2	131.3	139.6	138.1	151.5	137.8	146.1	146.5	160.2
2.	28.0	30.4	29.6	31.7	32.9	34.2	33.4	34.0	35.3	37.9	34.7	36.2
3.	7.1	9.5	9.2	7.5	11.0	12.5	11.1	6.9	11.6	14.4	10.9	9.5
4.	-0.4	10.3	13.7	15.9	6.2	13.0	12.3	19.0	4.3	16.8	12.9	21.0
5.	-6.4	2.1	3.6	6.2	-7.4	3.8	0.2	7.9	-7.4	5.4	0.1	7.6

	1964				1965				1966			
	I	II	III	IV	I	II	III	IV	I	II	III	IV
1.	148.3	157.1	156.2	170.1	157.2	168.2	168.1	187.7	175.3	186.1	183.9	198.0
2.	38.3	40.3	39.4	40.0	42.9	45.4	42.5	44.3	51.7	48.3	45.5	51.2
3.	13.5	15.1	14.8	11.1	17.8	19.3	15.4	12.9	21.3	22.6	17.3	15.7
4.	5.9	17.2	14.6	20.6	10.2	18.7	12.5	26.5	13.1	19.4	11.8	20.4
5.	-6.2	4.1	1.6	7.9	-7.1	-5.2	1.3	10.4	-7.9	7.1	-5.2	8.5

CHAPTER 4

Second Proof Based on Bank Credit Range

Section 1. The Second Proof

In 1960, this author has furnished a different full proof concerning the development in the monetary turnover, in his essay The Changed Structure, A Different Picture of the Monetary Economy [201]. This abbreviated proof was based only on the credit range of the Federal Banking System. This author proceeded from the standpoint that, leaving out the Federal Reserve System, the credit range in other sectors of the economy can only change in consequence of genuine saving. All changes in the monetary turnover, apart from this saving, must, therefore, be reflected in the credit range of the Federal Reserve and the commercial banks. In this manner, all important phenomena in the monetary circuit, such as the formation of demand deposits, credit creation, reserve positions and others, as well as the monetary policy of the Federal Reserve could be investigated. Admittedly, this approach is more complicated, and the examination is more difficult to follow than in the comprehensive presentation in the preceding chapters of the present book. But in the 1950's, a computation of credit ranges of the remaining economy on a quarterly basis was not yet available, so that another computation was not possible. Besides, our present calculation had to be conducted by means of computers.

Although the abbreviated proof is as valid as that based on the Flow-of-Funds accounts, and its results should have been equally relevant, they have been virtually disregarded. Unfortunately, in economic thinking there is little patience with the theories of others, and in this case pains had to be taken with a rather complex problem; since one was in advance inclined to doubt that some traditional, fundamental theorems might be wrong, a closer examination ceased virtually before it began. One is also unprepared in economics to consider and to accept proofs; it is against the customary mode of thinking!

In the following sections, we will present the second proof with some abridgments, but also with some additional observations concerning the development during recent years.

Section 2. The Credit Range

First we wish to consider mainly statistics. We want to examine how the range of money disposal of the Federal Reserve System has developed since World War II and what limit was set to the supply of money and credit.

We shall make use of credit ranges, i.e., we shall examine how in the course of the years, from month to month, the possibility of granting credit and of investments, separately for the Federal Reserve and for the commercial banks, rose or fell. (1) For this purpose the statements of condition and transactions of the entire System have to be analyzed.

However, it must be emphasized that in our calculations we shall meet with difficulties which are expressed in the fact that many factors to be reconsidered have been unsuitably or insufficiently defined, and often represent only in part what was to be expressed by the respective concepts. Apart from this, some terms are vague and some quantities are difficult to compute. This applies to such terms, for instance, as money supply, demand deposits, time deposits, velocity.

The statistical data in Tables 1 B and 2 B are based on financial statements and on statements of condition of Federal Reserve Banks and of all commercial banks, reported in the Federal Reserve Bulletins. The credit range for each month has been computed in the last column. Monthly figures have been given because these data will also be useful for our other calculations. In addition, annual averages for all positions and the credit ranges are listed.

By credit range claims and obligations of the respective institutions or of the respective sector are to be understood. (2) The money disposal range, mostly of the remaining economy, shall comprise credit range and the disposable currency.

1. The statistics of the Federal Reserve Banks comprise average daily figures for the period from 1946. The monthly fluctuations of the credit range within single years reflect mainly seasonal changes in the circulation of currency.

2. The statistics of all commercial banks comprise data for the last Wednesday of each month for the period beginning July 1947. Data for the period before that date are not available to the same extent, yet the partially available data render a similar picture. Also, due to the incomplete data available for the period beginning in July 1947, a few quite unimportant gaps in the statistics of the commercial banks were unavoidable.

---

1. R. Stucken [198] writes on this in a similar sense: "To this range of money creation we are inclined to attribute a central importance for the study of money and credit; in our opinion it is the decisive factor."

2. The credit range of the Federal Reserve will not comprise currency in circulation, although it really must be regarded as an obligation of the Federal Reserve. Yet in this case gold also would have to be included, which can equally be considered as a means of payment and which serves as a covering of the currency. The result of our investigations and the conclusions would naturally be the same, even if we were to use a different division.

ad 1. The annual average of the average daily figures of
the credit range of the Federal Reserve Banks fluctuated from 6.3
billion dollars in 1946, 0.5 billion dollars in 1949, to 24.5 billion dollars in 1966. The set-offs to these figures comprise
roughly currency in circulation and capital accounts, less gold
reserves and Bank premises.

Since in the course of these years the Federal Reserve had
no influence on fluctuation in the gold reserve, nor upon changes
in currency in circulation, (3) it is clearly evident from the
data listed above that the Federal Reserve during this period was
not in a position to change its credit range on its own initiative.

ad 2. The annual average of the credit range of all commercial banks (semi-annually for 1947) grew gradually from 10.3
billion in 1947 to 41.6 billion in 1966. The set-offs comprise
roughly total capital accounts and interbank settlements less cash
in vault and bank premises.

This growth of credit range is explained mainly by the increase of capital accounts. In Table 3 B, the respective data are
listed. The average grew from 10 billion dollars in 1947 to 31.1
billion dollars in 1966. Thus, apart from increases of capital
accounts and quite minimal shifts, commercial banks also are unable to change their credit range.

As far as the relationship between the Federal Reserve and
the commercial banks is concerned, the mutual shifts affect solely
deposits of banks in the Federal Reserve and they, therefore, neither change the two credit ranges, nor the relationship to the remainder of the economy. They possess only internal importance
within the System.

3. Our above statements should be sufficient for the time
being, yet we wish to remain with this topic a bit longer and to

---

3. *The Bank for International Settlements [11] remarks in
its Annual Report for 1959: "Money that is held idle is, as a
rule, not in the form of currency but in the form of deposits."*

*E. A. Goldenweiser [80]: "The volume of currency has ad-
justed itself sensitively to changes in public demand, from day to
day, from month to month, and from year to year."*

*H. L. Lutz [133]: "Any excess of currency above ordinary
needs will not stay in circulation, but will return to the banks.
Thus, the principal source of additional money supply must be the
commercial banks."*

*M. Nadler [156]: "Other factors influencing reserves -
such as the movements of gold, currency in circulation, and the
float - are beyond the control of the Reserve and the banks."*

*T. Wilson [221]: "The amount of notes in circulation is
determined by the demand for them."*

examine, on the one hand, what happened during this period to investments and loans of commercial banks after changes in reserve
requirements, and on the other hand, how the transactions of government securities between the Federal Reserve and the commercial
banks developed.

It is claimed that the banks in this case "rather quickly"
expand their earning assets and deposits in relation to changes in
the reserve requirements, the proportion being 5 to 1.

The actual development contradicts these claims, since
four times in this period, in 1949, 1953, 1954, and 1958, after a
decrease of reserve requirements, the commercial banks did not
even increase their credits to the economy by the amount of the
freed money. Thus, there can be no question of a multiple increase
in credit. On the other hand, during 1948 and 1951, after an increase of reserve requirements, the loans of the commercial banks
rose from month to month, although they should have diminished by
many billion dollars, according to the theory of credit creation.
The data of our statistics give the following picture (in billion
dollars):

A. Increase in Reserve Requirements of Demand Deposits
(1) February 27, 1948 to September 24, 1948: Central reserve city banks from 20% to 26% = by 30%. Reserve city banks
from 20% to 22% = by 10%. Country banks from 14% to 16% = by 14%.

Data Compared: Banks - Last Wednesday in February 1948
and in September 1948; Federal Reserve - February 1948 and October
1948 (for the increase of September 24, 1948 would not be fully
taken into account, since the statistics of the Federal Reserve
comprise averages of daily figures).

Commercial Banks. Reserve requirements rose from 16.8 to
19.9 = by 3.1. Total loans and investments declined from 115.5 to
113.6 = by 1.9 (they rose once more to 114.3, by 0.7, until December 1948). The difference was covered mainly by government deposits, which rose from 1.8 to 2.8 = by 1.0. Seasonal adjusted demand deposits decreased from 84.8 to 84.1 = by 0.7, or by 0.8%.

The Federal Reserve used the increase of reserve requirements from 16.8 to 19.8 = by 3.0 (computed in daily averages) for
the greatest part, i.e., from 20.7 to 23.2 = 2.5, to purchase government securities sold through the commercial banks in this period.

(2) January 11, 1951, to February 1, 1951: Central reserve city banks from 22% to 24% = by 9%. Reserve city banks from
18% to 20% = by 11%. Country banks from 12% to 14% = by 17%.

Data compared: Banks - Last Wednesday in December 1950
and in February 1951; Federal Reserve - December 1950 and February
1951.

Commercial Banks. Reserve requirements rose from 17.2 to
19.1 = by 1.9. Total loans and investments declined from 127.5 to
125.0 = by 2.5. They rose to 126.2, by 1.2, until June 1951.

Seasonal adjusted demand deposits increased from 89.8 to 90.5 = by 0.7, or by 0.8%.

The Federal Reserve used the increase in reserve requirements (from 17.4 to 18.9 = by 1.5, computed in daily averages) to purchase government securities (from 20.3 to 21.7 = 1.4) sold through the commercial banks in this period.

B. Decrease in Reserve Requirements of Demand Deposits

(1) May 1, 1949 to September 1, 1949: Central reserve city banks from 26% to 22% = by 18%. Reserve city banks from 22% to 18% = by 18%. Country banks from 16% to 12% = by 25%.

Data compared: Banks - Last Wednesday in April 1949 and September 1949; Federal Reserve - April 1949 and September 1949.

Commercial Banks. Reserve requirements decreased from 19.0 to 16.0 = by 3.0. Total loans and investments rose from 112.5 to 118.5 = by 6.0. The difference of 3.0 is covered by an increase in demand deposits by 0.7, government deposits by 1.6, time deposits by 0.1, and expansion of the credit range by 0.6.

Seasonal adjusted demand deposits decreased from 83.8 to 83.3 = by 0.5, or by 0.6%.

Federal Reserve. The lowering of reserve requirements from 19.2 to 16.1 = by 3.1 (computed in daily averages) was covered by the sale of government securities to the banks by 4.0 (from 21.4 to 17.4). The difference of 0.9 was mainly caused by the purchase of gold (24.3 to 24.6 = 0.3) and the lowering of government deposits (1.1 to 0.6 = 0.5).

(2) July 1, 1953 to July 9, 1953: Central reserve city banks from 24% to 22% = by 8%. Reserve city banks from 20% to 19% = by 5%. Country banks from 14% to 13% = by 7%.

Data compared: Banks - Last Wednesday in June 1953 and July 1953; Federal Reserve - June 1953 and July 1953.

Commercial Banks. Reserve requirements decreased from 20.8 to 19.6 = by 1.2. Total loans and investments rose from 138.1 to 143.2 = by 5.1. The difference of 3.9 is mainly covered by an increase of government deposits by 3.7 (from 3.8 to 7.5).

Seasonal adjusted demand deposits decreased from 98.8 to 98.7 = by 0.1, or by 0.1%.

Federal Reserve. The lowering of reserve requirements from 20.3 to 19.7 = by 0.6 (computed in daily averages) was mainly covered by an increase in government deposits by 0.4 (from 0.1 to 0.5).

(3) June 6, 1954 to August 1, 1954: Central reserve city banks from 22% to 20% = by 9%. Reserve city banks from 19% to 18% = by 5%. Country banks from 13% to 12% = by 8%.

Data compared: Banks - Last Wednesday in May 1954 and August 1954; Federal Reserve - June 1954 and August 1954.

Commercial banks. Reserve requirements decreased from 19.7 to 18.4 = by 1.3. Total loans and investments rose from 145.7 to 149.5 = by 3.8. The difference of 2.5 is covered by an increase in demand deposits by 0.7, government deposits by 0.3, time deposits by 1.1, and expansion of credit range by 0.4.

Seasonal adjusted demand deposits rose from 100.1 to 101.0 = by 0.9, or by 0.9%.

Federal Reserve. The lowering of reserve requirements from 19.5 to 18.5 = by 1.0 (computed in daily averages) was mainly covered by the sale of government securities to the commercial banks by 0.7 (from 24.7 to 24.0).

(4) February 27, 1958 to April 24, 1958: Central reserve city banks from 20% to 18% = by 10%. Reserve city banks from 18% to 16.5% = by 8%. Country banks from 12% to 11% = by 8%.

Data compared: Banks - Last Wednesday in February 1958 and in April 1958; Federal Reserve - February 1958 and May 1958 (the decrease of April 24, 1958 would not be fully taken into account, since the Federal Reserve statistics comprise averages of daily figures).

Commercial banks. Reserve requirements decreased from 18.9 to 18.3 = by 0.6. Total loans and investments rose from 168.6 to 175.6 = by 7.0. The difference is mainly covered by an increase in government deposits by 1.7 (from 3.5 to 5.2), time deposits by 2.4 (from 57.8 to 60.2), and demand deposits by 1.6 (from 105.6 to 107.2).

Seasonal adjusted demand deposits rose from 105.5 to 107.2 = by 1.7, or by 1.6%.

Federal Reserve. The lowering of reserve requirements from 19.0 to 18.2 = by 0.8 (computed in daily averages) was almost matched by the sale of gold (22.8 to 21.8 = 1.0). (4)

---

4. H. Hellwig [100] reports that in Germany, from the end of 1950 to the end of 1956, deposits in the central bank and cash in credit institutions rose from 1.9 to 7.3 billion DM, i.e., by 5.4 billion DM. The rate of minimum reserve requirements for this period amounted to 8%, and therefore the coefficient of money creation to 12.5. Hence, 67.5 billion DM were to be expected as money creation, yet actually the growth of demand deposits amounted to 9.3 billion DM.

Hellwig computes further that from the end of 1956 to the end of October 1957 the deposits and cash of the credit institutions increased by 4.3 billion DM. The average rate of reserve requirements for this period amounted to 8% to 9%, the coefficient to 11 to 12.5. But the demand deposits of the credit institutions rose only by 0.6 billion DM, instead of by ca.50 billion DM, i.e., "not 'to the utmost limit of bank money creation,' as was to be expected," according to E. Schneider [187].

E. Kellenberger [120] states that in Switzerland in 1949 the required minimum relationship between liquid means and short-

Changes in reserve requirements in 1960 are not considered because, although in this year reserve requirements of central reserve city banks fell by 1 1/2 per cent, those of country banks increased by 1 per cent.

---

term liabilities of banks amounted to 3.7% or 303 million francs, but the relationship was actually fivefold, i.e., 18.46% or 1518 million francs. "The banks, as a whole, could therefore put 1.2 billion francs additionally in circulation, i.e., grant more credit by this amount."

Table 1 B

FR's Credit Range. Averages of daily figures (in billions of dollars)

		Reserve Bank credit outstanding			Deposits				
		U. S. govt. securities	Discounts and advances	Total [1]	Member bank reserves	Treasury	Non-member banks	Total	Credit range
1.	1946	23.6	0.2	24.3	15.9	0.6	1.3	17.8	6.5
2.	1946	23.1	0.4	23.9	15.7	0.9	1.2	17.8	6.1
3.	1946	22.5	0.6	23.5	15.5	0.8	1.2	17.5	6.–
4.	1946	22.3	0.4	23.1	15.5	0.4	1.1	17.–	6.1
5.	1946	22.7	0.2	23.4	15.7	0.6	1.1	17.4	6.–
6.	1946	23.2	0.2	23.9	16.–	0.7	1.1	17.8	6.1
7.	1946	23.5	0.2	24.2	16.–	0.6	1.3	17.9	6.3
8.	1946	23.6	0.2	24.3	16.–	0.5	1.3	17.8	6.5
9.	1946	23.6	0.3	24.4	16.2	0.5	1.2	17.9	6.5
10.	1946	23.5	0.3	24.1	16.2	0.4	0.9	17.5	6.6
11.	1946	23.7	0.4	24.5	16.3	0.6	1.–	17.9	6.6
12.	1946	23.8	0.3	24.7	16.5	0.6	0.9	18.–	6.7
	Yearly averages	23.3	0.3	24.–	16.–	0.6	1.1	17.7	6.3
1.	1947	23.6	0.3	24.4	16.4	0.8	1.–	18.2	6.2
2.	1947	23.8	0.3	24.6	16.–	1.9	0.8	18.7	5.9
3.	1947	23.–	0.3	23.7	16.–	1.3	1.1	18.4	5.3
4.	1947	22.1	0.2	22.7	15.9	0.7	1.1	17.7	5.–
5.	1947	21.8	0.1	22.3	16.–	0.6	1.–	17.6	4.7
6.	1947	21.7	0.2	22.2	16.2	0.6	0.9	17.7	4.5
7.	1947	21.9	0.1	22.3	16.3	0.7	1.–	18.–	4.3
8.	1947	22.1	0.2	22.5	16.5	1.–	1.1	18.6	3.9
9.	1947	22.1	0.2	22.6	16.9	0.6	1.–	18.5	4.1
10.	1947	22.1	0.2	22.8	17.1	0.9	0.9	18.9	3.9
11.	1947	22.1	0.3	22.9	17.–	1.3	1.–	19.3	3.6
12.	1947	21.9	0.3	22.9	17.3	1.–	1.–	19.3	3.6
	Yearly averages	22.3	0.2	23.–	16.5	0.9	1.–	18.4	4.6
1.	1948	21.6	0.2	22.4	17.4	1.1	1.–	19.5	2.9
2.	1948	20.7	0.4	21.6	16.8	1.3	1.–	19.1	2.5
3.	1948	20.6	0.4	21.4	17.1	1.1	1.1	19.3	2.1
4.	1948	20.4	0.3	21.1	16.9	1.2	1.–	19.1	2.–
5.	1948	20.3	0.3	21.–	16.9	1.4	0.9	19.2	1.8
6.	1948	20.8	0.3	21.5	17.4	1.5	0.9	19.8	1.7
7.	1948	21.3	0.3	22.–	17.5	1.8	1.–	20.3	1.7
8.	1948	21.4	0.3	22.–	17.7	1.8	0.9	20.4	1.6
9.	1948	21.6	0.4	22.4	18.5	1.3	0.9	20.7	1.7
10.	1948	23.2	0.4	23.9	19.8	1.6	1.–	22.4	1.5
11.	1948	23.–	0.4	23.8	19.8	1.6	1.–	22.4	1.4
12.	1948	23.–	0.3	24.–	20.–	1.4	1.1	22.5	1.5
	Yearly averages	21.5	0.3	22.3	18.–	1.4	1.–	20.4	1.9
1.	1949	22.3	0.3	23.1	20.–	1.–	1.2	22.2	0.9
2.	1949	22.3	0.3	23.–	19.6	1.5	1.2	22.3	0.7
3.	1949	21.6	0.3	22.3	19.4	1.–	1.3	21.7	0.6
4.	1949	21.4	0.2	22.–	19.2	1.1	1.2	21.5	0.5
5.	1949	20.–	0.3	20.6	18.1	0.9	1.1	20.1	0.5
6.	1949	19.4	0.2	19.9	18.1	0.4	1.–	19.5	0.4
7.	1949	18.8	0.2	19.3	17.6	0.4	1.–	19.–	0.3
8.	1949	18.1	0.2	18.6	16.9	0.5	1.–	18.4	0.2
9.	1949	17.4	0.2	18.–	16.1	0.6	1.–	17.7	0.3
10.	1949	17.6	0.1	18.1	16.1	0.6	1.2	17.9	0.2
11.	1949	17.7	0.2	18.2	16.1	0.5	1.3	17.9	0.3
12.	1949	18.3	0.2	19.–	16.3	0.7	1.3	18.3	0.7
	Yearly averages	19.6	0.2	20.2	17.8	0.8	1.1	19.7	0.5

[1] Includes float, industrial loans and acceptances

Table 1 B (continued)   75

FR's Credit Range. Averages of daily figures (in billions of dollars)

	Reserve Bank credit outstanding			Deposits				Credit range
	U. S. govt. securities	Discounts and advances	Total [1]	Member bank reserves	Treasury	Non-member banks	Total	
1. 1950	18.1	0.1	18.6	16.5	0.5	1.4	18.4	0.2
2. 1950	17.7	0.2	18.3	16.1	0.6	1.5	18.2	0.1
3. 1950	17.7	0.2	18.2	16.1	0.6	1.3	18.–	0.2
4. 1950	17.6	0.1	18.1	15.9	0.7	1.2	17.8	0.3
5. 1950	17.5	0.1	18.–	15.9	0.6	1.3	17.8	0.2
6. 1950	17.8	0.1	18.3	16.2	0.5	1.4	18.1	0.2
7. 1950	18.1	0.1	18.7	16.3	0.5	1.5	18.3	0.4
8. 1950	18.3	0.2	18.9	16.3	0.7	1.4	18.4	0.5
9. 1950	18.9	0.1	19.6	16.6	0.7	1.2	18.5	1.1
10. 1950	19.4	0.1	20.–	16.7	0.6	1.4	18.7	1.3
11. 1950	19.4	0.1	20.2	16.7	0.4	1.3	18.4	1.8
12. 1950	20.3	0.1	21.6	17.4	0.6	1.3	19.3	2.3
Yearly averages	18.4	0.1	19.–	16.4	0.6	1.3	18.3	0.7
1. 1951	20.7	0.2	21.8	18.1	0.4	1.2	19.7	2.1
2. 1951	21.7	0.3	23.3	18.9	0.8	1.3	21.–	2.3
3. 1951	22.3	0.2	23.7	19.2	0.6	1.2	21.–	2.7
4. 1951	23.–	0.2	24.–	19.3	0.6	1.3	21.2	2.8
5. 1951	22.4	0.4	23.7	18.9	0.6	1.2	20.7	3.–
6. 1951	22.8	0.2	23.9	19.3	0.3	1.2	20.8	3.1
7. 1951	23.1	0.2	24.3	19.2	0.4	1.2	20.8	3.5
8. 1951	23.1	0.3	24.3	19.2	0.5	1.1	20.8	3.5
9. 1951	23.3	0.3	24.7	19.4	0.6	1.1	21.1	3.6
10. 1951	23.8	0.1	25.–	19.9	0.5	1.–	21.4	3.6
11. 1951	23.4	0.3	24.8	19.8	0.4	0.9	21.1	3.7
12. 1951	23.4	0.7	25.4	20.3	0.3	0.8	21.4	4.–
Yearly averages	22.7	0.3	24.1	19.3	0.5	1.1	20.9	3.2
1. 1952	23.2	0.2	24.4	20.5	0.1	0.7	21.3	3.1
2. 1952	22.6	0.4	23.8	20.–	0.4	0.8	21.2	2.6
3. 1952	22.6	0.3	23.9	20.2	0.3	0.8	21.3	2.6
4. 1952	22.4	0.4	23.7	19.8	0.5	0.9	21.2	2.5
5. 1952	22.3	0.6	23.7	19.8	0.6	0.8	21.2	2.5
6. 1952	22.6	0.6	24.1	20.1	0.3	0.8	21.2	2.9
7. 1952	22.8	1.1	24.8	20.5	0.3	1.–	21.8	3.–
8. 1952	23.–	1.1	24.8	20.3	0.5	1.1	21.9	2.9
9. 1952	23.5	0.7	25.1	20.5	0.3	1.–	21.8	3.3
10. 1952	23.7	1.1	25.7	20.6	0.5	1.–	22.1	3.6
11. 1952	23.6	1.6	26.2	20.7	0.6	1.–	22.3	3.9
12. 1952	24.4	1.6	27.3	21.2	0.6	1.–	22.8	4.5
Yearly averages	23.1	0.8	24.8	20.4	0.4	0.9	21.7	3.1
1. 1953	24.2	1.4	26.6	21.–	0.6	1.–	22.6	4.–
2. 1953	23.9	1.3	26.1	20.5	0.5	0.8	21.8	4.3
3. 1953	23.9	1.2	26.–	20.4	0.2	0.9	21.5	4.5
4. 1953	23.9	1.2	25.9	20.–	0.4	1.–	21.4	4.5
5. 1953	24.–	1.–	25.7	19.9	0.4	0.9	21.2	4.5
6. 1953	24.7	0.4	26.–	20.3	0.1	0.8	21.2	4.8
7. 1953	25.–	0.4	26.1	19.7	0.5	0.7	20.9	5.2
8. 1953	25.–	0.7	26.3	19.5	0.7	0.9	21.1	5.2
9. 1953	25.2	0.5	26.4	19.6	0.5	0.9	21.–	5.4
10. 1953	25.3	0.4	26.5	19.5	0.6	0.9	21.–	5.5
11. 1953	25.2	0.5	26.4	19.7	0.5	0.8	21.–	5.4
12. 1953	25.6	0.4	27.1	19.9	0.6	0.9	21.4	5.7
Yearly averages	24.7	0.8	26.3	20.–	0.5	0.9	21.3	4.9

[1] Includes float, industrial loans and acceptances.

Table 1 B (continued)

FR's Credit Range. Averages of daily figures (in billions of dollars)

	Reserve Bank credit outstanding			Deposits				Credit range
	U. S. govt. securities	Discounts and advances	Total [1]	Member bank reserves	Treasury	Non-member banks	Total	
1. 1954	25.3	0.1	26.2	20.2	0.2	0.9	21.3	4.9
2. 1954	24.8	0.3	25.7	19.6	0.6	0.9	21.1	4.6
3. 1954	24.6	0.2	25.6	19.6	0.5	0.9	21.–	4.6
4. 1954	24.6	0.2	25.5	19.4	0.6	0.9	20.9	4.6
5. 1954	24.7	0.2	25.5	19.5	0.5	0.9	20.9	4.6
6. 1954	25.–	0.2	25.9	19.7	0.6	0.9	21.2	4.7
7. 1954	24.8	0.1	25.6	19.2	0.5	1.–	20.7	4.9
8. 1954	24.–	0.2	24.9	18.5	0.6	1.–	20.1	4.8
9. 1954	23.9	0.2	24.8	18.4	0.5	0.9	19.8	5.–
10. 1954	24.5	0.3	25.4	18.9	0.6	0.9	20.4	5.–
11. 1954	24.7	0.3	25.8	19.2	0.5	0.8	20.5	5.3
12. 1954	24.9	0.4	26.3	19.3	0.4	0.8	20.5	5.8
Yearly averages	24.6	0.2	25.6	19.3	0.5	0.9	20.7	4.9
1. 1955	24.2	0.4	25.4	19.1	0.3	0.9	20.3	5.1
2. 1955	23.8	0.5	25.–	18.8	0.5	0.9	20.2	4.8
3. 1955	23.6	0.6	25.–	18.6	0.7	0.8	20.1	4.9
4. 1955	23.6	0.6	25.1	18.8	0.5	0.9	20.2	4.9
5. 1955	23.7	0.4	24.9	18.7	0.4	0.8	19.9	5.–
6. 1955	23.6	0.5	25.–	18.7	0.3	0.7	19.7	5.3
7. 1955	24.–	0.6	25.5	18.8	0.5	0.8	20.1	5.4
8. 1955	23.9	0.8	25.4	18.7	0.6	0.8	20.1	5.3
9. 1955	23.7	0.9	25.5	18.7	0.5	0.8	20.–	5.5
10. 1955	24.–	0.9	25.8	18.9	0.5	0.8	20.2	5.6
11. 1955	24.–	1.–	26.1	18.9	0.5	0.8	20.2	5.9
12. 1955	24.6	0.8	26.9	19.2	0.4	0.9	20.5	6.4
Yearly averages	23.9	0.7	25.5	18.8	0.5	0.8	20.1	5.3
1. 1956	23.9	0.8	25.9	19.1	0.4	0.8	20.3	5.6
2. 1956	23.4	0.8	25.2	18.7	0.5	0.8	20.–	5.2
3. 1956	23.5	1.–	25.5	18.9	0.5	0.6	20.–	5.5
4. 1956	23.4	1.1	25.4	18.8	0.5	0.6	19.9	5.5
5. 1956	23.3	1.–	25.2	18.7	0.6	0.6	19.9	5.3
6. 1956	23.5	0.8	25.5	18.9	0.5	0.6	20.–	5.5
7. 1956	23.6	0.7	25.6	18.8	0.5	0.6	19.9	5.7
8. 1956	23.5	0.9	25.4	18.8	0.5	0.6	19.9	5.5
9. 1956	23.7	0.8	25.7	19.–	0.5	0.6	20.1	5.6
10. 1956	23.8	0.7	25.7	18.9	0.5	0.6	20.–	5.7
11. 1956	24.–	0.7	26.1	19.2	0.5	0.6	20.3	5.8
12. 1956	24.8	0.7	27.2	19.5	0.5	0.6	20.6	6.6
Yearly averages	23.7	0.8	25.7	18.9	0.5	0.6	20.1	5.6
1. 1957	24.1	0.4	25.9	19.3	0.3	0.6	20.2	5.7
2. 1957	23.1	0.7	24.9	18.8	0.3	0.6	19.7	5.2
3. 1957	23.1	0.9	25.–	18.9	0.4	0.5	19.8	5.2
4. 1957	23.2	1.–	25.4	19.1	0.4	0.6	20.1	5.3
5. 1957	23.–	0.9	25.–	18.8	0.5	0.7	20.–	5.–
6. 1957	23.–	1.–	25.2	19.–	0.5	0.7	20.2	5.–
7. 1957	23.4	0.9	25.5	19.1	0.5	0.7	20.3	5.2
8. 1957	23.1	1.–	25.2	18.8	0.5	0.6	19.9	5.3
9. 1957	23.3	1.–	25.5	19.–	0.5	0.7	20.2	5.3
10. 1957	23.3	0.8	25.3	19.–	0.5	0.6	20.1	5.2
11. 1957	23.4	0.8	25.4	19.–	0.5	0.6	20.1	5.3
12. 1957	24.–	0.7	26.2	19.4	0.4	0.5	20.3	5.9
Yearly averages	23.3	0.8	25.4	19.–	0.4	0.6	20.1	5.3

[1] Includes float, industrial loans and acceptances.

Table 1 B (continued)   77

FR's Credit Range. Averages of daily figures (in billions of dollars)

		Reserve Bank credit outstanding			Deposits				
		U. S. govt. securities	Discounts and advances	Total [1]	Member bank reserves	Treasury	Non-member banks	Total	Credit range
1.	1958	23.6	0.5	25.2	19.3	0.5	0.5	20.3	4.9
2.	1958	23.4	0.2	24.6	19.0	0.4	0.6	20.0	4.6
3.	1958	23.5	0.1	24.6	18.7	0.5	0.6	19.8	4.8
4.	1958	23.6	0.1	24.7	18.4	0.5	0.7	19.6	5.1
5.	1958	23.9	0.1	24.9	18.2	0.5	0.7	19.4	5.5
6.	1958	24.7	0.1	25.9	18.6	0.4	0.6	19.6	6.3
7.	1958	25.2	0.1	26.3	18.6	0.5	0.7	19.8	6.5
8.	1958	25.4	0.3	26.6	18.6	0.5	0.6	19.7	6.9
9.	1958	25.1	0.5	26.5	18.4	0.4	0.6	19.4	7.1
10.	1958	25.3	0.4	26.8	18.5	0.4	0.7	19.6	7.2
11.	1958	25.6	0.5	27.2	18.5	0.4	0.7	19.6	7.6
12.	1958	26.3	0.6	28.4	18.9	0.5	0.6	20.0	8.4
Yearly averages		24.6	0.3	26.0	18.6	0.5	0.6	19.7	6.2
1.	1959	25.8	0.6	27.6	18.9	0.4	0.7	20.0	7.6
2.	1959	25.5	0.5	27.1	18.6	0.4	0.7	19.7	7.4
3.	1959	25.4	0.6	27.1	18.4	0.5	0.7	19.6	7.5
4.	1959	25.7	0.7	27.3	18.7	0.5	0.6	19.8	7.5
5.	1959	25.9	0.8	27.7	18.6	0.5	0.7	19.8	7.9
6.	1959	26.0	0.9	27.9	18.5	0.5	0.7	19.7	8.2
7.	1959	26.4	1.0	28.4	18.7	0.5	0.6	19.8	8.6
8.	1959	26.6	1.0	28.5	18.6	0.5	0.6	19.7	8.8
9.	1959	26.7	0.9	28.7	18.6	0.5	0.7	19.8	8.9
10.	1959	26.5	0.9	28.6	18.6	0.5	0.7	19.8	8.8
11.	1959	26.7	0.9	28.7	18.6	0.5	0.7	19.8	8.9
12.	1959	27.0	0.9	29.4	18.9	0.5	0.7	20.1	9.3
Yearly averages		26.2	0.8	28.1	18.6	0.5	0.7	19.8	8.3
1.	1960	25.9	0.9	28.2	18.9	0.5	0.7	20.1	8.1
2.	1960	25.3	0.8	27.3	18.2	0.5	0.6	19.3	8.0
3.	1960	25.3	0.6	27.0	18.0	0.5	0.5	19.0	8.0
4.	1960	25.5	0.6	27.2	18.1	0.6	0.6	19.3	7.9
5.	1960	25.8	0.5	27.4	18.2	0.5	0.5	19.2	8.2
6.	1960	26.1	0.4	27.8	18.3	0.5	0.6	19.4	8.4
7.	1960	26.6	0.4	28.2	18.5	0.5	0.6	19.6	8.6
8.	1960	27.0	0.3	28.2	18.5	0.5	0.6	19.6	8.6
9.	1960	26.7	0.2	28.1	18.6	0.5	0.6	19.7	8.4
10.	1960	27.1	0.2	28.5	18.7	0.5	0.6	19.8	8.7
11.	1960	27.9	0.2	29.3	19.0	0.5	0.7	20.2	9.1
12.	1960	27.2	0.1	29.1	19.3	0.5	0.7	20.5	8.6
Yearly averages		26.4	0.4	28.0	18.5	0.5	0.6	19.6	8.4

1. Includes float, industrial loans, and acceptances.

Table 1 B (continued)

FR's Credit Range. Averages of daily figures (in billions of dollars)

		Reserve Bank credit outstanding			Deposits				Credit range
		U. S. govt. securities	Discounts and advances	Total [1]	Member bank reserves	Treasury	Non-member banks	Total	
1.	1961	26.9	0.1	28.5	16.7	0.5	0.6	17.8	10.7
2.	1961	26.8	0.2	28.1	16.5	0.5	0.6	17.6	10.5
3.	1961	26.8	0.1	28.0	16.4	0.5	0.6	17.5	10.5
4.	1961	26.7	0.1	27.9	16.5	0.4	0.5	17.4	10.5
5.	1961	26.7	0.1	28.0	16.4	0.5	0.5	17.4	10.6
6.	1961	26.9	0.1	28.3	16.5	0.5	0.5	17.5	10.8
7.	1961	27.0	0.1	28.5	16.5	0.5	0.5	17.5	11.0
8.	1961	27.4	0.1	28.7	16.7	0.5	0.5	17.7	11.0
9.	1961	27.6	0.0	29.1	16.8	0.5	0.6	17.9	11.2
10.	1961	28.0	0.1	29.5	17.1	0.5	0.6	18.2	11.3
11.	1961	28.6	0.1	30.1	17.2	0.5	0.5	18.2	11.9
12.	1961	29.1	0.2	31.2	17.3	0.5	0.4	18.2	13.0
Yearly averages		27.4	0.1	28.8	16.7	0.5	0.5	17.7	11.1
1.	1962	28.5	0.1	30.5	17.2	0.4	0.5	18.1	12.4
2.	1962	28.4	0.1	29.8	16.9	0.4	0.5	17.8	12.0
3.	1962	28.6	0.2	30.1	16.9	0.4	0.5	17.8	12.3
4.	1962	29.1	0.1	30.6	17.1	0.5	0.6	18.2	12.4
5.	1962	29.5	0.1	31.0	17.1	0.6	0.6	18.3	12.7
6.	1962	29.6	0.2	31.3	17.2	0.5	0.6	18.3	13.0
7.	1962	29.6	0.1	31.5	17.3	0.5	0.6	18.4	13.1
8.	1962	30.1	0.1	31.6	17.1	0.5	0.5	18.1	13.5
9.	1962	29.9	0.1	31.8	17.2	0.5	0.5	18.2	13.6
10.	1962	30.2	0.1	32.1	17.4	0.5	0.5	18.4	13.7
11.	1962	30.2	0.1	32.1	16.7	0.5	0.5	17.7	14.4
12.	1962	30.5	0.3	33.2	16.9	0.6	0.5	18.0	15.2
Yearly averages		29.5	0.1	31.3	17.1	0.5	0.5	18.1	13.2
1.	1963	30.2	0.1	32.7	16.9	0.8	0.5	18.2	14.5
2.	1963	30.5	0.2	32.3	16.7	0.8	0.5	18.0	14.3
3.	1963	30.6	0.2	32.5	16.7	0.9	0.4	18.0	14.5
4.	1963	30.9	0.2	32.7	16.7	0.9	0.4	18.0	14.7
5.	1963	31.1	0.2	33.0	16.8	0.9	0.4	18.1	14.9
6.	1963	31.5	0.2	33.5	16.8	0.8	0.4	18.0	15.5
7.	1963	32.2	0.3	34.3	17.0	0.9	0.4	18.3	16.0
8.	1963	32.2	0.4	34.1	16.7	0.8	0.4	17.9	16.2
9.	1963	32.3	0.4	34.4	16.9	0.9	0.3	18.1	16.3
10.	1963	32.6	0.3	34.6	16.9	0.9	0.4	18.2	16.4
11.	1963	33.1	0.4	35.4	17.0	0.9	0.3	18.2	17.2
12.	1963	33.7	0.4	36.6	17.3	0.9	0.4	18.6	18.0
Yearly averages		31.7	0.3	33.8	16.9	0.9	0.4	18.1	15.7

---

1. *Includes float, industrial loans, and acceptances.*

Table 1 B (continued)   79

FR's Credit Range. Averages of daily figures (in billions of dollars)

		Reserve Bank credit outstanding			Deposits				Credit range
		U. S. govt. securities	Discounts and advances	Total [1]	Member bank reserves	Treasury	Non-member banks	Total	
1.	1964	33.2	0.3	35.8	17.2	1.0	0.4	18.6	17.2
2.	1964	33.0	0.3	35.0	17.0	0.9	0.3	18.2	16.8
3.	1964	33.4	0.3	35.5	17.1	0.9	0.4	18.4	17.1
4.	1964	33.5	0.2	35.6	17.1	0.9	0.3	18.3	17.3
5.	1964	33.9	0.3	36.0	17.1	1.0	0.3	18.4	17.6
6.	1964	34.6	0.3	36.8	17.4	0.9	0.3	18.6	18.2
7.	1964	34.9	0.3	37.1	17.4	0.8	0.3	18.5	18.6
8.	1964	35.1	0.3	37.2	17.3	0.9	0.3	18.5	18.7
9.	1964	35.3	0.3	37.6	17.6	0.9	0.3	18.8	18.8
10.	1964	35.3	0.3	37.7	17.7	0.9	0.3	18.9	18.8
11.	1964	36.0	0.4	38.4	17.8	0.6	0.3	18.7	19.7
12.	1964	37.1	0.3	39.9	18.0	0.9	0.4	19.3	20.6
Yearly averages		34.6	0.3	36.9	17.4	0.9	0.3	18.6	18.3
1.	1965	36.7	0.3	39.2	18.0	0.9	0.4	19.3	19.9
2.	1965	37.1	0.4	39.2	17.8	0.9	0.4	19.1	20.1
3.	1965	37.3	0.4	39.5	17.8	0.9	0.3	19.0	20.5
4.	1965	37.6	0.5	39.9	18.0	0.9	0.4	19.3	20.6
5.	1965	38.1	0.5	40.3	18.1	0.9	0.3	19.3	21.0
6.	1965	38.8	0.5	41.2	18.2	0.8	0.3	19.3	21.9
7.	1965	39.2	0.5	41.7	18.3	0.8	0.4	19.5	22.2
8.	1965	39.3	0.6	41.5	18.1	0.9	0.4	19.4	22.1
9.	1965	39.1	0.5	41.6	18.1	1.0	0.4	19.5	22.1
10.	1965	39.6	0.5	42.0	18.3	1.0	0.4	19.7	22.3
11.	1965	40.1	0.5	42.6	18.2	0.9	0.4	19.5	23.1
12.	1965	40.9	0.5	43.9	18.7	0.7	0.4	19.8	24.1
Yearly averages		38.6	0.5	41.1	18.1	0.9	0.4	19.4	21.7
1.	1966	40.6	0.4	43.4	18.8	0.7	0.4	19.9	23.5
2.	1966	40.6	0.5	43.1	18.5	0.8	0.4	19.7	23.4
3.	1966	40.4	0.6	42.9	18.4	0.5	0.4	19.3	23.6
4.	1966	40.6	0.6	43.3	18.8	0.3	0.5	19.6	23.7
5.	1966	41.1	0.7	43.9	18.8	0.7	0.5	20.0	23.9
6.	1966	41.7	0.7	44.5	18.7	0.8	0.5	20.0	24.5
7.	1966	42.2	0.8	45.7	19.2	1.1	0.6	20.9	24.8
8.	1966	42.3	0.7	45.3	18.8	1.1	0.5	20.4	24.9
9.	1966	42.7	0.8	45.6	19.3	0.9	0.5	20.7	24.9
10.	1966	42.8	0.7	45.6	19.4	0.8	0.6	20.8	24.8
11.	1966	43.3	0.6	46.1	19.2	0.7	0.6	20.5	25.6
12.	1966	43.8	0.6	46.9	19.6	0.3	0.6	20.5	26.4
Yearly averages		41.8	0.6	44.7	19.0	0.7	0.5	20.2	24.5

1. *Includes float, industrial loans, and acceptances.*

Table 2 B

Credit Range of All Commercial Banks. Last Wednesday of the month (in billions of dollars)

		Claims					Liabilities					
		Loans and investments			Member bank reserves	Total	Demand deposits [1]	U.S. govt. deposits	Time deposits	Discounts and advances	Total	Credit range
	Total	Loans	U.S. govt. securities	Other securities								
7. 1947	113.4	34.–	70.7	8.7	16.4	129.8	83.–	1.4	35.–	0.1	119.5	10.3
8. 1947	114.–	34.9	70.3	8.8	16.5	130.5	83.3	1.7	35.1	0.1	120.2	10.3
9. 1947	115.2	35.5	70.8	8.9	16.8	132.–	84.1	1.9	35.2	0.1	121.3	10.7
10. 1947	116.3	36.8	70.5	9.–	16.9	133.2	85.4	1.8	35.4	0.4	123.–	10.2
11. 1947	116.6	37.6	70.1	8.9	17.1	133.7	85.9	1.9	35.1	0.4	123.3	10.4
12. 1947	116.3	38.1	69.2	9.–	17.9	134.2	87.1	1.5	35.4	0.1	124.1	10.1
¹/₂yearly averages	115.3	36.1	70.3	8.9	16.9	132.2	84.8	1.7	35.2	0.2	121.9	10.3
1. 1948	116.6	38.2	69.4	9.–	17.3	133.9	86.8	1.3	35.3	0.3	123.5	10.4
2. 1948	115.5	38.7	67.9	8.9	16.8	132.3	84.6	1.8	35.6	0.3	122.3	10.–
3. 1948	113.6	38.9	65.5	9.3	16.6	130.2	81.5	2.4	35.6	0.4	119.9	10.3
4. 1948	114.3	38.8	66.3	9.2	17.–	131.3	82.7	2.5	35.6	0.3	121.1	10.2
5. 1948	114.6	39.5	65.9	9.2	16.9	131.5	82.8	2.4	35.6	0.3	121.1	10.4
6. 1948	113.9	39.9	64.8	9.2	17.4	131.3	82.7	2.2	35.9	0.3	121.1	10.2
7. 1948	114.8	40.1	65.3	9.3	17.5	132.3	83.3	2.4	35.8	0.3	121.8	10.5
8. 1948	115.1	40.6	65.1	9.4	17.7	132.8	83.8	2.4	35.8	0.3	122.3	10.5
9. 1948	113.6	41.7	62.5	9.4	19.9	133.5	83.9	2.8	35.8	0.4	122.9	10.6
10. 1948	114.1	41.6	63.3	9.2	20.–	134.1	85.1	2.3	35.8	0.3	123.5	10.6
11. 1948	114.2	42.3	62.8	9.1	19.9	134.1	85.2	2.2	35.6	0.6	123.6	10.5
12. 1948	114.3	42.7	62.5	9.1	20.2	134.5	85.8	2.1	35.7	0.3	123.9	10.6
Yearly averages	114.6	40.3	65.1	9.2	18.1	132.7	84.–	2.2	35.7	0.3	122.3	10.4
1. 1949	114.5	42.4	63.–	9.1	20.–	134.5	85.4	2.–	35.9	0.5	123.8	10.7
2. 1949	113.4	42.–	62.2	9.1	19.4	132.8	83.4	3.–	36.–	0.3	122.7	10.1
3. 1949	112.5	42.4	60.9	9.2	19.–	131.5	81.1	3.4	36.1	0.3	120.9	10.6
4. 1949	112.5	41.3	62.–	9.2	19.–	131.5	82.4	2.1	36.2	0.3	121.–	10.5
5. 1949	113.4	40.9	63.2	9.3	18.–	131.4	82.5	1.9	36.2	0.2	120.8	10.6
6. 1949	113.7	41.2	63.–	9.5	18.–	131.7	82.2	2.2	36.3	0.2	120.9	10.8
7. 1949	114.8	40.5	64.4	9.8	17.5	132.3	83.1	1.5	36.3	0.4	121.3	11.–
8. 1949	117.9	41.2	66.7	10.–	16.5	134.4	83.4	3.1	36.3	0.5	123.3	11.1
9. 1949	118.5	41.7	66.7	10.1	16.–	134.5	83.1	3.7	36.3	0.3	123.4	11.1
10. 1949	119.5	41.8	67.6	10.1	16.1	135.6	84.3	3.6	36.2	0.1	124.2	11.4
11. 1949	119.7	42.7	66.9	10.1	16.–	135.7	85.–	3.2	35.9	0.3	124.4	11.3
12. 1949	120.8	43.3	67.3	10.2	16.3	137.1	86.7	3.–	36.1	0.1	125.9	11.2
Yearly averages	115.9	41.8	64.5	9.6	17.7	133.6	83.6	2.7	36.1	0.3	122.7	10.9
1. 1950	121.2	42.9	68.–	10.3	16.4	137.6	86.4	3.3	36.3	0.1	126.1	11.5
2. 1950	120.6	43.1	67.1	10.4	16.2	136.8	84.5	4.2	36.4	0.1	125.2	11.6
3. 1950	120.3	43.7	65.8	10.8	15.8	136.1	83.2	4.3	36.6	0.4	124.5	11.6
4. 1950	120.3	43.8	65.5	11.–	15.9	136.2	84.3	3.2	36.8	0.2	124.5	11.7
5. 1950	121.2	44.1	66.1	11.–	15.8	137.–	85.–	3.2	36.8	0.3	125.3	11.7
6. 1950	122.1	44.9	66.–	11.2	16.–	138.1	85.4	3.8	36.8	0.1	126.1	12.–
7. 1950	122.3	46.–	64.9	11.4	16.4	138.7	86.5	3.6	36.6	0.3	127.–	11.7
8. 1950	123.3	47.3	64.2	11.8	16.3	139.6	87.4	3.8	36.4	0.1	127.7	11.9
9. 1950	123.6	48.9	62.5	12.1	16.7	140.3	88.–	3.6	36.4	0.1	128.1	12.2
10. 1950	124.4	49.8	62.5	12.1	16.6	141.–	89.2	3.1	36.3	0.1	128.7	12.3
11. 1950	125.4	51.5	61.7	12.1	16.8	142.2	90.3	3.–	36.1	0.2	129.6	12.6
12. 1950	127.5	52.8	62.4	12.3	17.2	144.7	93.2	2.8	36.2	0.3	132.5	12.2
Yearly averages	122.7	46.6	64.7	11.4	16.3	139.–	86.9	3.5	36.5	0.2	127.1	11.9

[1] Demand deposits other than interbank and U. S. govt., less cash items reported as in process of collection.

Table 2 B (continued)   81

Credit Range of All Commercial Banks. Last Wednesday of the month (in billions of dollars)

	Claims						Liabilities					Credit range
	Loans and investments				Member bank reserves	Total	Demand deposits [1]	U.S. govt. deposits	Time deposits	Discounts and advances	Total	
	Total	Loans	U.S. govt. securities	Other securities								
1. 1951	125.1	52.7	60.–	12.4	19.–	144.1	91.6	2.8	36.2	0.8	131.4	12.7
2. 1951	125.–	53.5	59.1	12.4	19.1	144.1	90.6	4.2	36.2	0.4	131.4	12.7
3. 1951	125.7	54.4	58.8	12.5	19.–	144.7	89.–	6.4	36.4	0.5	132.3	12.4
4. 1951	125.4	54.3	58.5	12.6	19.2	144.6	89.5	5.8	36.4	0.1	131.8	12.8
5. 1951	125.1	54.5	58.1	12.5	18.5	143.6	89.5	4.8	36.5	0.5	131.3	12.3
6. 1951	126.2	55.–	58.6	12.6	19.1	145.3	89.5	6.2	36.8	0.2	132.7	12.6
7. 1951	126.1	54.6	58.7	12.8	19.1	145.2	90.7	4.6	37.–	0.1	132.4	12.8
8. 1951	127.–	55.2	59.1	12.7	18.9	145.9	91.4	4.1	37.3	0.3	133.1	12.8
9. 1951	128.6	56.–	59.7	12.9	19.4	148.–	92.–	5.1	37.4	0.2	134.7	13.3
10. 1951	130.5	56.7	60.9	12.9	19.6	150.1	95.–	3.7	37.8	0.2	136.7	13.4
11. 1951	131.8	57.3	61.6	13.–	19.6	151.4	96.3	3.8	37.5	0.5	138.1	13.3
12. 1951	133.4	58.3	61.9	13.2	20.2	153.6	98.1	3.4	37.9	0.8	140.2	13.4
Yearly averages	127.5	55.2	59.6	12.7	19.2	146.7	91.9	4.6	36.9	0.4	133.8	12.9
1. 1952	132.8	57.5	62.–	13.3	20.–	152.8	97.9	2.8	38.3	0.2	139.2	13.6
2. 1952	132.2	57.6	61.3	13.4	19.7	151.9	95.7	3.9	38.5	0.4	138.5	13.4
3. 1952	132.5	57.8	61.1	13.6	20.3	152.8	94.8	5.8	38.7	0.2	139.5	13.3
4. 1952	132.3	58.2	60.4	13.7	19.9	152.2	95.1	4.5	38.9	0.7	139.2	13.–
5. 1952	133.1	58.5	60.7	13.8	19.7	152.8	95.3	4.4	39.1	0.8	139.6	13.2
6. 1952	134.8	59.6	61.2	14.–	20.–	154.8	95.8	5.9	39.4	0.3	141.4	13.4
7. 1952	136.8	59.7	62.9	14.1	20.4	157.2	95.7	7.–	39.7	1.4	143.8	13.4
8. 1952	136.6	60.2	62.–	14.4	19.8	156.4	95.8	6.2	39.9	0.9	142.8	13.6
9. 1952	137.1	61.2	61.6	14.3	20.6	157.7	96.4	6.5	40.1	0.4	143.4	14.3
10. 1952	139.4	62.4	62.9	14.2	20.4	159.8	98.6	5.3	40.4	1.2	145.5	14.3
11. 1952	141.7	63.4	64.1	14.2	20.9	162.6	99.4	7.–	40.3	1.6	148.3	14.3
12. 1952	141.6	64.2	63.3	14.1	19.9	161.5	101.5	5.3	41.–	0.2	148.–	13.5
Yearly averages	135.9	60.–	62.–	13.9	20.1	156.–	96.8	5.4	39.5	0.7	142.4	13.6
1. 1953	140.8	63.9	62.8	14.2	20.5	161.3	100.5	4.2	41.1	1.3	147.1	14.2
2. 1953	140.1	64.1	61.9	14.1	20.–	160.1	98.3	5.4	41.3	0.8	145.8	14.3
3. 1953	140.–	65.2	60.5	14.3	20.1	160.1	97.4	5.8	41.5	0.7	145.4	14.7
4. 1953	138.5	65.3	58.9	14.3	19.8	158.3	98.–	2.9	41.8	1.2	143.9	14.4
5. 1953	138.1	65.4	58.3	14.4	19.8	157.9	97.5	2.9	42.–	0.6	143.–	14.9
6. 1953	138.1	65.5	58.4	14.2	20.8	158.9	97.2	3.8	42.4	0.3	143.7	15.2
7. 1953	143.2	65.6	63.2	14.3	19.6	162.8	97.4	7.5	42.6	0.6	148.1	14.7
8. 1953	143.1	66.–	62.6	14.5	19.4	162.5	97.5	7.–	42.8	0.5	147.8	14.7
9. 1953	143.–	66.3	62.2	14.5	19.4	162.4	97.7	6.2	43.1	0.3	147.3	15.1
10. 1953	144.–	67.1	62.3	14.5	19.5	163.5	100.3	3.8	43.5	0.3	147.9	15.6
11. 1953	145.5	67.2	63.7	14.6	19.8	165.3	100.2	5.7	43.2	0.5	149.6	15.7
12. 1953	146.4	68.3	63.6	14.5	20.1	166.5	103.3	4.1	43.8	0.2	151.4	15.1
Yearly averages	141.7	65.8	61.5	14.4	19.9	161.6	98.8	4.9	42.4	0.6	146.7	14.9
1. 1954	145.3	66.5	64.2	14.7	20.4	165.7	102.3	3.1	44.1	0.1	149.6	16.1
2. 1954	144.9	66.9	63.–	15.–	19.6	164.5	99.6	4.2	44.3	0.2	148.3	16.2
3. 1954	142.8	67.–	60.7	15.1	19.5	162.3	96.7	5.1	44.8	0.2	146.8	15.5
4. 1954	144.1	66.8	62.1	15.2	19.6	163.7	98.6	4.2	45.–	0.1	147.9	15.8
5. 1954	145.7	67.1	63.3	15.3	19.7	165.4	98.7	4.8	45.4	0.2	149.1	16.3
6. 1954	146.4	67.3	63.5	15.5	19.2	165.6	98.1	5.6	46.–	0.2	149.9	15.7
7. 1954	147.3	67.3	64.3	15.7	19.–	166.3	100.–	3.6	46.3	0.2	150.1	16.2
8. 1954	149.5	66.5	67.3	15.7	18.4	167.9	99.4	5.1	46.5	0.2	151.2	16.7
9. 1954	150.6	67.3	67.3	16.–	18.2	168.8	101.2	4.1	46.7	0.2	152.2	16.6
10. 1954	154.–	67.7	70.2	16.1	18.9	172.9	103.1	5.7	47.–	0.3	156.1	16.8
11. 1954	155.7	69.4	70.1	16.2	19.2	174.9	104.–	6.6	46.6	0.3	157.5	17.4
12. 1954	156.8	71.1	69.5	16.2	19.3	176.1	106.9	4.3	47.–	0.4	158.6	17.5
Yearly averages	148.6	67.6	65.5	15.6	19.2	167.8	100.7	4.7	45.8	0.2	151.4	16.4

[1] Demand deposits other than interbank and U. S. govt., less cash items reported as in process of collection.

Credit Range of All Commercial Banks. Last Wednesday of the month (in billions of dollars)

	Claims						Liabilities					
	Loans and investments											
	Total	Loans	U.S.govt. securities	Other securities	Member bank reserves	Total	Demand deposits¹	U.S.govt. deposits	Time deposits	Discounts and advances	Total	Credit range
1. 1955	156.2	70.6	69.–	16.7	18.9	175.1	107.–	3.5	47.2	0.4	158.1	17.–
2. 1955	154.8	71.2	66.8	16.8	18.5	173.3	104.5	4.3	47.3	0.4	156.5	16.8
3. 1955	153.5	72.3	64.2	17.–	18.4	171.9	102.4	4.1	47.6	0.7	154.8	17.1
4. 1955	155.5	72.9	65.6	17.–	18.7	174.2	104.5	4.6	47.6	0.5	157.2	17.–
5. 1955	155.6	73.9	65.–	16.7	18.6	174.2	103.3	5.1	47.8	0.5	156.7	17.5
6. 1955	155.5	75.7	63.–	16.8	18.6	174.1	103.4	4.9	48.1	0.7	157.1	17.–
7. 1955	157.–	76.6	63.7	16.7	18.9	175.9	103.9	5.7	48.–	0.5	158.1	17.8
8. 1955	156.7	77.3	62.5	16.9	18.4	175.1	103.9	4.9	48.3	0.5	157.6	17.5
9. 1955	157.3	78.4	62.–	16.9	18.5	175.8	104.9	4.2	48.4	0.7	158.2	17.6
10. 1955	158.9	79.2	62.9	16.8	18.9	177.8	106.1	4.5	48.5	1.–	160.1	17.7
11. 1955	159.4	81.4	61.4	16.6	18.5	177.9	106.9	4.2	48.1	0.6	159.8	18.1
12. 1955	161.1	82.8	61.8	16.5	18.9	180.–	109.7	3.7	48.5	0.5	162.4	17.6
Yearly averages	156.8	76.–	64.–	16.8	18.6	175.4	105.–	4.5	48.–	0.6	158.1	17.4
1. 1956	159.4	82.–	60.9	16.5	18.7	178.1	108.9	2.–	48.6	0.8	160.3	17.8
2. 1956	158.3	82.5	59.2	16.6	18.4	176.7	105.6	3.6	48.9	0.6	158.7	18.–
3. 1956	159.9	84.7	58.6	16.6	18.6	178.5	104.4	6.2	49.2	0.7	160.5	18.–
4. 1956	160.1	85.3	58.2	16.6	18.5	178.6	106.1	4.1	49.1	0.9	160.2	18.4
5. 1956	159.7	86.–	57.3	16.4	18.2	177.9	104.2	5.4	49.3	0.6	159.5	18.4
6. 1956	160.5	87.7	56.4	16.4	18.6	179.1	105.1	5.1	49.8	0.5	160.5	18.6
7. 1956	159.6	87.1	56.2	16.3	18.3	177.9	105.2	3.3	50.–	0.5	159.–	18.9
8. 1956	161.–	87.5	57.2	16.4	18.3	179.3	104.5	5.5	50.2	0.5	160.7	18.6
9. 1956	162.–	88.5	56.9	16.6	18.7	180.7	105.4	5.1	50.4	0.6	161.5	19.2
10. 1956	162.5	88.8	57.4	16.3	18.7	181.2	107.4	3.5	50.6	0.5	162.–	19.2
11. 1956	164.–	89.5	58.2	16.3	18.9	182.9	108.3	4.9	50.–	0.4	163.6	19.3
12. 1956	165.7	91.2	58.3	16.2	19.1	184.8	110.7	3.9	50.6	0.6	165.8	19.–
Yearly averages	161.1	86.7	57.9	16.4	18.6	179.6	106.3	4.4	49.7	0.6	161.–	18.6
1. 1957	162.8	88.9	57.7	16.2	18.9	181.7	109.5	1.6	51.6	0.7	163.4	18.3
2. 1957	162.5	89.3	56.8	16.3	18.6	181.1	107.–	2.5	52.1	0.5	162.1	19.–
3. 1957	162.9	90.6	55.7	16.5	18.3	181.2	105.2	3.5	52.9	0.6	162.2	19.–
4. 1957	165.1	91.–	57.5	16.7	18.9	184.–	107.3	4.–	53.3	0.7	165.3	18.7
5. 1957	165.1	91.2	57.1	16.8	18.7	183.8	104.8	5.–	53.9	1.–	164.7	19.1
6. 1957	165.6	93.3	55.5	16.8	18.6	184.2	105.6	4.5	54.3	0.8	165.2	19.–
7. 1957	165.4	92.3	56.3	16.8	18.6	184.–	106.6	3.4	54.7	0.4	165.1	18.9
8. 1957	165.9	92.8	56.2	16.9	18.6	184.5	105.1	4.1	55.1	0.8	165.1	19.4
9. 1957	166.3	93.4	55.9	17.–	18.6	184.9	105.5	3.6	55.4	0.8	165.3	19.6
10. 1957	167.9	93.–	57.3	17.6	18.8	186.7	107.2	3.2	55.8	0.8	167.–	19.7
11. 1957	167.3	93.–	56.8	17.4	18.7	186.–	107.2	3.–	55.3	0.6	166.1	19.9
12. 1957	169.8	94.3	57.8	17.7	19.4	189.2	108.9	4.2	55.8	0.8	169.7	19.5
Yearly averages	165.5	91.9	56.7	16.9	18.7	184.3	106.7	3.7	54.2	0.7	165.1	19.2

¹ Demand deposits other than interbank and U. S. govt., less cash items reported as in process of collection.

Table 2 B (continued)   83

Credit Range of All Commercial Banks
(Last Wednesday of month, in billion dollars)

		Claims						Liabilities					
		Loans and Investments											
				U.S. Govt. sec.	Other sec.	Memb. bank res.	Total	Dem. dep. (1)	U.S. Govt. dep.	Time dep.	Dis. and adv.	Total	Credit Range
		Total	Loans										
1.	1958	167.6	92.0	57.7	17.9	19.0	186.6	107.6	2.1	56.8	0.3	166.8	19.8
2.	1958	168.6	92.1	58.3	18.2	18.9	187.5	105.6	3.5	57.8	0.2	167.1	20.4
3.	1958	171.4	93.0	59.5	18.9	18.4	189.8	104.6	5.6	59.1	0.1	169.4	20.4
4.	1958	175.6	93.5	62.8	19.3	18.3	193.9	107.2	5.2	60.2	0.2	172.8	21.1
5.	1958	175.4	92.9	63.1	19.4	18.0	193.4	105.8	5.4	61.0	0.2	172.4	21.0
6.	1958	179.9	95.6	64.2	20.1	18.6	198.5	106.2	9.2	61.8	0.1	177.3	21.2
7.	1958	177.6	93.6	64.1	19.9	18.2	195.8	108.1	4.0	62.6	0.1	174.8	21.0
8.	1958	180.0	93.8	66.1	20.2	18.2	198.2	107.5	5.5	63.0	0.2	176.2	22.0
9.	1958	179.5	94.2	64.7	20.6	18.1	197.6	108.1	4.2	63.0	0.3	175.6	22.0
10.	1958	181.7	95.0	66.2	20.5	18.3	200.0	111.0	3.4	63.2	0.4	178.0	22.0
11.	1958	184.1	96.1	67.7	20.3	18.9	203.0	111.9	5.6	62.4	1.0	180.9	22.1
12.	1958	185.2	98.2	66.4	20.6	18.5	203.7	115.5	4.2	63.5	0.1	183.3	20.4
Yearly averages		177.2	94.2	63.4	19.7	18.5	195.7	108.3	4.8	61.2	0.3	174.6	21.1
1.	1959	185.6	97.7	67.5	20.4	18.5	204.1	113.8	4.5	63.7	0.5	182.5	21.6
2.	1959	183.8	97.9	65.5	20.4	18.2	202.0	111.3	4.1	64.0	0.6	180.0	22.0
3.	1959	182.9	99.2	63.2	20.6	18.2	201.1	110.3	3.6	64.4	0.6	178.9	22.2
4.	1959	185.7	101.2	63.6	20.9	18.4	204.1	112.5	4.3	64.9	0.5	182.2	21.9
5.	1959	185.8	102.4	62.6	20.8	18.1	203.9	110.7	4.9	65.3	0.6	181.5	22.4
6.	1959	185.9	104.4	60.9	20.6	18.2	204.1	110.7	4.4	65.7	0.9	181.7	22.4
7.	1959	187.7	105.9	61.1	20.6	18.1	205.8	112.7	4.7	65.6	0.6	183.6	22.2
8.	1959	188.2	107.4	60.3	20.5	18.0	206.2	111.1	5.9	65.9	0.6	183.5	22.7
9.	1959	187.8	107.8	59.2	20.7	17.8	205.6	111.4	6.1	66.0	0.3	183.8	21.8
10.	1959	188.4	108.2	59.6	20.6	18.4	206.8	112.7	5.2	65.8	0.9	184.6	22.2
11.	1959	188.3	109.5	58.5	20.3	18.1	206.4	113.1	4.4	65.1	0.6	183.2	23.2
12.	1959	190.3	110.8	58.9	20.5	18.3	208.6	115.4	5.0	66.2	0.4	187.0	21.6
Yearly averages		186.7	104.4	61.7	20.7	18.2	204.9	112.1	4.8	65.2	0.6	182.7	22.2
1.	1960	187.8	109.5	58.0	20.3	17.9	205.7	114.0	3.5	65.5	0.5	183.5	22.2
2.	1960	186.5	110.2	56.2	20.1	17.5	204.0	110.5	4.5	65.6	0.4	181.0	23.0
3.	1960	185.7	111.4	54.2	20.1	18.0	203.7	108.8	4.4	66.3	0.8	180.3	23.4
4.	1960	188.8	113.0	55.8	20.0	18.2	207.0	111.5	4.5	66.5	0.5	183.0	24.0
5.	1960	188.6	113.6	55.1	19.8	17.9	206.5	107.7	6.9	66.8	0.4	181.8	24.7
6.	1960	188.9	114.8	54.2	19.9	17.9	206.8	107.8	7.1	67.7	0.3	182.9	23.9
7.	1960	190.9	114.2	56.7	20.0	18.4	209.3	110.1	6.2	68.2	0.3	184.8	24.5
8.	1960	191.2	114.7	56.6	20.0	18.4	209.6	108.9	5.4	69.1	0.4	183.8	25.8
9.	1960	193.3	115.4	57.7	20.2	19.0	212.3	109.3	7.4	69.7	0.6	187.0	25.3
10.	1960	195.6	114.8	60.4	20.4	19.3	214.9	112.2	6.0	70.3	0.9	189.4	25.5
11.	1960	195.5	115.0	60.2	20.3	19.4	214.9	111.9	5.4	70.3	0.1	187.7	27.2
12.	1960	199.5	117.6	61.0	20.9	19.6	219.1	115.1	5.9	71.6	0.1	192.7	26.4
Yearly averages		191.0	113.7	57.2	20.2	18.5	209.5	110.7	5.6	68.1	0.4	184.8	24.7

---

1. *Demand deposits other than interbank and U. S. Government, less cash items reported as in process of collection.*

Table 2 B (continued)

Credit Range of All Commercial Banks
(Last Wednesday of month, in billion dollars)

		Claims						Liabilities					
		Loans and Investments				Memb. bank res.	Total	Dem. dep. (1)	U.S. Govt. dep.	Time dep.	Dis. and adv.	Total	Credit Range
		Total	Loans	U.S. Govt. sec.	Other sec.								
1.	1961	197.0	114.2	61.9	20.9	19.2	216.2	114.7	3.3	72.0	0.1	190.1	26.1
2.	1961	199.3	116.7	61.3	21.3	19.2	218.5	110.6	5.8	73.6	0.3	190.3	28.2
3.	1961	198.0	116.6	59.7	21.7	18.7	216.7	110.3	4.2	74.5	0.1	189.1	27.6
4.	1961	199.7	117.2	60.7	21.8	18.7	218.4	113.6	2.0	75.3	0.0	190.9	27.5
5.	1961	201.2	117.8	61.5	21.9	18.8	220.0	110.6	4.8	78.2	0.1	193.7	26.3
6.	1961	201.8	118.0	61.8	22.1	19.0	220.8	110.3	6.4	79.4	0.1	196.2	24.6
7.	1961	205.1	118.1	64.7	22.3	19.1	224.2	113.0	5.5	79.8	0.1	198.4	25.8
8.	1961	205.1	118.4	64.2	22.5	19.0	224.1	111.5	5.3	80.5	0.1	197.4	26.7
9.	1961	209.9	120.5	66.1	23.3	19.7	229.6	112.4	8.2	81.1	0.1	201.8	27.8
10.	1961	210.3	120.5	66.6	23.2	20.2	230.5	115.7	5.7	81.7	0.2	203.3	27.2
11.	1961	211.3	121.7	66.2	23.4	19.8	231.1	116.2	5.5	81.5	0.1	203.3	27.8
12.	1961	215.4	124.9	66.6	23.9	21.2	236.6	120.5	5.9	82.4	0.6	209.4	27.2
Yearly averages		204.5	118.7	63.4	22.4	19.4	223.9	113.3	5.2	78.3	0.2	197.0	26.9
1.	1962	213.7	122.4	67.2	24.1	19.9	233.6	117.0	4.9	84.5	0.1	206.5	27.1
2.	1962	214.3	123.8	66.0	24.5	19.7	234.0	114.8	5.1	86.1	0.1	206.1	27.9
3.	1962	215.2	125.4	64.4	25.4	19.8	235.0	113.0	6.3	88.0	0.2	207.5	27.5
4.	1962	217.4	126.6	64.7	26.1	20.0	237.4	116.9	3.9	88.9	0.3	210.0	27.4
5.	1962	218.0	127.5	64.4	26.1	19.6	237.6	112.6	7.2	90.4	0.2	210.4	27.2
6.	1962	220.7	129.2	64.4	27.0	20.3	241.0	112.1	9.6	92.0	0.4	214.1	26.9
7.	1962	220.4	128.7	64.2	27.5	19.8	240.2	114.7	5.5	92.3	0.1	212.6	27.6
8.	1962	222.1	130.4	63.8	27.9	20.1	242.2	112.1	7.4	93.3	0.1	212.9	29.3
9.	1962	225.3	132.8	64.3	28.2	20.3	245.6	114.1	8.1	94.2	0.8	217.2	28.4
10.	1962	228.6	134.4	65.6	28.6	20.1	248.7	117.1	6.4	95.3	0.2	219.0	29.7
11.	1962	229.3	134.8	65.6	28.8	19.8	249.1	117.6	6.1	95.6	0.1	219.4	29.7
12.	1962	235.8	140.1	66.4	29.3	20.2	256.0	122.3	6.8	97.7	0.2	227.0	29.0
Yearly averages		221.7	129.7	65.1	27.0	20.0	241.7	115.4	6.4	91.5	0.2	213.6	28.1
1.	1963	232.0	136.3	66.2	29.5	19.7	251.7	119.2	4.3	99.3	0.1	222.9	28.8
2.	1963	233.6	138.4	65.3	29.9	19.8	253.4	116.5	6.4	100.8	0.1	233.8	29.6
3.	1963	234.9	139.4	64.8	30.7	19.6	254.5	115.4	7.3	102.4	0.2	225.3	29.2
4.	1963	234.9	139.5	64.0	31.4	20.0	254.9	118.2	3.8	103.3	0.9	226.2	28.7
5.	1963	236.5	141.8	63.0	31.7	19.6	256.1	114.2	6.8	104.7	0.1	225.8	30.3
6.	1963	241.0	145.0	63.5	32.4	20.0	261.0	115.3	11.1	105.9	0.6	232.9	28.1
7.	1963	241.0	145.6	62.5	32.9	20.4	261.4	117.8	7.1	106.8	0.3	232.0	29.4
8.	1963	240.4	145.8	60.9	33.7	19.6	260.0	115.8	5.9	107.9	0.3	229.9	30.1
9.	1963	244.8	148.9	61.8	34.2	20.1	264.9	117.0	8.8	108.3	0.5	234.6	30.3
10.	1963	246.1	149.7	62.0	34.4	20.2	266.3	120.8	3.6	110.2	0.2	234.8	31.5
11.	1963	249.1	152.7	62.3	34.1	20.1	269.2	121.6	4.4	110.4	0.6	237.0	32.2
12.	1963	254.2	156.0	63.2	35.0	21.1	275.3	124.6	6.7	111.1	0.1	242.5	32.8
Yearly averages		240.7	144.9	63.3	32.5	20.0	260.7	118.0	6.4	105.9	0.3	230.6	30.1

1. *Demand deposits other than interbank and U. S. Government, less cash items reported as in process of collection.*

Table 2 B (continued)   85

Credit Range of All Commercial Banks
(Last Wednesday of month, in billion dollars)

		Claims					Liabilities					
		Loans and Investments										
			U.S.		Memb.		Dem.	U.S.		Dis.		
			Govt.	Other	Bank		dep.	Govt.	Time	and		Credit
		Total	Loans	sec.	sec.	res.	Total	(1)	dep.	dep.	adv.	Total	Range
1.	1964	249.8	153.1	62.1	34.6	20.4	270.2	122.8	2.8	113.9	0.3	239.8	30.4
2.	1964	250.6	154.0	61.5	35.1	20.6	271.2	118.8	5.7	115.0	0.6	240.1	31.1
3.	1964	253.9	156.8	61.5	35.6	20.1	274.0	118.8	7.9	116.1	0.1	242.9	31.1
4.	1964	254.6	158.7	60.1	35.8	20.2	274.8	121.0	4.2	117.3	0.4	242.9	31.9
5.	1964	255.7	160.9	59.1	35.7	20.1	275.8	117.6	7.2	118.6	0.2	243.6	32.2
6.	1964	260.2	164.5	59.3	36.4	20.7	280.9	120.3	10.3	119.6	0.1	250.3	30.6
7.	1964	258.6	163.8	58.3	36.5	20.7	279.3	121.0	5.1	120.5	0.3	246.9	32.4
8.	1964	260.3	164.4	58.8	37.1	20.2	280.5	119.8	6.0	121.4	0.1	247.3	33.2
9.	1964	266.2	167.7	60.7	37.8	20.9	287.1	122.7	9.2	122.4	0.1	254.4	32.7
10.	1964	266.6	167.2	61.4	38.0	21.3	287.9	125.2	4.8	123.8	0.5	254.3	33.6
11.	1964	271.1	170.3	62.7	38.1	20.9	292.0	125.0	7.1	124.2	0.2	256.5	35.5
12.	1964	277.4	175.6	63.0	38.8	22.2	299.6	132.3	6.5	126.7	0.4	265.9	33.7
Yearly	averages												
		260.4	163.1	60.7	36.6	20.7	281.1	122.1	6.4	120.0	0.3	248.7	32.4
1.	1965	274.0	173.4	61.5	39.1	21.8	295.8	127.4	4.1	129.4	0.2	261.1	34.7
2.	1965	275.2	175.5	60.0	39.7	20.7	296.0	123.1	6.7	131.2	0.1	261.1	34.9
3.	1965	278.3	179.0	59.0	40.3	21.2	299.5	123.0	8.3	133.1	0.1	264.5	35.0
4.	1965	281.2	181.5	58.3	41.4	21.4	302.6	125.6	6.8	134.4	0.3	267.1	35.5
5.	1965	282.2	183.9	57.2	41.1	21.0	303.2	121.6	9.9	135.6	0.3	267.4	35.8
6.	1965	287.7	188.6	56.9	42.2	22.2	309.9	124.4	11.8	137.4	0.7	274.3	35.6
7.	1965	285.9	187.1	56.3	42.6	21.9	307.8	125.1	6.9	139.0	0.6	271.6	36.2
8.	1965	287.8	188.9	55.5	43.4	21.7	309.5	123.6	7.2	140.6	0.5	271.9	37.6
9.	1965	291.5	191.7	55.9	43.8	21.8	313.3	126.3	7.4	142.0	0.1	275.8	37.5
10.	1965	295.3	192.8	58.4	44.1	21.6	316.9	129.5	4.1	144.0	0.4	278.0	38.9
11.	1965	297.1	194.6	58.8	43.8	22.1	319.2	128.8	5.4	144.5	0.8	279.5	39.7
12.	1965	306.1	201.7	59.5	44.9	23.4	329.5	138.3	5.5	146.7	0.5	291.0	38.5
Yearly	averages												
		286.9	186.6	58.1	42.2	21.7	308.6	126.4	7.0	138.2	0.4	271.9	36.7
1.	1966	302.2	198.1	59.6	44.4	22.8	325.0	134.0	3.9	147.8	0.9	286.6	38.4
2.	1966	302.0	199.6	57.3	45.1	21.3	323.3	128.5	5.4	148.7	0.7	283.3	40.0
3.	1966	304.3	203.5	55.4	45.4	22.2	326.5	130.3	5.1	151.2	0.6	287.2	39.3
4.	1966	307.1	205.2	55.4	46.5	22.8	329.9	133.2	5.0	152.8	0.2	291.2	38.7
5.	1966	308.1	207.4	53.5	47.1	22.0	330.1	127.3	7.8	154.4	0.4	289.9	40.2
6.	1966	314.2	212.0	53.5	48.8	22.8	337.0	131.0	11.0	155.0	0.6	297.6	39.4
7.	1966	312.4	211.0	52.7	48.6	22.9	335.3	129.7	6.2	156.8	1.0	293.7	41.6
8.	1966	314.0	211.8	53.7	48.4	21.9	335.9	129.9	4.7	157.4	0.4	292.4	43.5
9.	1966	314.9	212.5	53.6	48.8	22.6	337.5	129.3	6.0	157.1	1.0	293.4	44.1
10.	1966	314.2	212.0	53.6	48.6	23.3	337.5	131.6	4.7	156.5	0.6	293.4	44.1
11.	1966	315.8	213.5	54.4	47.9	24.0	339.8	133.5	3.8	156.0	0.5	293.8	46.0
12.	1966	322.7	217.7	56.2	48.8	24.9	347.6	139.3	5.0	158.8	1.0	304.1	43.5
Yearly	averages												
		311.0	208.7	54.9	47.4	22.8	333.8	131.5	5.7	154.4	0.7	292.2	41.6

1. *Demand deposits other than interbank and U. S. Government, less cash items reported as in process of collection.*

Table 3 B

Total Capital Accounts of All Commercial Banks

(Last Wednesday of month, in billion dollars)

Months	1947	1948	1949	1950	1951	1952	1953	1954	1955	1956
1.		10.1	10.5	11.0	11.6	12.2	12.9	13.6	14.6	15.3
2.		10.1	10.6	11.0	11.6	12.3	12.9	13.7	14.7	15.5
3.		10.2	10.6	11.1	11.7	12.3	13.0	13.7	14.7	15.5
4.		10.2	10.6	11.1	11.7	12.5	13.1	13.9	14.8	15.7
5.		10.3	10.7	11.2	11.8	12.5	13.2	13.9	14.9	15.8
6.		10.3	10.8	11.4	12.0	12.6	13.3	14.0	14.9	15.9
7.	9.9	10.3	10.8	11.4	12.0	12.6	13.3	14.1	15.0	15.9
8.	9.9	10.4	10.8	11.5	12.1	12.6	13.3	14.1	15.1	16.0
9.	9.9	10.4	10.9	11.5	12.1	12.7	13.5	14.2	15.1	16.3
10.	10.0	10.5	10.9	11.6	12.2	12.8	13.6	14.4	15.3	16.3
11.	10.0	10.5	11.0	11.6	12.2	12.8	13.6	14.6	15.4	16.4
12.	10.1	10.5	11.0	11.6	12.2	12.9	13.6	14.6	15.3	16.3
Averages	10.0	10.3	10.8	11.3	11.9	12.6	13.3	14.1	15.0	15.9

Months	1957	1958	1959	1960	1961	1962	1963	1964	1965	1966
1.	16.4	17.5	18.6	19.6	21.1	22.5	23.8	25.4	27.6	30.2
2.	16.5	17.6	18.6	19.7	21.2	22.6	24.0	25.7	27.7	30.3
3.	16.5	17.7	18.7	19.9	21.0	22.6	24.1	25.7	28.1	30.4
4.	16.6	17.8	18.9	20.0	21.2	22.7	24.2	26.1	28.2	30.7
5.	16.7	17.9	19.0	20.1	21.5	22.9	24.4	26.4	28.5	30.8
6.	16.7	18.2	19.0	20.3	21.7	23.2	24.6	26.8	29.5	31.3
7.	17.0	18.2	19.2	20.4	21.7	23.0	24.5	26.6	29.3	31.1
8.	17.1	18.3	19.3	20.6	21.9	23.2	24.6	26.8	29.4	31.4
9.	17.1	18.4	19.4	20.7	22.2	23.3	24.7	27.1	29.6	31.5
10.	17.4	18.5	19.5	20.8	22.1	23.6	24.9	27.2	29.9	31.6
11.	17.4	18.5	19.6	21.0	22.3	23.7	25.0	27.4	30.1	31.9
12.	17.5	18.5	19.6	21.0	22.5	24.1	25.7	27.8	30.3	32.1
Averages	16.9	18.1	19.1	20.3	21.7	23.1	24.5	26.6	29.0	31.1

Section 3. The Changed Structure
Only after World War II did the United States economy really expand and diversify, which is evident from the immense increase in the GNP. We have experienced in this country an almost uninterrupted boom with generally high and rising outlays for housing, business plant and equipment, and public works. Our economy can be regarded almost as a closed unit for our purposes. This continuous development on the largest goods and capital market in the world finally furnishes us with sufficient material for studying the conditions. Only in the most recent years, after the development continued for a while, has it become possible to subject our economy and thereby particularly the prevailing theory of capital to an effective investigation.

Section 4. The Money Supply and Its Substitutes
The money supply represents the quantity of money or circulating medium. (5) It thus encompasses, first of all, money in the hand of the public, and further, as is generally assumed, demand deposits in the banks, since these deposits serve the purposes of turnover, too. This is formally correct, yet such formal statements are useless for practical considerations if they do not correspond to actual conditions and development.
The Federal Reserve Bank of Richmond [56] has the following comments on this:
"A quandary exists as to whether one should include time deposits and short-term highly liquid securities.... The dilemma is usually resolved by using the Federal Reserve's published statistics, 'demand deposits, adjusted, plus currency outside banks,' as a measure of money supply.... Short-term liquid assets and time deposits are not included because they must be converted into money before being 'spent.'"
Yet nothing is clarified by such an attitude. One can proceed in this manner in a theoretical treatise where, at the very beginning, an arbitrary assumption is made upon which all calculations are then based; our economic reasoning may be sharpened by such a practice. For practical purposes, however, such a procedure is inadvisable, since it can, as in this case, lead to faulty conclusions.
The substitutes for money supply over which the economy disposes are manifold. The most important of these are bills of the Treasury. If no bills were in circulation, investors would have had to keep ready the largest part of this amount in demand deposits. Recently the same applies to certificates of deposits.

---

5. *C. Warburton [214] lists four methods for measuring the money supply, each of which comprises other items.*

This stock of bills and certificates of deposits in the hand of investors is sufficient by itself to show how misleading any statistics and all comparisons must be if they operate with the concept of "money supply." In comparing statistical tabulations of two dates usually a difference of a few hundred million dollars is shown, but bills and certificates of deposits may constitute a difference of many billion dollars, and they are not taken into consideration at all.

G. Katona, A. Lauterbach, and S. W. Steinkamp [119] thus report on the basis of inquiries that at a short-term rate of interest of three percent or more business invests its extra money in short-term securities, such as Treasury notes, bills, commercial paper, tax anticipation notes; yet when the rate is beneath this level the money is rather left with the banks. In the first half of 1958, for example, with a falling rate of interest, bills of "other" investors decreased by 5.4 billion dollars, and marketable securities, due within one year, by 7.7 billion dollars. E. V. Bell [14] once called bills "interest-bearing cash."

The Federal Reserve further lists currently the amount of money supply, including time deposits. In this manner yet another incidental element is included in the tables, for it is irrelevant for the economy whether a saver leaves his savings as time deposits in a bank or somewhere else. The picture is further confused by this and the value of the statement is further reduced.

Beside bills, likewise certificates, bonds and notes, which are soon due, and short-term paper can be held in readiness as a reserve. Also increased loans to small business have to be considered another substitute or supplement for demand deposits; it is estimated that one half of small business inventory requirements is financed in this manner. It is further reported that especially in the fur and canning industries trade acceptances are widely used; they constitute a full substitute for payment between business.

In recent times the practice has been established that banks oblige their debtors to keep deposited with them at all times twenty per cent of granted loans. These amounts are frozen for a long time and have no turnover; they are to be written off, in reality, against loans. They do not constitute money supply and only add to the vagueness of this concept.

Finally, it has to be taken into consideration that credit lines reduce the necessity of keeping ready larger demand deposits. In a period of prosperity, as we have experienced it since World War II, with steadily rising savings and an expansion of enterprises, credit lines may be regarded as a potential substitute for demand deposits.

The respective currency and demand deposits will probably have to be accepted as one of the data of the economic system, since we are not in a position to make any calculation which is only partly reliable regarding their fluctuations. (6)

Section 5. The Velocity of Circulation
1. The problem of the velocity of circulation belongs to
the most debated problems of economics. The differences of opinion are so great that the demand is made "to eliminate, once and
for all, the phrase 'velocity of circulation' from our vocabulary."
It is "unfortunate because those who employ it tend to make an independent entity out of it and imbue it with a soul." (7) Another
economist inquires: "Has the time not come finally to abolish
definitely the concept of velocity of circulation on which hardly
two authors agree?" (8)
The decisive question in the discussion appears to be
whether the Federal Reserve System is in a position to influence
or, more specifically, to counteract the velocity. The theoretical aspect of this problem has not yet been examined. On the one
hand, it is emphasized that fluctuations in the turnover of money
are beyond the control of the credit authorities and there is no
effective way to hold them in check; there is nothing anyone can
do about it. On the other hand, it is maintained that "a further
rise in monetary velocity hardly constituted an effective avenue
of escape from credit restraint." (9)
2. Once we have found that the data regarding money supply
are not of much use, its velocity can also have only little meaning. We do not know anything about the transaction velocity of
currency and bills and of other substitutes and supplements for
demand deposits (discussed in previous chapters); all this is not
measurable under the given circumstances, and thus we cannot obtain any total picture of it.
3. Another difficulty consists in the fact that there
will always be a lag between the increase of demand deposits and
the rise of the GNP, since in order to achieve a higher turnover,
business has to prepare and to use higher demand deposits during
a certain period of time before (the GNP only refers to finished
goods and services). This period will vary depending on the
branch of business and on other circumstances. The same data are
thus not comparable for both magnitudes, since they do not refer
to corresponding situations. Hence, the concept "income velocity"
has little meaning if this lag is not considered in the calculations.

---

6. *H. G. Johnson [111] remarks: "The money supply in the
future will likely be a passive result rather than an active de-
terminant of other developments."*
7. *A. H. Hansen [92].*
8. *H. W. H. Wijnholds [218].*
9. *Federal Reserve Bank of New York [55].*

Since we know so little about the velocity of circulation and cannot hope to learn more about it in the foreseeable future, the application of this concept is even less justified than that of money supply. (10)

Section 6. The Turnover
The transaction-velocity of demand deposits can give us an idea of the velocity of the turnover of money in the checking accounts of the commercial banks. Here it is used only as a data in an estimated order of magnitude, and it thus has only an indicative meaning for us.

We shall assume that checks drawn against demand deposits in the course of a year amount to twenty-five times the average volume of deposits. If we assume, again only in approximate figures, that the demand deposits increase by 2.5 per cent annually, it follows that with every disbursement only one per mil on the average is retained by the same bank, and the remainder, i.e., 99.9 per cent, is used for the creation of new values, i.e., for "values in production," as we shall henceforth refer to them.

Out of this 1/1000 growth, which takes place at the shift of the demand deposits across the accounts, a credit creation would thus have to result, which, according to the prevailing theory, is continuous. However, we shall not at this point enter into the usual discussion on how the demand deposits may grow when transferred from one bank to the other, how long this process will take, and whether such a development is at all materially possible. At present, we only want to discuss the situation as it actually exists in business life, proceeding from the standpoint of the individual bank.

Thus, for the time being, we are interested in the question whether the individual bank would be in a position - considering all factors and exercising due care - to grant out of this 1/1000 part five or six times as much in loans. It seems that this question can be answered in the negative in advance, for even advocates of the theory of credit creation are of the opinion that only if the velocity of circulation were much smaller might the theory be confirmed. (11)

---

10. H. Leuthner [128] points out that the concepts "velocity of circulation" and "quantity of money" are too undefined in theory and statistics to be employed in a realistic monetary circuit theory.

11. H. Ritterhausen [169] writes on this: "Within the framework of payment, i.e., of money with a high velocity of circulation, there exists no creation of money or credit."

It must be assumed that each bank will normally recognize the risk it runs by proceeding to a multiple credit creation on the basis of this 1/1000 increase. It cannot count on any corresponding action from the other banks, and it will want to maintain its liquidity position within the customary frame. The fact that usually it does not leave itself any leeway also explains why a common planned action is impossible: no elbow room is created which would permit an eventual joint maneuver.

Section 7. Bank Reserves

It has already been mentioned that in the past years the development and changes of turnover in the monetary circuit have been insufficiently treated. In the statistical statements the Federal Reserve was assumed to be the pivot of the entire monetary activity, and all events were calculated and interpreted only from the standpoint of the financial conditions of the Federal Reserve Banks. The first pages of the financial and business statistics of each Federal Reserve Bulletin contain only data which are connected with these conditions. If data related to the Treasury are listed, they are soon subtracted, so that there is once more a return to the financial statements of the Federal Reserve Banks and their individual positions. Thus, reserve bank credit, required reserves, excess reserves, float and "related item" are computed as if these factors, before anything else, were responsible for the entire money circuit. Basically, they are only statements of condition of the Federal Reserve Banks, mostly for each week, represented in reverse order.

The actual development is in crass contrast to what is stated about bank reserves on the basis of the applied official statistics. It is obvious from our remarks in Section 2 that since World War II the Federal Reserve by its measures has not, by itself, changed its credit range, that of the banks and of the remainder of the economy, and that, under existing conditions, the banks equally were unable to grant additional credit to the economy. Those positions in the statement of conditions of the Federal Reserve (gold reserve and currency in circulation) which had caused fluctuations within its credit range could not normally be influenced by the Federal Reserve. (This will be discussed later.) Thus, the Federal Reserve could do as little to change the range of money disposal of the commercial banks as that of other financial institutions or nonbank investors which admittedly are not under its control. Hence, the Federal Reserve did not create any additional credit nor did it manipulate any credit during this period, so that the changes in bank reserves can be attributed only a subordinate role.

The Federal Reserve cannot by manipulating bank reserves reduce (or expand) the credit basis of the country, for amounts taken away from banks (or given to banks) must continue to be used

by the economy. Whatever more or less is lent or invested by
banks is supplemented by the Federal Reserve, and vice versa.
Through these fluctuations the Federal Reserve cannot withhold or
add anything, they do not change the range of disposable money of
the remainder of the economy, and this alone is the decisive factor.

The conflicting views on this question seem to consist
mainly in the opinion that, according to the traditional theory,
the Federal Reserve is excluded from the circuit, as if its movements counted for nothing. The Federal Reserve does not hold a
privileged position in this respect; it is incapable of acting in
any different and special manner, and it is technically unable,
similar to all other agents in the circuit, to cause a surplus or
a deficit to disappear. If the Federal Reserve does not increase
its loans to the banks, it has to use the amounts in question in
different ways in the economy, instead of using the instrumental-
ity of the banks. In the monetary circuit there are no "unused
funds" for the total economy in any form, and also not in that of
excess reserve balance.

It follows from this that the Federal Reserve is materially in no position to change its credit range or that of the banks
and of the remainder of the economy by manipulating bank reserves.
Thus, an increase or decrease of member bank reserves, factors
which are considered very important, are of no consequence to the
remainder of the economy.

Since manipulation of bank reserves does not change the
credit range of the Federal Reserve and of the commercial banks
among themselves and in relation to the remainder of the economy,
the relationship between the Federal Reserve and the commercial
banks is expressed only by the level of their deposits in the Federal Reserve, and shifts in these deposits merely influence the
internal relationship within the System.

Statistical data show that the excess reserves fluctuated
smoothly during the course of each year. There never were larger
shifts and the differences at any time amounted to only a few hundred million dollars. This means that the Federal Reserve did not
even influence the internal profit margin within the System, apart
from the reserve requirements rate. Hence, during the entire period, and independently of the prevailing trend, the Federal Reserve has not undertaken anything in the only direction in which
it was able to act.

It is assumed furthermore that the Reserve Banks can control the volume of reserve money merely by increasing and decreasing their assets. Reserve Banks can raise or lower the volume of
reserve money merely by increasing or decreasing their holding of
government securities (together with such acceptances, rediscounts,
advances, and industrial loans as are available).

However, it is not as simple to analyze the structure of

the statements of the condition of the Federal Reserve as that of
a private enterprise. The private businessman can alter, according to his judgment and depending on the business situation, the
individual debits and credits of his enterprise; the Federal Reserve, however, is bound by several factors which it cannot or may
not influence, and only on the basis of the existing conditions is
it in a position to form other elements of its statement of condition. The difficulty, which cannot be bridge, consists in the
word "merely." The Federal Reserve cannot increase and decrease
its assets at will because it does not control the amount of many
positions in its statements of condition; among these positions
belong, first of all, "gold certificates" and "Federal Reserve
notes." Those items, however, which can be changed, like the
"holding of government securities," are elements of the total circuit within the country and cannot influence the credit ranges.
They either have to be replaced by other assets or equivalent liabilities have to be liquidated, both, however, within the permitted framework which, besides, is always very limited. It makes no
difference whether the banks sell their securities to the Federal
Reserve or to other buyers, for the corresponding movements must
balance the effect in the entire circuit.
        The statistics on credit ranges and our discussion above
demonstrate that there can be no question of the commercial banks
having been obstructed at any moment by the Federal Reserve in
their freedom of movement or in their scope of function (apart
from changes in reserve requirements). The banks always have the
possibility to recover again within the circuit the amounts which
allegedly have been withdrawn from them; this is particularly true
in the same degree for the most frequently applied sales of bills
on the part of the Federal Reserve. Thus, the banks cannot expect
anything from the measures of the Federal Reserve which normally
can neither harm nor help them (see further discussion of the problem in Section 13).
        On the other hand, one might ask what purpose such measures
of the Federal Reserve could serve. If during the entire period
the commercial banks were unable to create additional credits, or
cancel existing ones, the measures directed at this by the Federal
Reserve would be useless.

        Section 8. The Formation of Demand Deposits
        We have to ask, above all, by what human dispositions do
increased amounts of money enter into the economy, and, furthermore, for what purpose are demand deposits formed. They serve
primarily the turnover of goods and the payment of services. The
keeping of demand deposits is too important a question for each
businessman to leave the decision to someone else. Each entrepre-
neur will keep that portion of his means in the form of demand deposits which he considers suitable at a given moment. On the av-

erage, this portion is relatively quite small. The businessman will calculate this very carefully, for, on the one hand, the keeping of demand deposits is expensive for him, since they bear no interest, and usually he could use this money profitably somewhere else. On the other hand, he will not permit his transactions and his economic plans to be thwarted by setting too low an amount. He will often revise his calculations and increase or decrease the demand deposits accordingly.

It should be considered, for instance, that during 1963-67, gross investment of nonfinancial business amounted to 57.3, 59.5, 69.7, 71.9, and 72.6 billion dollars, respectively, and at the end of these years demand deposits and currency of nonfinancial business amounted to 50.0, 48.2, 46.5, 47.2, and 46.5 billion dollars, respectively. From this follows that it would have been sufficient to divert only a small portion of the amount for gross investment to demand deposits in order to obtain a tremendous increment in money supply. It must be assumed that each corporation would have carried out the switch of the desired amount without much hesitation if it had appeared that its turnover money was insufficient. No firm probably would have risked the fruits of its investments because of a small difference.

It is emphasized in the discussion that one cannot control the rate at which people reach for their checkbooks. Yet in the same manner, it is impossible to dictate how much money the individual or the business are to keep in their checking accounts - if we stop thinking incoherently and begin to consider the total picture. The amounts which are not needed, or not needed temporarily, can be converted without any difficulty into other investment - even if only into certificates of deposits or time deposits at the same or another commercial bank or into deposits at a savings bank. Nobody can likewise prevent the businessman from buying Treasury bills for his demand deposits and, thus, decrease the money supply in the usual meaning of the term.

Seen from this point of view, the amount of demand deposits or currency in circulation is subject to the same determinants which affect the levels of savings or consumption. The public decides how much is to be consumed or saved, and, thus, it is also the decision of the public and of business how much demand deposits and currency are to be in circulation. Only as much as is needed by the economy is used; the remaining currency is deposited in the banks, and the remaining demand deposits are used somewhere else.

If one were to tell an unprejudiced businessman, who is unfamiliar with theoretical speculations, that someone determines and fixes the amount of demand deposits or even that he can be restricted in his freedom of decision to divert amounts from his own funds to demand deposits, he would certainly be surprised. He would reply that so far he had not noticed this, and he would -

correctly - refuse to believe this to be the case. Besides, it would be strange if in a free, modern economy a measure of general nature were possible which could limit to such a degree the natural freedom of action and the valid rights of businessmen. The question of how much currency and demand deposits are needed for turnover is essential; indeed, without the ability to determine it any planned business activity would be impossible. This question can therefore be decided by no one but the mature business which alone directs the economy. "Neither the Federal Reserve nor the Treasury is strong enough to override the forces of the grassroots that are there in this economy," (12) so that it is a misinterpretation of the entire economic process to assume that its sequence is different.

The remarks so far has demonstrated that there can be no question of a creation of additional credits by the banks, for in the modern economy no one can "create" anything in money matters. It seems to us that the correct term for this is "compensate." We have to visualize in what manner the businessman and the bank will proceed in this respect: if the businessman believes that he must increase his demand deposits for the purpose of mastering his turnover, he will either take up a loan in the desired amount from a bank (in terms of accounting, the bank will charge his loan account and credit his checking account) or, if for any reason he does not wish, or is unable, to go into debt, he will transfer the corresponding amount from his "values in production" to his checking account. In this second case, the bank usually will grant a loan in the amount of the increased demand deposits to another customer. In both cases, the bank will increase its loans by the same amount by which the demand deposits of the entire economy have been, or had to be, raised. Thus the action of the bank consists in compensating the amounts which the economy needs additionally for turnover purposes, so that in the end result the economy does not have to divert these amounts from the "values in production." If, on the other hand, during a recession business decreases its activity and, at the same time, its demand deposits, the banks also had to decrease their loans by a corresponding amount, i.e., "discompensate" the sinking demand deposits. At best, the banks can also compensate their cash items in process of collection because the respective amounts, upon which the checks have been drawn, still exist in terms of accounting and form an element of the statement of condition of the bank in question. The amounts falling to the share of this, however, are relatively small, fluctuate constantly, and can thus be disregarded in the end result.

_____

12. W. McC. Martin, J. [135].

The actual development confirms that business always maintained demand deposits only to the extent of its needs at a given moment, and no one else could interfere in this process. (13) As appears from our calculation in Section 2, under B, the demand deposits decreased after each lowering of the reserve requirements or rose by a few per mil, although, according to the theory of credit creation, they should have risen by 5 to 25 per cent.

---

13. A. Gambino [73] points out: "This does not signify that the credit system can decide at its own discretion the volume of financial assets to be held by the public; that it can 'force' the public to include in its budget the increases of financial assets. The public...is also free to choose where those holdings capacities should be used.... They end by having an influence on the real total of the assets themselves. The public can never be forced to take on an amount of financial assets...beyond the limits corresponding to its holding capacities and its choices. Robertson...and Keynes...have not realized...that the public can influence not only the value but also the volume of deposits, just as it can influence, in general, the volume of the other financial assets and of their whole."

H. J. Köhler [123] remarks that the influence of the central bank on the quantity of circulating money is in any case not very large, but, in addition, the concept of the quantity of money is, for itself, highly problematical...when one does not know what money is, and also cannot know how much of it exists.

H. G. Moulton [152]: "Many writers have used the expression 'pumping additional money into the channels of circulation' ...as though it were somehow forced into the hands of the public by bankers or government officials. The money supply is assumed to be independently expanded - without regard to the requirements of production and trade, and without association with the financial operations of business. The supply of money in the channels of circulation at any given time is simply the amount employed in organizing and carrying out productive operations. The magnitude of the money supply thus used is determined by the aggregate volume of production and the level of costs per unit of output. The supply of money and the supply of goods...rather both originate in, grow out of, productive operations in a pecuniary economy. These normally depend upon quite other factors than the supply of gold or bank reserves or fiscal and monetary policies."

A. Murad [153]: "The Federal Reserve authorities...need not trouble themselves to determine 'the volume of money appropriate to a given economic situation,' a task 'requiring continuous examination and study,' according to W. McC. Martin, Jr. The volume of money appropriate to a given economic situation is the vol-

The period during World War II further furnished us an ex-
cellent example of the process just described. Although in this
essay we are dealing with the development in the subsequent period, particularly during World War II the banks compensated demand
deposits without at the same time granting credits to business,
so that we discover here a kind of "pure," "dissected" illustra-
tion of the process. Thus extraordinary conditions may sometimes
permit us a view of actual interrelationships which otherwise
would be difficult to see.
     From December 1939 to December 1945, deposits in all com-
mercial banks rose from 47.8 billion dollars (demand deposits 32.5
and time deposits 15.3 billion) to 136.1 billion dollars (demand
deposits 105.9 and time deposits 30.2 billion), i.e., by 88.3 billion dollars (demand deposits by 73.4 and time deposits by 14.9
billion). At the same time, loans of all commercial banks increased only by 8.9 billion dollars (from 17.2 to 26.1 billion);
government securities, however, by 74.3 billion dollars (from 16.3
to 90.6 billion). It thus appears that during the war the economy formed 90 per cent of the demand deposits independently, and
received, at most, only 10 per cent of them in the form of loans
from banks. One can imagine that particularly during this period
when profit opportunities were very considerable, business was increasing demand deposits only very reluctantly by the tremendous
amount of 73.4 billion dollars, and maintaining it without interest; for instance, it could have transferred a part of this amount
as time deposits with its banks (if all other investment opportunities are disregarded). However, businessmen were forced to maintain such high demand deposits, for otherwise they would have been
unable to keep up with the increased turnover. We may assume that
a smaller amount would not have been sufficient.
     The demand deposits were increased, or actually had to be
increased out of the funds of business itself, as we have shown
above. Supposedly money was deposited only seldom directly for
this purpose; it is probable that the increase of demand deposits
resulted mainly by gradually leaving additional amounts on the
accounts. If this had not happened, the increased GNP necessary
for war production could not have been achieved.
     At this time, businessmen were not debtors but creditors,
and it is evident that the initiative was exclusively theirs, and

---

ume of money which the community wants to hold in that situation."
     G. Shea [193]: "It is business itself, in its own thrifty
way, which is keeping the money supply where it is. People who
seek to hold the Federal Government or the Reserve Board responsible for the fact the money supply hasn't grown any faster are looking in the wrong direction."

that the banks remained quite passive. The banks also followed
their interest in this period, always within reasonable limits,
compensating the additional demand deposits and investing the resulting amounts in government securities. If one were to assume
a reversed process, i.e., that the banks had granted credits to
the government before, and only then found covering for them in
demand deposits, they soon would have had to abolish this practice,
namely, if businessmen would not have increased their turnover and
consequently their demand deposits and had not become creditors of
the banks. (14)

World War II involved an expenditure approximating 380
billion dollars and in economic literature it is stated that a
quarter of this amount "was financed by creation of money through
the banking system" and that "the deposits on which the checks are
drawn are largely created through expansion of bank credit - bank
loans and investments." (15) The actual situation contradicts
such views. The strongest increase of demand deposits took place
during these years (by more than fifty per cent of the present-day
amount), and it is incorrect that they were "created through expansion of bank credit," for business alone supplied them directly. This fact cannot be ignored. Further, there was no "creation
of money through the banking system," for the banking system merely passed on the money deposited with it. According to the opposite and unjustified concept of the process, the banks would have
to present business with this allegedly created money in some way.

As far as the role of the Federal Reserve in this development is concerned, however, it can only be stated that the Federal
Reserve equally used all the means at its disposal, and especially
the deposits left with it on the basis of reserve requirements,
for the purchase of government securities, so that its stock of
these securities rose by 21.8 billion dollars (from 2.5 to 24.3
billion) from December 1939 to December 1945. Thus, it also
promptly compensated the counter-value of the part of demand deposits falling to its share. These data are sufficient to regard
the attitude of the Federal Reserve during this period as passive.
(16)

---

14. With regard to Germany, H. Hellwig [100] states that
for the sale of government obligations to the banks the government
did not receive any bank deposits, which it ceded to its suppliers,
but that the banks purchased the obligations of the Reich with the
money which their depositors had obtained by supplying the state
or individuals.

15. E. A. Goldenweiser [79] and Federal Reserve Bank of
New York, Bank Reserves [54].

16. A. Copeland [40] writes on this: "The analysis illus-

Section 9. Credit Creation

It has already been stated that during the past years the commercial banks have not created any additional credits, nor were they in a position to do so. They merely lent additionally those amounts which increased with them as demand deposits; the increase, however, was smaller than the expansion of the total economy. These years were a period of an unprecedented prosperity in which the demand for new credit was tremendous, and, nevertheless, the banks were unable to find a single opportune moment to increase their deposits and their investment even relatively. No measure of the Federal Reserve could hinder this procedure, especially during the earlier years when prices of government securities were "pegged," even if the situation is judged in the light of the accepted theory. (17)

---

trates the proposition that the nonfinancial surpluses of all nonfederal sectors taken together were just large enough to advance exactly the amount of funds through financial channels needed by the federal government to finance the war.... When the government seeks to raise a large amount of money through financial channels to finance a war, one can ignore the fact that an excess of nonfinancial uses over nonfinancial sources of funds for the government means an equal excess of nonfinancial sources over nonfinancial uses of funds for the rest of the economy and a consequent equal amount of money that the rest of the economy will necessarily advance to the government through financial channels.... To the tune of 112.5 billion dollars the banking and monetary system was thus a mere financial intermediary.... Propositions...the validity of which I want to question...that the words "money creation" and "destruction" suggest that the federal government and the Federal Reserve System acting in concert can manipulate the sum of currency outside banks plus demand deposits adjusted, so that the variations in this quantity can be used as a means affectuating government credit policy in somewhat the same way that variations in the quantity of Federal Reserve credit can."

17. H. Hellwig [100] states that each individual bank was unable to grant more credits than the amount of its own and other means of which it disposes, so that all banks together cannot grant more credits than the amount of deposits which they received. For the individual banks, as well as for the banking system, the granting of credit is a function of the formation of deposits, not vice versa. The banking system's role in the money circuit is that of a mediator of credit, not of a creator of credit, and the importance of this role depends on the dispositions of the depositors, not on the granting of credit of the banks.

It follows from our discussion up to this point that two fundamental prerequisites are lacking for such a credit creation by the banks. First, the Federal Reserve is unable to throttle the position of the commercial banks in any way, and thus it is excluded from the entire process, with no fixed limits for the granting of additional credits by the banks. The situation looks, therefore, as if no reserve requirements existed. And second, the maintaining of demand deposits (and of their substitutes) does not depend upon the banking system but merely upon business. Business will not maintain additional and costly (because not bearing any interest) demand deposits merely to please the banks. For this reason, the banks do not have at their disposal the substance out of which further credits can be created, and, consequently, there can be no tendency in this direction on their part.

The commercial banks may have much greater freedom in forming their assets and liabilities than the Federal Reserve (see Section 7), yet they cannot "merely" increase or decrease their assets, for they do not control "the volume of deposit money" on the debit side. The relationship is exactly inverse: their loans and investments are a function of the demand deposits.

Yet leaving all these considerations aside, the powerful American economy and its continuous development in the last years permit the opportunity of a further and closer look into the interrelationships. For if we visualize how, by the transfer of demand deposits from one bank to another, additional credits can be increased, we follow only one movement without taking into account the total picture. We have to proceed step by step and always take into consideration the relationship of the banks among one another. It is correct to start with the individual bank, yet each process should be thought through, and for this purpose the mutual settlement of all bank accounts has to be considered at all times. If we do not do this, it appears that the conclusion at which we arrive is erroneous.

Thus, as we proceed, we shall have to stop from time to time to compare and to add together the statements of condition of all individual banks; then nothing can be omitted and the result will be exact. The large capital market in the United States, practically independent of foreign markets, and the published statistics on it greatly facilitate this. It is for this reason that in our Tables we have listed monthly data on transactions in the credit ranges of the past years. For instance, two dates can be compared after a change of reserve requirements, at intervals of a few weeks or a few months, as we have done in Section 2. In this manner, we can examine how relationships developed after sales or purchases of government securities by banks, after deficit-spending, etc.

If we juxtapose two such subsequent statements of condition of all commercial banks, it becomes evident that one and the

same amount cannot be used twice or even many times by one bank or
by all banks together, and no manipulation on the part of the
banks could change this. At this moment, no transfers from one
bank to another would be of any help, and no continuous multiplication is possible any more. Supposed interbank assets do not
suffice, for at each bank credit and debit must be covered.
Granted credits must be fully counterbalanced by actually existing,
seizable, continuously maintained demand deposits, which, at the
same time, also have been withheld from other uses. Credit creation would be possible only if demand deposits together with all
these qualities could be multiplied, which has never happened and
is also impossible to imagine.

     We always have to keep before our eyes that each bank and
all banks together at all times must be in a position to prepare
statements of condition, and at that moment all figures are reduced to a reasonable relationship. No in-between stages can exist (apart from the cash items of the banks in process of collection, in the simple relation of 1:1, as noted in Section 8). Already the first step in the direction of any additional credit is
impossible, thus the rest also is out of the question.

     In the light of the above presentation, the calculation of
the artificial expansion of demand deposits must be considered
naive. It is the worst application of the "ceteris paribus"
clause.

     The computation is taken at random, and one is led to im-
agine that only commercial banks move and multiply their money,
all other participants in the monetary circuit, business including,
complying or not counting at all.

     It is not correct that "the theory of multiple creation of
bank deposits has been repeatedly proved." Not a single example
of such a proof is known to the author. It is true that in the
past years it has been claimed on almost any occasion that credits
are created and cancelled in the proportion of 5:1 or 6:1, and it
could have been expected that data would be used to demonstrate
how this process worked in reality in terms of figures. Thus one
ought to have stated by approximately how much demand deposits
were raised or lowered in order for credit creation to be influenced, and approximately how much, on the basis of this, the expansion or contraction of bank credits amounted to. No such figures have been published during the past years. The cause of this
is to be found in the fact that nobody is able to show, for this
or for the previous periods, statements of condition or calculations which would prove credit creation, or which would at least
make it appear probable.

     All recently discussed models of multiple credit creation
through Special Drawing Rights or Eure-dollars equally are without
merit.

Section 10. Money Supply as a Means of Exchange
    It has already been said that if the commercial banks com-
pensate demand deposits, neither the credit range of the banking
system nor the range of money disposal of the remainder of the
economy is changed as a result. An increase (or decrease and
hoarding) of currency in circulation will have the same final result on the entire economy, yet the process formally is different.
    If, for instance, an amount of currency is hoarded, this
amount will soon be lacking in the economy for purposes of turnover, and the economy will therefore take it back from the Federal Reserve through the intermediation of the banks. Subsequently,
the Federal Reserve will purchase government securities, for example, for the same amount, for it is a participant in the circuit
and therefore has to use this amount in some way. If, then, the
hoarder also had originally invested his amount in government securities, the end result for the total economy would be the same;
by his action he only brought it about that, instead of himself,
the Federal Reserve profited from the interest on these government securities. Similarly (or, as the case may be, inversely),
this process will take place if the currency in circulation should
rise or fall as a result of expansion or contraction of the economy.
    In all these cases the credit range of the Federal Reserve
is increased or decreased; yet, since credits in the same amount
are simultaneously granted to or withdrawn from the economy, the
total money disposal range of the economy remains unchanged, similarly as in the case of compensation of demand deposits.
    Both in a compensation of the demand deposits and in an
increase of the currency in circulation, the range of money disposal of the entire economy remains unchanged, and the result consists merely in the economy being supplied with new money in circulation, in which case, however, it does not have to divert any
"values," so that its further force of expansion is not reduced;
this development is thus favorable to the economy. In a contraction, the situation is analogous, i.e., merely the money supply is
reduced. This state of affairs is of fundamental importance in
both cases.
    It is frequently assumed that for this development an ac-
tive banking policy is necessary. But this is not the case, for
this process takes place quite <u>automatically and continuously</u>, and
special help in this respect on the part of the Federal Reserve is
unnecessary, apart from its technical assistance. If this were
otherwise, the reactivation of these amounts would be quite incomplete, for the system would never have exact indicators in order
to take action to the necessary extent at the right time - apart
from the question whether an active banking policy is possible in
the modern economy.

The banks welcome every opportunity to increase the demand
deposits of their customers, since these deposits are the most important source of their profits. They promptly compensate any
such increase in their own interest, but they can only do so if
there is space for this. Similarly, the Treasury purchases further government securities if the circulation or hoarding of currency increases. In both cases the decision lies with the economy.

From this discussion it necessarily follows that no new
credits can be created out of money supply, and this is the chief
point of the development. (18) The actually existing, seizable,
continuously maintained demand deposits (see Section 9) and the
available currency resulted from savings and their reproduction
(compensation) cannot be an expansion of the credit range.

If, then, money supply is lacking to cover the current
turnover, the missing demand deposits are formed upon the initiative of business and compensated by the banks (see Section 8).
Business would never permit the economy to recede as a result of
lack of money in circulation, i.e., means of exchange; this is
practically beyond comprehension. Even if the Federal Reserve had
the potential to affect the amount of money in circulation, it
could achieve little under these circumstances, for business is in
a position to constantly renew its demand deposits. (19)

----

18. H. G. Moulton [152] writes: "There can be no independent 'inflating' or blowing up of the money supply; no automa-
tic 'pumping' or 'injecting' money into the channels of circulation. Accordingly, if we are to understand the price-changing
process, we must analyze the forces operating within the productive system.... Money enters the picture only after the productive
process has been completed."

19. T. G. Gaines [69, 70] writes: "Monetary analyses often seem to imply that the Federal Reserve is able to regulate
money supply growth to whatever target it might choose. The Fed
'creates' reserves, the banks 'create' credit, and the holders of
demand deposits passively absorb whatever deposits are generated.
In actual fact, demand deposits are only one among a variety of
financial claims and holders of demand deposits determine through
a rational allocation of resources the size of their demand deposits and therefore the size of the money supply. If fiscal and
monetary policies are successful in maintaining an orderly rate of
economic growth, the money supply will grow in some not easily
predictable relationship to the growth in the economy. But the
process runs from economic growth to a need for more money rather
than from monetary growth to economic advance.... There should be
no need for concern if money supply does not grow in pace with

In the case of changes in currency in circulation the situation is analogous.

In all these cases money supply played a mediator's role and could not influence, in terms of figures, the exchange of the "values in production." Only new means of exchange were created. In the modern economy money supply has no independent purchase power and by its increase neither additional short- nor long-term credits can be granted, nor can the purchasing power of the population be increased. (20) The money supply is "neutral," as it was proposed in the thirties.

---

some preconceived 'normal' rate of growth. And there should be no need for alarm at faster than 'normal' growth rate.... "

20. J. Ittensohn [108] maintains: "The monetary authorities have certainly not the slightest influence on the whole circuit of goods and services as far as it is settled in a money-less exchange, and indeed even in a transfer requiring payment in money .... These facts should show the utter nonsense of theories stating that measures of the monetary authorities may be charged with a deficient economic growth or with high unemployment. These theories are part of widely extended witch-stories of our century. The economy functions today, as ever, vastly by itself and has a course of its own. The theory of its dependence on monetary authorities is a pious self-deceit. Many bankers in Europe will deny today that credit creation by commercial banks is possible and real.... There is a critical error to which an astonishingly large number of economists hold stating that planned, farreaching economic measures are involved."

E. Wood [222]: "As a practical matter, the quantity of Federal Reserve money outstanding at a given time is largely beyond its control. The fact is that it is relatively easy for the members of the public to hold such cash as they choose.... The public can monetize such debts as they choose in given economic situation, with little change in the term of monetization.... The physical volume of trade and the cost-price structure are not malleable, and so the amount of balances is not either.... Each member of the economy feels free to adjust the size of his balance according to what seems in his best interest, within the possibilities of his wealth and income.... What is the nature of the process by which the amount of balances which the public choose to hold is maintained in equality with the amount which the banking system provides for? The members of the public (it is implied) have only an illusion that they determine the size of their balances as they wish; actually they determine only how a given volume of deposits shall be distributed. Changes in prices and in output, and to some extent changes in the willingness to hold substitutes for

Fluctuations in money supply can represent only a few per mil of personal consumption and would practically never have any weight. (21) In this case, too, money supply in its greatest part builds, as statistics indicate, a stationary, immovable mass and represents no purchasing power. (22)

Section 11. Open Market Operations
It is generally assumed that the Federal Reserve influences the ease or tightness of general money conditions mainly by its

----

deposits, occur continuously in such a fashion that the total deposits, as determined independently by the banking system, seems just right.... We are led to inquire whether the monetary authorities, following a routine which they have found practicable over the years, do not allow reserves to expand automatically - though not necessarily without changing the credit terms - in response to the public's attempts to strengthen their cash positions.... There is a flexibility in the availability of reserves; they can always be obtained in larger amounts.... The demand for deposits balances by the members of the economy is a basic factor influencing the rate of expansion, and during comparatively short periods it is the dominating influence.... Nor can (the authorities) control the amount of deposits at some predetermined figure; for the amount of deposits is geared to the general performance of the economy and to the standards for cash positions that the members of the public are trying to maintain."

21. H. G. Moulton [152] observes that, since increments in money supply "are commonly less than one per cent of aggregate wages and salaries, they are of negligible importance."

22. H. Feifel [59] remarks: "A part of sight deposits are completely motionless. The part of total bank deposits which are not disposed of and stand still, represents "inactive," respectively, "ineffective" money or <u>no</u> money at all.

R. Kerschagl [121]: "Deposits, before they are disposed of through a check, constitute only potential, and not virtual circulation money, and thus, so to say, a dormant and freezed purchasing power."

H. J. Köhler [123]: "Only the 'effective' quantity of money exerts influence on prices. There must be a distinction between mere possession of money (potential purchasing power) and employment of money (kinetic purchasing power)."

H. G. Moulton [152]: "Only such a portion of money as is actually exchanged against goods in the market affects prices. Money hoarded does not act on prices. Money kept in reserve by individuals to meet contingencies which do not occur, does not act on prices."

operations in the government security market, and that these operations "have become the chief instrument of credit control. The
Federal Reserve System, by selling government securities, can absorb banks' excesses or marginal reserves, which are available as
the basis for credit expansion, or can force member banks to borrow to maintain their required reserves. Similarly, by buying
government securities the System can provide the banks with funds
on the basis of which they can make additional loans or investments." (23)

    First of all, the statement must be doubted that the Fed-
eral Reserve can "force" banks or nonbank investors to purchase
bills from it or to sell them to it. If we speak of a countrywide
market, i.e., in aggregates, this fact may seem plausible; there
always should be someone who closes the transaction, if the price
is set correspondingly by the Federal Reserve. Yet in concrete
terms, i.e., from a micro-economic point of view, the question
arises which individual bank will feel itself compelled to purchase bills, if at the given moment loans to customers present a
more advantageous business for it. If banks often sell government
securities at substantial losses during long periods in order to
cater to their customers, they will not buy bills during this period because the Federal Reserve desires it. It is not correct
that the Federal Reserve is keeping the banks in check. Only the
appearance exists that this is the case, since the banks always
wish to be fully invested and tend toward the limit of their possibilities. It is only their own position which puts barriers in
their way. Precisely as the banks cannot dictate the amount of
demand deposits to business, so the Federal Reserve cannot dictate
to the banks what their behavior in this case should be.

    Apart from this, the transactions of the nonbank investors
with the Federal Reserve should influence the position of the
banks in the same manner, for they correspondingly change the
amount of the demand deposits. Yet it has to be considered that
each of these nonbank investors as a rule follows his own plan
which he adopts at least many weeks in advance. He estimates what
monetary arrangements will be necessary, and a subsequent opportunity of a purchase or sale of bills will not change his plans.
Besides, the transaction will not offer sufficient appeal, since
the difference can amount to only a few dollars.

    In order to assess the situation correctly one has to re-
member that the bill market is imperfect to a high degree. Many
buyers invest in bills almost regardless of rate, and any interest
rate will be acceptable to them, since otherwise they receive no
interest at all on their deposits. On the other hand, if in the

---

23. *Federal Reserve Bank of New York [54].*

meantime the buyers need cash, they will sell the bills on the market, and the price is incidental for them. Thus, supply and demand very often are rigid.

States, municipalities, public authorities, as well as public funds and various large private corporations are investing the proceeds of issued bonds and other securities in bills. Industry and insurance companies attempt to buy up bills for all their temporary surpluses. The intention is to profit from interest, even for very short periods, until future use of these assets. The development on the market is therefore unpredictable and accidental, and dependent on very temporary influences. (24) This development on the market is, of course, also influenced by the appearance of the Treasury, which is guided by its own considerations. These transactions, as well as the surpluses and deficits of the Treasury and its deposits and withdrawals, form another unstable element in the money market.

The appearance of several, or even of one buyer who intends to invest his free money for a few weeks, is capable of throwing the market into disorder. Thus it is reported, for example, that at the beginning of 1956 the presence on the market of the Ford Foundation, the Illinois Toll Road Authority, and the Home Loan Bank System noticeably disturbed the situation for some time. When in the fall of 1955 American Telephone and Telegraph temporarily invested 650 million dollars, the price was depressed by about seven per cent (from 2.15 to 2%), i.e., a demand amounting to less than 1/4 per cent of the government debt is capable - due to the thinness of the market - of lowering the interest rate to such a degree. Thus, decisions of private corporations on timing and procedure regarding their investments often are of greater importance than measures of the authorities.

As a result of the element of chance and of the irregularity of the appearance on the market of the nonbank investors, it is very difficult to predict what amount will be offered or demanded, so that the Federal Reserve has to be very careful in its behavior on the market. It often occurs that either no bills are available or no buyers can be found, or, last of all, the price

---

24. How much the rate of interest for bills fluctuates week by week can be seen from the fact that, for instance, in July 1958 it decreased in one week from 1.006% to 0.768%, i.e., by 23%, and in another week, in April 1960, the rate on 13-week bills rose from 2.731% to 3.622%, or by 33%, and on 26-week bills from 2.927% to 3.854%, or by 32%. It is often added in this connection that the fluctuations were chiefly technical, resulting from special circumstances affecting the short-term money market.

might be unreasonable. By every purchase or sale, the Federal Reserve may cause considerable fluctuations and handicap the market behavior, and the mere readiness of the Federal Open Market Committee to intervene sometimes brings about changes of several points, so that a hasty intervention can often cause complications without achieving the desired result. Therefore, the Federal Reserve always tries to make certain in advance whether buyers or sellers are present on the market; and it is mainly in this direction that all its efforts tend. (25)

On the basis of this situation, it appears that the Federal Reserve is battling only the daily problems of accidental changes on the "only-bill" market, for the bills constitute merely a purely "defensive" weapon. The Federal Reserve is unable to act at will on the market, and only the market dictates what is to happen and in which way the Federal Reserve itself must behave.

Section 12. Idle Balances

In dealing with this question, a false conclusion has been reached for decades, and the contradiction is not cleared up, although nobody expresses doubts as to the correctness of Cassel's famous statement on the subject. (26)

---

25. These facts follow from numerous unofficial comments on the bill market, and also from many explanations on the part of the authorities. A. Hayes [96] states, e.g.: "A group of money market specialists works constantly at forecasting the additions to or withdrawals of funds from the national money market." W. Thomas [203]: "Because of various temporary factors affecting the supply of bank reserves, demands for reserve funds often vary by hundreds of millions of dollars within a few days. Most of the Federal Reserve operations are concerned with adjusting the availability of reserves to these short-term variations." Federal Reserve Bank of New York [55]: "Open market operations were almost continuously undertaken to smooth out seasonal and other temporary swings in bank reserve positions."

26. G. Cassel [31] indicated: "A possessor of income... cannot leave his income unused for some time, as is popularly supposed. He may fancy that he is doing so, but in reality he puts his money in the banks, and therefore puts it at the disposal of business or, in more general terms, the demand for capital. The idea that is common in financial journalism, and unfortunately not uncommon in science that capital in the abstract sense can be stored up and not used for the formation of real capital until a later date, is clearly...false; it is simply based upon a defective analysis of the real processes of the economic exchange."

L. A. Hahn [88] writes about this very convincingly: "If

The vague manner in which the question is posed is responsible for the view that the banking system can create credit and
that the Federal Reserve supplies "powerful" dollars. Some of our
theories still date back to the time of the coin-clipping kings,
and thus it is believed that the authorities are able to print as
much money as they wish; yet even then this money could only be
put into circulation if the people accepted it or were forced to
accept it. There exists a vague concept that the Federal Reserve
arranges the irregularities in monetary matters and somehow regulates the relationship between savings and investment.

It is often emphasized in the financial press that on the
basis of a corresponding monetary policy money and private credit
"quickly came out of hiding" and that in this there can be found
"a logical starting point" for a recovery of the economy; or that
by reducing member bank reserve requirements funds are released
for productive use and that these funds were previously immobilized
and "must remain idle to back deposits." (27) However, for the
economy as a whole there exists no such thing as idle balances or
hidden money, and no amounts are lost for it. Further, it is not
at all necessary that owners of funds "are willing to lend" them,
(28) for the economy will use them in any case.

The error concerning the total economy seems to consist
mainly in the fact that the movements of the Federal Reserve in
the money circuit are judged incorrectly (cf., discussion in Chapter 3, Section 3). The Federal Reserve can only pour from one
bucket into the other, and it can neither lend one amount twice
nor can it normally deactivate any money, i.e., render it unable
to affect the total circuit of money. All the money of the Federal Reserve is fully occupied all the time, and thus it cannot
maintain idle balances. It cannot serve as a buffer to the economy and is technically unable to advance future savings or to form
reserves of savings in order to stock past savings.

When the Federal Reserve purchases government securities
on the market, the deposits of the banks with the Federal Reserve
will increase and the banks will soon demand an equivalent for
them, for they always endeavor to keep their money fully occupied.
If, on the other hand, the Federal Reserve sells government securities, it will receive an equivalent which it has to use somehow.
Since it cannot give it away and is bound to act according to its
regulations, it will in any case have to introduce this equivalent

---

one went to the moon with this money, serious difficulties would
arise.... "

27. J. T. Chippendale, Jr. [34], Journal of Commerce, December 2, 1957, and February 21, 1958.

28. W. Thomas [203].

into the circuit. In other transactions of the Federal Reserve, the process will take a similar course and the result will remain the same. In these calculations it is not enough to take one door into account, for thus we lose sight of the other door through which the compensation takes place. If the compensation on the part of the Federal Reserve, in the case of the hoarding of currency, is not taken into account, one link in the chain is left out, and we arrive at the erroneous conclusion that "hoarded currency constitutes unused funds."

It is further claimed in financial literature that the central bank or the government are in a position to sterilize amounts of money in order to avoid the allegedly "potentially inflationary effects of gold purchases." But it becomes immediately evident from the clear separation which was made between "values in production" and "money supply" as means of exchange that such a procedure is impossible within the modern economy. On the one hand, there are no technical measures on the money market by which the authorities would be able to create or to destroy "values in production," and, on the other hand, the volume of the means of exchange depends on business and the economy, and nothing could be gained by this manipulation.

No sterilization or desterilization of amounts takes place, and the assumption of such a process can only be based on an unprecise evaluation of the circuit. The corresponding purchases or sales of government securities by the Federal Reserve take place automatically, by force, for the Federal Reserve must somehow use its surpluses or cover its deficits. Thus, it is incorrect to maintain that the effects of flow of gold "can easily be offset by the monetary tools available." (29) The Federal Reserve must offset it, this process is compulsory. The same is true of the banks which compensate or dis-compensate the demand deposits of foreign countries, if the payment in the gold exchange is made by these demand deposits. All these processes belong to the common transactions in the money circuit which do not change the total situation, so that no countermeasures are necessary - or possible.

Section 13. Reasonable Behavior
In Section 7 we have already arrived at the conclusion that the measures of the Federal Reserve only affect the internal relationship within the System and are expressed in excess reserves which, on principle, it can determine. We shall now investigate the means at the disposal of the Federal Reserve in order to carry out an active policy within this framework, and what form this takes in practice.

_____

29. W. McC. Martin, Jr. [140].

a) The Federal Reserve would be in the position to raise its assets at will, for it can purchase government securities in unrestricted amounts (i.e., restricted only by law) for currency or for deposits with it, without running the risk of finding itself in payment difficulties. For the currency could be paid at best only on deposits, and all deposits, again, could be transferred only for the benefit of third persons, and this would not at all change the over-all situation of the Federal Reserve.

This state of affairs makes it possible for the Federal Reserve to support the operations of the Treasury at all times, and probably is chiefly responsible for the belief in the almost unlimited power of the Federal Reserve, which for this reason is not included in the general circuit in the discussion of monetary matters. But in doing so, it is forgotten that this special position is quite limited in time. (30)

This advantage of the Federal Reserve, incidentally, also has its counterpart. For if the Federal Reserve sells government securities, it cannot in this case, as any other contractor, wait for a while and buy back these securities at will at a later date, for it does not have anyone to hold deposits for it in the meantime. In this case, the banks will also make their appearance soon, and they will wish to get rid of the surplus of government securities purchased.

b) The authorities put the currency in circulation and they can very well limit its issue. Yet the Federal Reserve is bound to issue currency for amounts deposited with it, so that a direct connection exists between these deposits and currency. But the Federal Reserve could also limit the volume of these deposits. For example, it could sell part of its government securities or fail to renew the government securities which are due, and in this manner it could reduce the total deposits with it. If, then, it refuses all purchases, even at continually lower prices, it would be in a position to keep its total deposits at the desired decreased level.

ad a) and b) Such a procedure on the part of the central bank, however, can probably not even be seriously taken into consideration in a modern economy. It is possible neither to a large nor to a small extent. The Federal Reserve would only disturb the market by increased purchases or sales. It must be pondered that

---

30. *The Federal Reserve raised its holdings of one-year certificates, for instance, at the beginning of June 1958, in support of the Treasury's 16.2 billion dollar refunding, by about 1.5 billion, and then, one month later, had to sell gradually bills of about the same amount, i.e., of about 1.3 billion dollars. This development could be predicted with certainty.*

the markets in government securities are very thin and that the
demand is inelastic, so that every somewhat more energetic action
of the Federal Reserve in one or the other direction would be
bound to cause disturbances and tensions in the current business.

In the case of an increase or decrease of reserve requirements, if the Federal Reserve should refuse to invest or to disin-
vest the difference, similar complications would also have to
arise.

ad a) In the event of an expansion of the deposits by the
Federal Reserve, the banks would wish to get rid of these deposits,
since they do not profit by them. Idle deposits in the Federal
Reserve are as expensive for the banks as idle demand deposits of
business in the banks. They would search intensively government
securities and other securities on the market and intervene in
bills auctions in order to dispose of their excesses, and competition between the banks in this respect would be the result. In
such a situation, the Federal Reserve would be unwilling to sell
government securities bought previously, in fact, with the money
of its member banks. It would be a kind of suspension of payments
on the part of the Federal Reserve.

ad b) If during prosperity - for only then would this usually apply - the Federal Reserve sold larger positions of government securities and then stopped all purchases and left the market
to its fate, the banks would be unable to obtain deposits with the
Federal Reserve. Thus, in the event of an eventual increase of
their demand deposits, they would not be able to meet their reserve requirements. This, according to the traditional opinion,
is the only way to prevent an expansion of bank credits. By the
procedure we described under ad a), the Federal Reserve could increase its profits and lower those of the banks, so that the direct result would be only an internal shift within the framework
of the System. But in this case the Federal Reserve would be able
to cause a much more incisive effect of a general nature by its
action.

In terms of aggregates, this entire concept seems to be
convincing. The problem is easily solved if one sets up the principle that the totality of banks is forced to reduce their demand
deposits. However, if we dissect the aggregates, it is seen at
once that this conception is practically infeasible. Each of the
14,000 banks would attempt not to reduce its own deposits in the
Federal Reserve in order not to have to reduce its own demand deposits. If only one or a few commercial banks existed, much would
be possible. Yet with thousands of banks, each bank will keep its
own interest at heart, for particularly the level of demand deposits is the most important factor in the banking business.

In the event of a greater throttling by the Federal Reserve, however, an even greater competition between the banks
would develop. A struggle for deposits with the Federal Reserve

would arise, which would destroy all regular monetary transactions on the market. It would result in a derailment on the bond market and on the money market with incalculable consequences for the entire economy. (31)

However, the behavior of the Federal Reserve is reasonable from the very beginning; it always proceeds in a very cautious

---

31. A. Murad [153] indicates: "The simple device by which the banks were able to accomplish...expansion despite "restrictive" Federal Reserve policies, was to borrow additional reserves from the Federal Reserve banks. If the Federal Reserve banks should ever refuse to privide the required reserves, they would precipitate a financial crisis. Equally wrong is the notion that the function of reserves is to serve as regulator of the quantity of bank deposits. Even as the bank balances of business firms do not regulate the volume of business, but on the contrary are regulated largely by the volume of business, so bankers' balances, i.e., reserves, do not regulate the volume of business done by banks and more particularly the amount of their deposit obligations, but on the contrary are regulated largely by the volume of banking business and by the amount of deposits. What the experience actually did demonstrate was that reserves are regulated by the banks' deposits obligations, together with reserve requirements, and that they are not the regulators of the quantity of deposits.... At no time has credit been denied to the community by refusal of Federal Reserve banks to lend to banks."

E. Wood [222]: "At any given time the members of the economy have their own ideas as to the cash position they want to maintain, and it would cause crisis and ruin if the authorities did not permit them to have that amount on some sort of tolerable terms.... This mechanical theory of the way the Federal Reserve influences the banking system and the economy is not at all realistic. If, in a given economic situation, the demand for balances should increase and there were no means by which the deposits could be obtained, the money market would tighten instantly; if the deficiency in balances were great, money rates would go to panic levels. As a matter of operating procedure the banks do permit the public to adjust their aggregate balances to requirements, and the Federal Reserve permits the banks in turn to adjust reserves to requirements. The banks requirements are in fact a reflection of those of the public. The Federal Reserve makes no attempt to force the banking system to conform to a predetermined amount of reserves, and it could not do so.... There is continuity in the rate of expenditure in the economy; it is not determined statistically by the amount of money at a given moment."

manner in order not to cause any irregularities in the market. This scope of its operations is described in detail in official publications, and it can be seen from them that the Federal Reserve follows the trend of the market in this respect very carefully and that it promptly takes measures accordingly, as we have already mentioned.

We shall now broach the question whether the pressure which the Federal Reserve would exert, in order to keep low or to reduce the demand deposits in the banks, would indeed be effective. In our examination of the problem we shall at once disregard the theoretical possibility of a completely irresponsible behavior of the Federal Reserve.

Let us assume that a Board of Governors decides to lower the demand deposits by, say, five billion dollars, which would be substantial. At first we must remember that we are not operating here with a mathematical formula in which a small shift would make the entire equation untenable. We are dealing with a living organism of the economy which in the past has demonstrated at all occasions its admirable ability for adjustment and its irrepressible power of expansion. In life there are thousands of complications which cannot be predicted by any formula and thousands of opportunities of avoiding the obstacles in order to continue the further development.

In order to prevent the increase of demand deposits by five billion dollars, the Federal Reserve, according to the prevailing theory, would have to decrease the reserves of the member banks by about one billion dollars. If debits to demand deposits accounts amount in 1968 to about 8000 billion dollars annually, and if there are 300 days with six banking hours each, this one billion dollars will have an average rate of turnover of 13.5 minutes. With only a little understanding of proportions in economic life, it is easy to see that such a measure by the Federal Reserve could not have any effect at all.

It should also be mentioned that if the banks had met with any obstruction in increasing their deposits in the Federal Reserve, they would never have made such frequent and urgent demands that their customers maintain a portion of the granted loans in the form of compensatory deposits (cf., discussion in Section 3) - which amounts to an indirect increase in the lending rate charged to their customers. For the banks have to transfer a fraction of these demand deposits to the Federal Reserve, and if this created any difficulties for them, they would certainly have found other ways to preserve their advantage. The amounts saved in this manner could have been used by the banks for loans to further customers, if this were of any practical importance.

The theoretical possibility of decreasing the money supply may exist for the central bank, if the destruction of the existing monetary system is accepted. Yet it would be unreasonable to de-

scribe the possibility of an absurd conduct as freedom of decision
or as power. Similarly, one might assume that the Federal Reserve
would be able not to supply sufficient currency for circulation,
e.g., during Christmas, and would thus throttle economic life.
The sphere of the efficacy and power of the Federal Reserve in
both cases is without any practical importance.

The application of the theory of credit creation by the
banks and of money supply by the Federal Reserve is a strange continuation of an illogical and formalistic idea which has no relation to reality. A few members of the Board of Governors are unable to dictate actions to many million enterprises and to tens of
million owners of demand deposits. Both credit creation and a
senseless behavior of the Federal Reserve must be disregarded in
practical considerations.

Section 14. Statements of Condition

According to the prevailing theory, it is assumed that our
central banking regulates the money supply merely by increasing
and decreasing its assets and that "the reserve money is a function of the volume of these assets" (cf., Section 7).

The increasing or decreasing of assets is relatively easy
for a private enterprise, but not for a central bank which always
has to act within the framework of the obligations imposed upon
it. In order to change the statements of condition, the Federal
Reserve simultaneously has to keep in mind the formation of assets
and liabilities, any excess and any deficiency demands countercov-
ering - and this is the core of the problem. Any increase or decrease of the reserve requirements or of the currency in circulation must, by force of circumstances, lead to an investment or
disinvestment, mainly in government securities; this can be seen
from the statements of condition of the Federal Reserve for the
entire period of the past years. Thus, it cannot be correct if it
is stated that the reserves deposited with the Federal Reserve by
the member banks are not used for the purchase of government securities. (32) From where, then, did the Federal Reserve take the
funds, apart from the equivalent for currency, for the purchase of
its great stock of government securities? What else can the Federal Reserve do with the surplus after an increase in the reserve
requirements?

Any change in the assets of the Federal Reserve must be
balanced by a counterposition, but the amount of currency and the

-----

32. W. McC. Martin, Jr. [135] stated, e.g.: "It is most
important to note here that contrary to a widespread misunderstanding, the Federal Reserve System does not use the reserves deposited
with it by the member banks to buy government securities."

reserve requirements, apart from the valid percentage, are independent of the Federal Reserve. At this point the causal process
must start.

In this connection, it should be emphasized that in the
event of a compensation (and "dis-compensation") of demand deposits (see Section 6 and 8) the banks as a whole also maintain only
a passive attitude; i.e., this compensation (and "dis-compensation") does take place in reality in any case, even without the
collaboration of the banks. This is at once evident if the situation is seen from the point of view of accountancy. For if the
demand deposits increase (decrease), the total indebtedness of the
remainder of the economy with respect to the banks, ceteris paribus, i.e., with unchanged deposits in the Federal Reserve, currency, capital accounts, premises, etc., must also increase (decrease)
simultaneously. If the individual bank does not compensate its
increasing demand deposits, it will suffer a loss of profit; another bank, however, will draw profit from it, to wit, technically
by interbank-settlement, and it will thus carry out the compensation. In this manner, compensation and dis-compensation are accomplished precisely. The previous tentative explanation as to how
each bank proceeds concerning an alleged credit creation, is considered here from a different aspect of this question, in the aggregate.

For example, it was proposed in the fall of 1957 that the
reserve of the Federal Reserve be used to finance small business.
Such reserves "are now idle and not used for any purpose - and
there is no prospect that they will be used." (33) One version of
the Sparkman-O'Mahoney bill and another of the Patman-Johnson bill
existed about this. (34) In the light of our discussion, it becomes clear that all funds of the Federal Reserve are occupied at
all times, and in order to use them for the desired purpose one
would have to do without their present use in the same amount.
(We are not concerned here with the problem of whether this would
be indicated.)

Another example: It is claimed that the Federal Reserve
authorities "could in principle force a sufficient reduction of
commercial bank assets to compensate for the growth in the assets
of other institutions." (35) In this case, the Federal Reserve
again would have to sell government securities in great amounts
and at very attractive prices. Since the business world, ceteris
paribus, could not use its "values in production" for this purpose
for it would subsequently be unable to find buyers for these "val-

---

33. W. Patman [160].
34. Wall Street Journal, March 19, 1958.
35. A. F. Burns [29].

ues," it would have to use its demand deposits and it would, thus, have to consent to give up, to a large extent, the continuation of its current business! On the other hand, commercial banks would be obliged to dis-compensate those demand deposits and to sell their government securities for an equivalent amount.

All these constructions are only possible if the transactions of the Federal Reserve are not included in the money circuit.

Section 15. Two Policies at Once

It is generally assumed that the Federal Reserve has two goals in mind - on the one hand, to smooth out temporary and seasonal swings in the money exchange, and on the other, to control the cost and the availability of credit in order to further, at the given moment, the desired growth of the economy.

In a paper issued by the Federal Reserve Bank of New York, R. V. Roosa [179] describes the measures of the Federal Reserve in these two directions as dynamic or defensive. Roosa remarks that the defensive job of the Federal Reserve is to provide fuel that the money machine needs, and to distribute and allocate the market's stock in trade within any given period. This part of the task of the Federal Reserve is described in great detail, and we obtain an exact and also interesting picture of the subject.

Yet we are confronted with a different picture when looking at the dynamic objectives of the Federal Reserve. Roosa writes that the dynamic aim consists in varying the quantity of reserves by such amounts and through such methods as to make the banking system an active force - promoting growth, resisting depression, and limiting inflation. He remarks further that defensive operations frequently are of real importance in the implementation of dynamic policy. Yet he excludes from his discussion the question of what "such methods" are, as well as the entire problem of the dynamic policy.

On the basis of our analysis, we claim that in the modern economy any dynamic policy on the part of the Federal Reserve is impossible. This is demonstrated by two main arguments: (1) no idle balances for the total economy exist and the banking system is therefore normally unable to increase or decrease capital or money; and (2) the banking system does not determine the money supply.

Quite characteristic is the explanation of those cases in financial literature where the measures of the Federal Reserve move in an opposite direction to the intended dynamic policy. Roosa reports that in the second half of 1955 purchases were undertaken almost exclusively when the dynamic policy was actually one of restraint. He explains that the secret was in keeping close watch on the absorption of reserves by other factors, and then taking action day by day to offset only enough of the reserve absorption to prevent the creation of even tighter conditions. He states further that "paradoxically enough the restraint was in fact achieved." (36)

Our explanation for the above process is that the technical conditions of the bill market forced the Federal Reserve to undertake purchases on the market during six months, and since the seasonal, or the defensive measures, as Roosa defines them, are the only determinants, no other approach could be considered. The restraint had its origin in the boom which prevailed in the market during the entire period, and there were no other factors which caused the restraint. The situation described in the footnote arose in a recession. This time the Federal Reserve was forced to take opposite seasonal measures, and the supposed easing of credit was not observed. One cannot speak of a paradox when the situation for many months was directly opposite to that which the Federal Reserve assumed to be existing. This fact cannot be denied and must somehow be explained.

Thus, the Federal Reserve is not in a position - if it wishes to avoid any serious complications on the money market - to pursue any plans by continuous transactions on the open market and to observe some sort of timing for this purpose. It would soon lose its breath and be forced to retrace its steps, regardless of the dynamic objective.

Besides, it appears very doubtful whether it is at all possible to carry out two different policies with the same means and on the same market. As a principle, it may sound plausible that a definite goal should be pursued, "after allowing for seasonal variations," as Roosa [179] writes. Yet it is very questionable whether such a directive can be of any practical value. The theory of probability teaches us that two different, independent objectives will require, in 50% of the cases on the average, measures in opposite directions and almost always of different intensity, and must, thus, be incompatible. It is impossible, for example, to inform the market that one will buy today in order to pursue a long-term policy, and that one will sell the next day in order to compensate for seasonal fluctuations. In such opposite cases one will have to decide on one measure, or none of the two goals will be reached.

---

36. *Two years later, G. Shea [192] interpreted a reverse situation in a similar manner: "Some observers are arguing that ...the Reserve holdings of governments have increased less since early November than in the corresponding two-month period a year earlier. It reflects too limited a perspective. What counts is the overall effort of Reserve policies. The Board sometimes reduces its bill holdings even when it is easing credit, by making sure the reduction offsets only a part of an easing that is taking place from other causes."*

It appears from the available descriptions and, what is
more important, from the actual results, that the Federal Reserve
decided on the defensive measures and is entirely absorbed with
this objective. (This solution seems to be the only correct one,
for the Federal Reserve has to devote itself, above all, to this
task.) All descriptions of the development on the open market indicate that there is only a question of day-to-day transactions,
and that everything is provided for the time being. The "feel" of
each day's market, about which there is so much talk, is simply a
sense for the events which may happen during the next few hours.
What may happen within a week is of no interest any more, for in
the meantime the situation will still change several times.

It is sometimes claimed in financial literature that the
formulation and execution of central bank policy is an art (cf.,
for example, W. R. Burgess [25] and L. R. Seltzer [190]). This
opinion has no validity. Certainly, long-time experience and much
adroitness are necessary for the effective execution of seasonal
measures, yet, in any case, no particular inventiveness is needed
for this. It should rather be compared to a craft.

Section 16. The Reserve Requirements
The respective statistical data have already been quoted
and partially discussed in Section 2. It appears that during
these years neither the theory on credit creation was borne out by
reality nor did, or could, the System supply any additional credits to the economy in this or another form.

We thus find ourselves seriously in error if we believe
that the reserve requirements are an instrument of monetary policy
and that the Federal Reserve can influence the money market situation outside of the banking system through their changes. Each of
the cited examples shows that the range of money disposal of the
remainder of the economy had to remain unchanged.

The profits of each commercial bank are chiefly dependent
on the amount of its demand deposits which constitute its "raw
material." That part of these deposits which has been ceded, free
of cost, to the Federal Reserve will only lower these profits.
This is practically the only function of the reserve requirements.

Transactions in securities between the Federal Reserve and
the commercial banks in the course of the years have, above all,
the purpose of leveling the seasonal fluctuations of the currency
in circulation. In this respect, the Federal Reserve usually arranges its measures in such a manner that the banks have to maintain as little cash as possible and can use, instead, short-term
earning assets as secondary reserves. When, particularly at the
end of the year, the banks have to pay out great amounts in currency, they are in a position to sell a part of these assets or
not to renew them at maturity. The certainty that the Federal Reserve is standing at their side and will, if necessary, purchase

these assets, gives them the opportunity to considerably narrow
the margin of their nonearning assets. If this certainty did not
exist, the banks would constantly have to maintain large reserves
of cash, and lower their profits correspondingly. The difference
would benefit the Federal Reserve, which invests the equivalent of
the issued currency. This does not mean that the readiness of the
Federal Reserve to purchase short-term government securities is
out of place. It is probably the most proper means of assuring an
orderly circulation of money. We only wish to emphasize that, by
its behavior, the Federal Reserve works to a great extent for the
advantage of the commercial banks.

Section 17. The Reserve Positions

It is claimed that bank reserves govern the amount of money banks have to lend. However, in Section 7 we stated that
changes in bank reserves have only a very subordinate role because
they can merely influence the internal relationship within the
System. Regarding the credit range of the Federal Reserve and of
the commercial banks as a whole, fluctuations in reserve bank
credit are merely a shifting from one pocket to the other, a process which cannot have any effect on the amount of available money
for the remainder of the economy. The excess reserves also have
to be used in the circuit by the Federal Reserve, and it is without importance for the remainder of the economy where the credits
come from. But, as it was argued, even within the internal range
of profits, the Federal Reserve has caused almost no changes.

Nevertheless, the fluctuations in reserve positions of the
banks are described in all details in the daily newspapers, as if
the public were particularly interested in the fluctuations of
bank profits in their total amount. One observes a small technical segment of the whole picture and develops the most sophisticated considerations on this topic.

The published data can only give us information on how the
turnover is technically executed within the money circuit. Yet,
from a general point of view, such details have no importance for
the economy. The behavior of the banks in this day-to-day picture
is not interesting, since we know its directives in advance.

Section 18. The "Pegging"

It can be seen from our statistics on the development within the credit ranges that before the Accord between the Treasury
and the Federal Reserve in March 1951 the availability of credit
of the System also had not changed. This situation resulted, although, as it is generally admitted, interventions of the Federal
Reserve during this period of "pegging" had to be without effect.
On the basis of this state of affairs, it must be argued that if
the measures of the Federal Reserve are discontinued, the situation within the money circuit is not changed, and that consequent-

ly these measures exert no influence on the availability of credit
(cf., also discussion under a) in Chapter 2).

Furthermore, "pegging" was regarded as a cause of the inflation, although in this respect any connection must be excluded.
For if the money circuit and the credit ranges behaved similarly
before and after the Accord, it is difficult to understand why any
responsibility for the loss in value of the dollar should be as-
cribed to the fact of "pegging."

The discussion on the 1951 Accord has brought up the question of the independence of the Federal Reserve. On its part it
was stated that "independence for the monetary authority is important, because, and only because, it permits better...to manage the
money supply in the public interest." (37) Yet in the light of
our discussion, the debate which arose seems to have little meaning. If during "pegging" and "nonpegging," and during recession
and boom, the Federal Reserve is unable to change anything in the
total monetary development by the measures taken on its own initiative, the question of whether it ought to be more or less independent is unimportant. The present policy of the freedom for the
Federal Reserve System could thus be revised without much damage.

Further remarks:
Tight and Easy Money. The Federal Reserve seems to believe
that it directs the economy and that it is alternately carrying
out a tight or an easy money policy, yet it only always turns, together with the System, in its narrow circle, and the economy develops and grows almost independently of it. The Federal Reserve
assumes the merit, or, in a given situation, the blame for this
development, although it contributes to it only to a very significant degree. No measures with a view toward broad aims are undertaken, neither in boom nor in recession. The Federal Reserve
only acts from day to day and only the immediate result is taken
into consideration; it is unable to take into account what may or
should happen after weeks or months. The complete passivity of
the Federal Reserve in this respect can be proved in terms of figures.

All speculations based on the present or future action of
the Federal Reserve concerning tight or easy money are nothing but
pure predictions of future market trends and they have the same
value as any other of the usual predictions.

The Money Policy. The view must be rejected that the Federal Reserve exerts any "marginal degree" of influence or repre-

---

37. C. E. Allen [5].

sents "a determining marginal force" on the money market. (38)   In a thin market it is possible to be a leader with little ammunition. This is probably also possible concerning the level of interest because the price of money is subjected to different rules than the price of any other commodity. But in a free market comprising the entire American economy it is impossible to tip the scales, if one does not undertake anything in reality. Where nothing is done, nothing can be effected. Credit was not manipulated at all, and so it is impossible to achieve anything or to influence the market without having advanced or recalled money in the past.

In order to imagine the possibilities of the Federal Reserve in terms of figures one might consider the calculation made in Section 13. The 13.5 minutes given there in proportion to annual transactions, if the Federal Reserve were to abandon its reasonable behavior, may represent the relationship of the function of the Federal Reserve to the tremendous power of the American economy.

---

38. A. Murad [153] notes that the "prevailing fashion in this field of thought" is that: "The Federal System is a sort of central planning commission responsible for the proper functioning of the American economy. People who 'hold these truths to be self-evident' have no occasion to question them. Our monetary experts debate whether the kind, degree and timing of monetary policy actions were correct, whether the effects of those actions were good or bad, but they do not question whether such actions have any effects on prices and economic activity at all. An objective look at the evidence would disclose that monetary policy cannot control prices and economic activity; that it can do nothing and has done nothing to aid economic stability; nor to upset stability and boom." He maintains also that we have to give "primary attention to total expenditures and income, pushing money into the background where it may still exert some minor influence along with 'all other things.'"

R. Stucken [199] points out: "In view of the overheated conjuncture, the Federal Bank (in West Germany) has followed from the fall of 1959 to the fall of 1960 a distinct contraction policy, which the Bank changed subsequently, in the fall of 1960, despite an unchanged overstraining, and has operated with credit easing; in both cases, however, the Bank did not succeed in softening the trend.... With a convertible currency, we are yet quite at the beginning of the experience concerning price and exchange stability; a path through the difficulties must be yet found. This dilemma exists also in the United States and in Switzerland."

Interchangeability of Funds. Concerning interchangeability
of funds with different dates of maturity it has to be indicated
that the importance of such funds for the economy, as far as their
period of maturity is concerned, cannot be measured.

Although the interchangeability of funds is recognized,
not much attention is paid to this question in financial literature. As long as the view is held that the System regulates the
credit basis of the country, the problem of the interchangeability
of funds already seems to have been taken into consideration in
all measures of the Federal Reserve. Yet this problem always has
to be carefully considered whenever the supplementation and distribution of funds is being discussed.

It must be emphasized that these remarks refer only to the
interchangeability with regard to the availability of capital, and
not to the level of the interest rate. As far as interest rates
are concerned, great differences may develop between "pockets,"
even during small congestions; this is true especially for the
short-term market which is dominated by bills and where switches
between bills and demand deposits occur. The reason is to be
found in the special character of the formation of price in the
interest structure.

The Role of the Federal Reserve. Our statement that the
authorities can achieve nothing or very little should not be interpreted to mean that their efforts to form and to maintain an
orderly framework for the course of the economy should be considered as of little importance. We only wish to say that the function of the authorities is restricted to this regulatory task,
which is, however, important in itself.

It follows from our discussion that the Federal Reserve is
not in a position, even to a limited extent, to carry out the
tasks imposed on it by law. This is true also as far as price
stability is concerned. These regulations are entirely outdated
and ought to be dropped as soon as possible. Eventual new directives and regulations concerning the function and scope of activity of the Federal Reserve would have to be kept within an extreme-
ly restricted framework.

Chapter 5

The Principle of the Total Picture

Section 1
In economics, one often resorts to the classical example
of a Robinson Crusoe economy in order to expound many theoretical
or practical problems; in praxeology, for instance, the theory of
the solitary Crusoe is regarded as the first category. In such
comparisons, the process of production and consumption is precisely described step by step, and parallels are drawn, so that the
relevant situation can be clearer understood. But concerning the
turnover of money and values, no such examination is considered,
although it could in the most suitable way convince us as to the
real development in this field.

In the Robinson economy, it is not possible for the lone
person to consume something that has not been saved in the past.
First, it must actually be produced in a productive process, and
only then can it be used; one cannot avail oneself of the future.
If there are two Robinsons, the picture does not change. The same
obtains for a hundred Robinsons, a thousand Robinsons, and two
hundred million Robinsons. If this condition could change with
the number of participants, it should be possible to indicate at
what point one might take advantage of the not-yet-existing values.

Thus, in our economy it is equally impossible to employ
something - even for one dollar - that has not been produced previously in a regular manner. In this development, money or credit
can be helpful in the turnover, but it cannot be creative; out of
credit one cannot invest even one dollar, if this dollar was not
saved earlier by somebody. Capital, in the economic sense, is the
result of work performed beforehand, prepared in advance, and
therefore, ex definitione, its increment cannot take place subsequently. This is not a question of psychological conditions or
influence, because, for example, the authorities have granted credit in order to foster some development, and this may change the
situation; it is the matter of material fact, since the question
is simply whether values not yet produced can be disposed of.

Economic principles are often well understood and accepted
if a small number of units is dealt with (i.e., in microeconomics),
but are disregarded and ignored in a strange manner in relation to
the total economy for which many odd, eccentric, and haphazard
combinations seem to be possible.

The belief that by some devices it may be feasible to originate additional values is similar to the belief of alchemists of
the Middle Ages who imagined they could bring about miraculous
changes. In physics, the idea that more power could be created
beyond material possibilities would be ridiculed, but in economics,

124

"the dismal science," comparable ideas are maintained, and many economists hold that artificial contrivances can determine economic development. This is particularly puzzling because economics, in view of its subject matter, should be the most sober and realistic of sciences.

In the light of the above considerations - and before any other examination or analysis - we should exclude the possibility of additional credit, as well as shut out, a priori on this basis, the utilization of and profit from more values not yet in existence. (1)

Section 2
We have based our study, first, on the computation of the availability of credit, and this calculation comprises the turnover of the whole economy. In contemplating the resulting situation, we should always bear in mind that the availability of credit represents a fixed amount that cannot be changed by any artificial measures, as well as consider which factors influence it and how it develops in the course of years.

We have already described in Chapter 3, Section 4, that the increment in domestic availability of credit in any period for any sector is its own saving minus direct investment. The increment in domestic availability of credit is thus primarily dependent on saving, and secondly on the proportion in which economic units choose to invest directly. The remaining part of their saving invested in fixed-value assets constitutes the increment in the domestic availability of credit. We have also listed in Chapter 3, Section 4, some examples showing how the relation between net domestic saving-investment and the increment in domestic availability of credit developed during the course of different years. Analyzing this relationship in more detail, it has to be

---

1. W. Eucken [53] observes: "If it is correct that only what had been previously produced can be distributed, the first problem of all social reformers must be directed toward an economic order with the highest degree of economic efficiency."

H. Hellwig [100] cites A. Forstmann that one has "to relinquish the hocus-pocus theory of the possibility of disposing with 'money' of nonexistent goods, and thereby to return on the ground of economic reality marked by the primacy of the mediating credit granting."

A. Forstmann [63] also writes: "...the hocus-pocus theory of the possibility to put one's hand into the pocket of a naked man (because the paradox implied in the 'new' credit theory amounts indeed to the idea of being able with the created money to dispose of real capital not existing at all)."

considered, for instance, by how much those economic units decide
to pay off their indebtedness from their savings, in this manner
permitting the possible use of the relative amounts for granting
new credit.

        The most striking error concerning the availability of
credit is committed in evaluating the impact of the government
debts and the patterns of their maturity. It is contended that
short-term government securities facilitate expansion of bank
loans, especially during budget deficits, and that long-term indebtedness does not imply this risk. But a budget deficit only
raises the government debt, and not the money supply. No development in this respect can change the total availability of credit,
and a budget deficit reduces merely the amount of funds available
for current investment. (2)

----

        2. *The Wall Street Journal* reported, for instance, on
September 8, 1961: "Advance refunding helps avoid an increasingly
heavy concentration of the debt in short-term securities, which
banks can convert easily into cash to meet extra loan demand. Some
authorities - notably those in the Federal Reserve System - regard
this as potentially inflationary, especially when the Government
is running a budget deficit. Advance refunding helps keep part of
the debt in the hands of long-term investors, who ordinarily don't
convert the securities into cash."
        Other examples:
        R. V. Roosa [181] writes: "The contrasting risks, in
terms both of sustained growth and the amplitude of cyclical
swings, are (1) that the credit total may fall so far below this
range as to exert a serious downward pull of the economy, or (2)
that the credit total may rise so hugely or so fast as to feed or
propel an explosive boom. The 140 billion dollars of new credit
in 1957-59 was of unprecedented size. Any further enlargement of
new credit volume in 1960, through more money creation, would thus
have seemed to result in a virtually unbearable overloading of an
already over-stretched credit mechanism. The resurging total in
the second quarter of 1958 was attributable mainly to a spectacu-
lar increase in the volume of bank credit, and in its proportion
to total credit."
        As our computation shows, the increment in domestic avail-
ability of credit in 1957-59 amounted to about 110 billion dollars,
was 8.3 billion dollars in the second quarter of 1958, 29.7 bil-
lion dollars in 1960, and much steeper in the subsequent years.
The whole development can be only the result and not the cause of
cyclical swings. There is no danger that for this reason economic
growth could not be sustained or a downward pull might occur. The
amount of total credit should not raise any concern, and the vol-

Section 3

It follows from our discussion of the availability of credit that the actual demand deposits and the issued currency must be
in some way compensated. There exists namely, as described in
Chapter 4, Section 10, a stationary, immovable mass of money in
the form of demand deposits and currency, which does not represent
purchasing power, since only money supposed to be expended can exert pressure on the market of goods and services. The calculation
of increments in the availability of credit shows, however, that
any disposable money is absorbed by the economy, so that the monetary and banking system is bound to bring this money back into
use. This is, in fact, accomplished by compensation, as presented
in detail in Chapter 4.

Since in this chapter we wish to examine the situation from
the point of view of the total picture, we may also imagine that
there exists in the country only one bank in which all demand deposits are held. This bank would, to be sure, lend all its deposits or alternatively invest them, so that the whole immovable mass
would be compensated for; in the case of a direct withdrawal of
some amounts from demand deposits, these amounts would have to be
promptly discompensated. In real life, with many banks, not only
the current demand deposits, but also all demand deposits in the

---

ume of bank credit is irrelevant for the total picture.

*J. D. Daane [43], a member of the Board of Governors of
the Federal Reserve System, stated in October 1966 that the expansion of business credit had been a major factor behind current
inflationary pressures in the economy (New York Times, October 25,
1966). Thereupon, the American Bankers Association [6] pointed
out in a resolution: "It has become apparent in recent months
that the Federal Reserve is prepared...to apply a form of selective credit control designed to limit the growth in loans to business. This raises the question of whether attempts to impose upon
commercial banks arbitrary criteria for the allocation of credit
among various borrowers are consistent with the national interest.
In the short run business lending is no more inflationary than
other types of lending. In the long run, by facilitating expansion of productive capacity, lending to business is one of the
most effective instruments for stimulating increases in productivity and continuing economic growth.... It is highly questionable whether lending to business should be singled out for selective restraint." It appears, thus, that the Bankers Association
when its members had seemed to be restricted in their activity,
has abandoned suddenly the traditional view that bank credit had
a special character and has contended - and rightly so - that the
Federal Reserve should leave to the money market the allocation
of the available credit.*

past, are compensated for by commercial banks, and the counterbalance of the currency was invested by the Federal Reserve. If we view the turnover from this angle, the entire exchange should appear in a much clearer light.

This state of affairs can be adequately demonstrated as well on the basis of accountancy (cf., Chapter 4, Section 14). It can be shown that the compensation of demand deposits is carried out automatically, and the bank turnover may be regarded as based largely on bookkeeping transactions. Moreover, the compensation likewise includes cash items in the process of collection. (3)

In this manner, it is possible to link the proof based on Flow of Funds Accounts with the second proof based on bank credit range. From this joint presentation, one may conclude that when the problem of availability of credit is solved, the issue of who determines the total level of existing demand deposits is secondary. Since the Federal Reserve cannot influence the total availability of credit, why should it hinder business and consumers in keeping their demand deposits at a level which seems convenient to them?

Finally, it is possible to adopt quite a different standpoint. One can simply maintain that the monetary circuit develops exactly as stated in all particulars in Chapter 4, without entering into any reasons that bring about these conditions. Furthermore, one may point out that this situation prevails with current compensation and so on, as all circumstances indicate, urging to check carefully the whole description and find out where it does not correspond with reality. If there are some doubts and reservations, one should depict another pattern of monetary circuit which better fits the situation. For if there is dissent, one is obliged to define it and present another computation; one must finally compute and arrive at an overall calculation, because otherwise we can never succeed in our analysis. If, however, no divergencies can be detected in our picture, one ought to accept it and conform to it, at least for the time being.

Section 4
In spite of all this argument, there exists in the United States an influencial school of thought which contends that changes in the stock of money originate the ups and downs in the economy,

---

3. G. Garvy [74] notes: "Bank float is fairly large (about ten per cent) in relation to reported deposits, and the mail float may be even larger, but there are currently no means of measuring it.... The Federal Reserve Board's staff estimates that in recent years close to thirty per cent of corporate demand deposits, as shown on bank records, consisted of check float."

and that, hence, the money supply constitutes the central point of our economic mechanism.

In a work published in 1963, M. Friedman and A. Jacobson Schwartz [67] develop this theory in the extreme. In particular, in 120 pages they explain that during the Great Depression in 1929-33 and during the incomplete recovery in 1933-37, the monetary authorities could have restored prosperity by providing a greater money supply. Some economists have bestowed only praise upon this work. They hold that it is a monumental inquiry into the working of our monetary system; it is a scholarly accomplishment, above all, in the ingenuity that has been brought to bear on the solution of complex and subtle economic issues; it will be the classic reference on its subject for many years to come; this is one of those rare books that leave their mark on all future research on the subject. (4) Other critics are reproachful, however, stating that according to such a presentation the free market would go wrong; they ridicule pointing out that when income velocity is constant or at least regular, the change in the stock of money immediately tells us the change in GNP that will result in the future; that the lead of money supply is an arithmetic artifact which has no causal significance at all; that in this case changes in money supply lead national income. (5)

In conceiving this theory, the following apparent errors are committed:

a) It is assumed that people are glad to maintain large demand deposits, so that commercial banks are able to increase them at will. This is, however, not correct. If people cannot be induced to hold demand deposits and currency in increased quantities, the authorities are not in the position to pursue a policy which aims at manipulating the money supply. (6) The money supply serves only for turnover; it is impossible to use it for other purposes.

---

4. K. Brunner [24], H. G. Johnson [112], J. Tobin [204].

5. L. Keyserling [122], L. S. Ritter [167], R. M. Solow [196], D. D. Hester [103].

G. Shea [194] remarks concerning the Great Depression: "The policies of the Reserve System were generous enough. How, then, can it be assumed that Reserve policies could engineer a rise in the stock of money in the face of declining business?"

6. T. C. Gaines [68] points out: "Changes in the money stock (demand deposits) probably are much more the consequence of independent, rational decisions by owners of financial assets than of Federal Reserve policy actions. That is to say, if private business chooses to economize on cash because of the income foregone when a demand deposit is held rather than a liquid earning

(But apart from this argument, if during the Great Depression people had maintained more money on their demand deposits, they would either have had to save these amounts previously or borrow them somewhere. In both cases, nothing could be changed, and the total availability of credit would not increase.)

b) The relationship concerning money supply is turned upside down. It is held that it is dependent in particular on the individuals and in general on the monetary authorities. What happens, then, when the monetary authorities do not agree with regard to the added up amounts of the money supply kept by individuals? The authorities would have to decree how much money everybody should have in hand. If one believes that business trends are contingent on the stock of money, an increase in it would amount to a simple order to business to enlarge the total production. (7) But, first of all, the followers of this theory should show when in the past monetary authorities have restrained people in keeping demand deposits at a level decided upon by individuals, and how the authorities have arranged it.

c) The money supply is considered to be a defined concept once and for all, and its substitutes are not taken into account

---

asset, there really is little the Federal Reserve can do to resist this shifting among financial asset forms, and there is no particular reason why they should attempt to do anything. The reverse, of course, is true when private business or individuals choose to add to their demand balances rather than hold other liquid assets .... This explanation of demand deposits changing as the result of conscious decisions of depositors rather than as the result of Federal Reserve manipulation of the reserve base may not have the intellectual fascination of a more abstract explanation, but it does square with the observed facts and is consistent with rational behavior.... It carries no implication that Federal policy has been 'too easy,' and it does not imply greater liquidity in the sense of balances that would be available for spending at a later time."

7. M. Friedman [65] recommends that one instructs "the System to use its open market powers to produce a four per cent per year rate of growth in the total of currency held by the public and adjusted deposits in commercial banks.... As a student of Henry Simons and Lloyd Mints, I shall follow them in recommending that the present system be replaced by one in which 100 per cent reserves are required...to keep reserves equal to 100 per cent of deposit liabilities whether demand or time in the form of either currency in vault or interest-bearing deposits with the Reserve System."

in the computation. (8) This artificial demarcation renders the whole procedure of little avail (see Chapter 4, Section 4). One may use this concept as an auxiliary device, yet at all times express reservations should be made regarding its precise meaning; otherwise it would be preferable to do without it. (9)

Concerning substitutes for the money supply, it is also held that government debt, and especially short-term debt, is necessary for the orderly market turnover. One maintains that the effect of debt removal on the money supply could result in a "catastrophic monetary deflation"; (10) "the liquidity of the nation's monetary system in part hinges on the supply of short-term governments"; (11) "the country does need a very substantial amount of short-term debt, which is really part of the money supply...and the country operates on that." (12) The fact, however, that the government has adopted its debt structure to the convenience of lenders in the course of time does not mean that this debt structure is now indispensable for the functioning of the money market. The market was able in the past and shall be able at any time in the future to develop tools for its operations which will satisfy its needs and assure its smooth and effective working. (13)

---

8. J. S. Duesenberry [49] remarks: "I had some difficulties in following his (Friedman's) argument because he deals with the demand for currency, demand deposits, and commercial bank time deposits without any reference to the demand for close substitutes for those things; e.g., deposits in mutual savings banks and savings and loan associations for households and holdings of Treasury bills for business. This does not seem consistent with the approach which he himself took in his restatement of the quantity theory in 'The Quantity Theory of Money. A Restatement' [64]."

9. O. Morgenstern [151] feels that "it is better to say nothing than to give wrong information which - quite apart from its practical abuse - in turn misleads hosts of later investigators; this is especially important if data are to be used in extensive aggregations."

10. J. E. Meade [146].

11. W. R. Burgess [26].

12. D. Dillon [46].

13. C. J. Anderson [7] observes: "It does not necessarily follow that in the absence of a large volume of short-term governments over-all liquidity would be less. In a modern credit economy, banks, financial institutions, and others are confronted with the problem of keeping their resources fully utilized despite seasonal and cyclical swings in financing needs and credit demands. When the volume of government securities was small, interbank balances, short-term paper, and call-loans were common meth-

Only a small minority of the profession is persuaded by
the argument of the theory discussed above (14), and it is rejected
by a great majority of businessmen as well. Many economists seem,
however, to be influenced to some degree by this theory, perhaps
because of the vigorous and insistent presentation by its adher-
ents. (15) It is disturbing that it could not be refuted on the
basis of the traditional argumentation; Friedman himself calls for
further investigations in this field (cf., footnote on p. 3).

Section 5
The foregoing discussion has already shown that the banking system is unable to guide or control the powerful forces of a
modern economy. Thus, the authorities are not in the position to
improve noticeably the existing condition in the money market,
but, in the negative, they may cause the monetary situation to de-
teriorate by an unreasonable policy. This is especially the case
in countries with undeveloped monetary markets, through government
indebtedness, embarking on excessive emission of currency, and
hence inflation. (16)

---

ods of adjusting reserve and cash positions.... Liquidity prefer-
ence would undoubtedly establish a pattern of market rates that
would afford a strong incentive for an increase in the volume of
private short-term credit instruments."
        14. R. M. Solow [196].
        15. G. Ackley [1] points out that monetary managers a
generation ago followed an "essentially perverse monetary policy.
From 1929 to 1933 they allowed the total money supply of the economy to decline 25 per cent when it could have and should have expanded." Today "we are much more sophisticated in our use of
monetary policy."
        J. M. Culbertson [42] notes that "in the future a more
even and higher rate of expansion of the money supply" should be
aimed at.
        A. H. Meltzer [147]: "There is the myth that fiscal poli-
cy has been the major expanding force bringing about the recovery
of the economy to the high levels of production in 1964 and 1965.
The fact is that the rate of economic expansion began shortly after the rate of monetary expansion increased, and the rate of
economic expansion has continued at a pace to be expected from the
combination of government deficits with monetary expansion."
        16. Nevertheless, it is often held that in communist coun-
tries flexible credit policies are pursued. The recent economic
literature in those countries confirms, however, that, after lengthy
experience, the command economies are now convinced that monetary
measures can have only little positive influence on the productive
process.

One might draw a parallel between money supply as a means of exchange and values in production, on the one hand, and the System and the total economy, on the other. The System can be regarded as the symbol of money supply as means of exchange. In a similar fashion, as money supply as a means of exchange is merely a servant of the market and as it cannot normally, and should not, cause changes in the production of values in a modern economy, so the System can and should not change the range of money disposal of the economy and disturb the proper course of the economy by actions whose consequences cannot be calculated in advance.

Our argument is mainly based on the following considerations:

Our analysis shows that the level of reserve requirements can in no way further or hinder the growth of the economy. As in the past, so also in the future the economy will determine how much demand deposits it needs for the current turnover, and the banking system will purposefully act accordingly.

Fluctuations in bank reserves are meaningless, so that there is little sense in paying particular attention to them or to regard them as the starting point of the analysis. The entire concept of the supply and absorption of bank reserves on the part of the Federal Reserve is artificial and misleading. A supply of reserves of nonexistent; it could be claimed with the same degree of justification that the economy supplies the Federal Reserve with securities or with other investment opportunities. There are no "powerful dollars" or magic bank reserves which regulate credit creation, which does not happen anyway.

If we wish to arrive at an intelligent explanation, the relevant factors have to be rearranged and put in correct order, i.e., those positions which normally are not influenced by the Federal Reserve must be treated as data, and only on this basis may further evaluations be made.

G. Hauge [95] points out, for instance: "Socialist governments abroad follow flexible credit policies as a matter of course when conditions call for them. Staunch spokesmen can be found for monetary discipline in Communist Poland, a fact I learned at first hand from the Polish finance minister in Warsaw.... From Salazar Portugal to Khrushchev Russia, flexible policy is a scientific technique of social control, not an ideological bone of contention."

H. Gestrich [77]: "The result of modern investigation is, in fact, very characteristic insofar as a market economy needs a centrally directed monetary credit policy, if it is to work well and smoothly, while in a command economy money has only a subsidiary function."

In order to visualize the course of transactions, a relevant separation of the credit ranges must be undertaken. It appears to be logical to delimit, on the one hand, the Federal Reserve and the commercial banks and, on the other hand, the remainder of the economy. If in this manner the banking system constitutes a separate sector, the picture becomes clearer, so that it
is easier to evaluate how credits can be granted out of this sector. Instead of this, the entire economy with the exception of
the Federal Reserve is regarded as a single sector, and no attention is paid to the movements of the Federal Reserve in the circuit. In consequence of this, such movements are regarded as addition or subtraction of funds, and their simultaneous compensation is not taken into account. It is therefore most important to
drop the concept that the Federal Reserve holds a privileged position within the circuit. Its transactions must be incorporated as
normal elements into the general money circulation.
    The theses of the theory of credit creation seem to be
built, above all, on the following faulty conclusions:
    Since the statements of condition of the Federal Reserve
were assumed to be the pivot of the money circuit, it was deduced
from this that bank reserves which are determined by the Federal
Reserve decide everything, and particularly the volume of credit.
It was then not considered necessary to examine whether the credit
creation on the part of the banks during the past years did indeed
take place - so firmly was the theory accepted as valid. It appears that the classic theory was right when it "conceived the
available credit as a rigid, limited stock." (17)
    The simple fact that the commercial banks are obliged to
transfer a percentage of their demand deposits to the Federal Reserve was explained that if they are only in a position to transfer this percentage to the Federal Reserve, their ability to multiply demand deposits and loans is infinitely great. (18) An examination of the actual relationships reveals that here cause and
result have been confused.
    It seems that in the case of credit being granted, the in-
terests of the bank and of the customers are identical. If the
bank is prepared to grant credits, it usually should find willing
recipients for them. Yet their interests soon part. For the bank
wishes that the lent money remains on the demand deposits, and the

---

17. H. Gestrich [76].
18. Similarly, there seems to exist the belief that the
Federal Reserve is able to lend further enormous amounts depending
on its judgment. For if their notes must be backed by a reserve
of 25 per cent in gold certificates, it would still be in a position to put into circulation currency above sixty billion dollars.

customer desires to invest it for the largest part and in the
quickest way possible in "values in production."

Only the unused and unusable demand deposits or currency
can possibly be increased, and this cannot alter the total availability of credit. Therefore, credit creation is materially impossible. Credit can be granted only from substance, dollar by
dollar. Nothing can be created from nothing, especially in money
matters. (19)

It cannot be correct that the position of the banks are
restricted by the sale of government securities by the Federal Reserve to nonbank investors, for the reason that by doing so, as is
claimed, the demand deposits of these nonbank investors in the
banks are reduced. Such a presentation only isolates one process
of the circuit and leaves out the proper relationships. That
which appears on the surface is accepted as something real.

It has to be considered that almost all transactions in
economic life are passed on by the demand deposits and that thus
gross-savings, which grow at the rate of over two billion dollars

----

*19. H. Feifel [59] writes: "According to the 'classic'
mediative credit theory, the banks exert only a mediating function;
they put only other people's money at the disposal of borrowers.
The opinions of V. F. Wagner, Bouniatian, Reisch, Cannan, Leaf,
Somary, De Viti de Marco are identical with the view of this theory.... Particularly in the English and American literature there
is a host of descriptions of the multiplication process of credit
creation, which, as a rule, differ only slightly from each other."*

*H. Hellwig [101]: "F. Somary decidedly rejects the modern
credit theory as false; we equally have a sharp refusal of this
theory by J. Goldschmidt.... The fact that one and the same amount
often functions infinitely as a means of exchange, is the main
source of all errors in the money and credit theory."*

*W. Stutzel [200] has "empirically tested" the theory of
the credit creation multiplicator, and reports on this: "From
1950 to 1958, the banks in West Germany have increased their liquid funds by about DM16 milliard. On the basis of a credit creation multiplicator of about 12 on the average of reserve rates,
and with a credit and money creation of DM192 milliard and the
given velocity of circulation of about 6, an increase in the gross
social product by about 1.2 billion, at market prices, results,
i.e., from DM100 milliard in 1950 to 1.3 billion in 1958. Taking
into account the development of the real gross social product,
this amounts to a sevenfold rise of the price level in 1950 or by
600 per cent. In reality, the gross social product was at market
prices in 1958 DM230 milliard; the price increase was on the order
of 20 per cent."*

Cf., also, footnotes on pp. 72-3.

per week and investments which are made with these savings, are
also transacted over demand deposits. We cannot select one movement and pursue it, for by doing so we lose sight of the general
picture. We have already spoken of such a pursuit, which does not
take into account other simultaneous changes (see p. 100). There
it was a matter of increased credits, here we are dealing with a
change in the credit range. If we proceeded in this manner, each
loan and each repayment by third persons would have to be described
in terms of shrinking or expansion of the position of the banks,
which would make any calculation impossible. This stream cannot
be defined or analyzed. The solution lies in the fact that, though
the current savings do indeed pass "dynamically" through the demand deposits, the demand deposits themselves change relatively
only very little. This permits us to shake off the ghost of the
rotating movement, to stop for a moment, and to use the average of
the demand deposits at a given time for purposes of comparison.
(20)

The amounts on the demand deposits which are used for investments in government securities do not form an element of the
constant demand deposits. They only pass through quickly and
would in any case be used up for other investment after a few
days. New amounts are put in their place, again only temporarily,
from gross-savings or from "values in production." This is the
nature of the money circuit. Only the substance which remains can
be counted, i.e., the amount which is usually maintained on the
demand deposits on the average.

We are best informed on this process by the data on the
financial assets of the nonbank investors. Cash and other liquid
assets of the insurance companies, for instance, at the end of the
years from 1950 to 1965 amounted to 4.1 to 4.6 per cent of all
other assets. A similar situation obtains for other nonbank investors.

Besides, the difficulties in evaluation of the situation
of selling government securities to nonbank investors arise also
as a result of the misleading division of the sectors, as described
on p. 134.

Unless the entire picture is kept before the eye, one soon
arrives at the most absurd conclusions. Thus, it would not be
possible for nonbank investors, for instance, to purchase government securities for larger amounts, for they would have exhausted
their demand deposits within a short time (yet they have constant-

---

20. *This seems to be the only possibility for obtaining a
basis for judging the situation, i.e., by a comparative statics
approach. An isolated study of an event in this case would only
be a stationary treatment of a dynamic process.*

ly been the biggest buyers of bills). Or it would be useless for
banks to sell securities to third persons, for by doing this they
would only reduce the demand deposits and lose interest (yet they
sell securities for many billions of dollars). In this second
case, only an exchange takes place. The nonbank investors purchase securities and by the same amount use so much less for other
investments, and the banks are able to grant loans to their customers for this amount.

Section 6
The Radcliffe Report in Great Britain [82] has confirmed
many results of our investigations, although the unanimity in its
conclusions could only be secured at the cost of vagueness on several important points. The Report makes it quite clear that the
conception of control of the banking system through the supply of
cash to the banks has no relevance to present-day conditions. The
money supply has been largely uncontrolled during the postwar period. "There has been no attempt in the postwar period to operate
on the banking position by limiting the supply of cash: the banks
have always been automatically provided with whatever was necessary to make their cash ratio fit the eight per cent rule imposed
since 1946" (par. 430). The orthodox view concerning the relation
between the money supply and the level of demand was rejected.
The Committee failed to find convincing evidence "of the operation
of an interest incentive effect," and holds that interest changes
have little effect on the volume of saving. It felt that there
was a tendency to attach rather too much importance to expecta-
tions "as independent market forces." Nowhere is it explicitly
put that the monetary policy should play a purely passive role in
the (short-term) regulation of the economy, though the Report contains plenty of passages indicating that something like this was
at the back of the Committee's mind. (21)
However, it is stated, too, that "the supply of Treasury
bills and not the supply of cash has become to be the effective
regulatory base of the domestic banking system" (par. 583). But
the Committee does not elaborate in more detail on this subject,
and has no definite recommendations to make. (22)

---

21. W. M. Dacey [44], J. G. Gurley [85], N. Kaldor [115],
and J. S. G. Wilson [220].
22. A. Gaskin [75] makes this quite philosophic remark:
"If control over the supply of money offers little hope...the answer must be in more direct measures of control over some of the
channels themselves. The problem is a formidable one, as the Report makes clear, but if we wish monetary policy to have anything
more than minor mildly pervasive influence, we have to start thinking along these lines."

The views of the Radcliffe Report encountered strong oppo-
sition, as could be expected. In a special volume, entitled Not
Unanimous, A Rival Verdict to Radcliffe's on Money, it has been emphasized that the Committee had underestimated the effectiveness
of monetary policy, and the importance of the supply of money has
been resolutely reasserted. (23) It was reproved that the formation stone of the British monetary theory had been abandoned. (24)
It was claimed, for instance, that, according to W. McC. Martin,
Jr. and P. Jacobsson, "the United States, by increasing the quantity of money...played a leading part in retrieving the whole world
from recession." The conclusions of the Report also met strong
dissension in the United States. (25)

----

23. *R. F. Harrod [93], R. F. Henderson [102], A. Seldon*
[189].

24. *R. F. Harrod [93].*

25. *T. Balogh [10] comments: "Monetary policy, whether*
in its traditional sense of regulating the price, or the more mod-
ern guise of regulating the quantity of money and credit, is power-
less to maintain stability at full employment by preventing...a
speculative inflationary boom.... If open market policy is no
longer effective - which may well be the case - it is...because of
the failure of the rate of interest as a regulator."

W. M. Dacey [44]: "While the Radcliffe Report has started
some new controversies, we can be thankful that it has settled
some old ones. In particular, it should finally be disposed of
one notion that has done perhaps more than any other to confuse
monetary discussion. This is the concept, given an extra thirty
years' lease of life by the Macmillan Report, that the effective
basic credit resides in the cash reserves of the banks, with its
implication that bank deposits may be expected to rise by a large
multiple of any addition to those reserves. The multiple would be
the reciprocal of the cash ratio. Since the banks now work to an
8 per cent ratio, the Macmillan concept, if it had any validity,
would mean that an increase of £ 10 million in bank cash would set
in train an expansion of no less than £ 125 million in deposits."

R. F. Harrod [93]: "The belittling reference to the sig-
nificance of the quantity of money must be wrong.... Control of
the money supply is the center-piece of monetary policy.... The
scepticism of the Report in relation to the potency of monetary
policy, and notably in relation to the effect of variations in the
quantity of money, goes quite against the current trend of think-
ing outside Britain.... Generally speaking, the Report appears to
be profoundly sceptical about the potency of monetary policy."

N. Kaldor [115]: "The Committee would not go so far as to
say that 'the supply of money is an unimportant quantity' but they

The Report of the Commission on Money and Credit [36] published in 1961, as well as the Commission's Research Studies [37],
did not bring any new elements into the discussion. They were only a repetition of the traditional views in the United States. In
a collective review-article of these studies, it was pointed out,
for example, that this volume is inadequate in dealing with the
impact of monetary policy. (26) P. L. Bernstein [17] finds only
one "article in the book written with any literary flair," and
many others "typical of what I found inadequate and disappointing
about this whole volume."

Section 7
All money is employed at all times, and in a modern economy there simply cannot exist any superfluous money which somehow

---

'view it as only a part of the wider structure of liquidity in the
economy.... We reject any suggestion that the rate of interest
weapon should be made more effective by being used much more vio-
lently than hitherto.' But if this is so, what remains of their
contention, that...manipulation of the structure of interest rates
must be 'the center-piece of monetary action?'"
      I. M. D. Little, R. R. Neild, and C. R. Roos [130]: "The
view that, if suitable techniques can be devised, monetary policy
can solve our present economic difficulties is mistaken and danger-
ous.... The role of monetary policy is essentially a subsidiary
one."
      J. Robinson [173,174]: "Monetary policy as a rational, im-
partial and effective means of controlling total demand always was
a myth, whether expressed in terms of a crude quantity theory or
in more subtle modern sophisteries. The Radcliffe Report, certainly, does not show much enthusiasm for the myth. If its authors
had followed systematically the clues entangled in their own
thought, it would have shown even less.... There is no such thing
as a purely quantative, overall financial policy. We are fortu-
nate in having had an official report that finally discards the
old mumbo jumbo (the Quantitative Theory of Money)."
      R. V. Roosa [180]: "The authorities should not only con-
trol the supply of money but also seek more broadly to effect the
liquidity of the economy.... If it is now possible in Britain almost completely to ignore the money supply...(it is)...a 'Monetary
System' without a Policy for Money...the denial of any special
place for money and for the related creation of bank credit...which
has been found crucially to the understanding and the use of commercial banking systems throughout the world."
      J. S. G. Wilson [220] speaks of "the near fanatical attack
on the concept of supply of money."
      26. L. V. Chandler [33].

later could raise the purchasing power. If perhaps it might sometimes seem - in our opinion unjustly so - that there exist too
many or too few demand deposits, they will always be compensated
or discompensated, so that in the total computation they do not
have to be taken into consideration. A similar situation exists
as far as currency is concerned; its countervalue is constantly
invested and disinvested by the Federal Reserve - usually in government securities, so that all demand deposits and currency are
tied up. The financial assets, however, constitute values in production; they are employed economically, and usually yield profits.
The economy would not pay any interest or shares of profit for un-
employed funds.

In this manner, all money is employed, directly or indi-
rectly, at any time. This is the crux of the theory of monetary
turnover, and without this thesis the theory is inconsistent and
unintelligible. Any balance is active for the total economy. The
concept of idle balances itself is <u>contradictio in adjecto</u>. (27)

The ratio of government securities and loans to deposits
in banks fluctuates depending on how far the banks endeavor - during an upswing - to grant more loans. In the case of a slackening
in credit demands, however, the loan ratio will decrease. (28)
Yet these fluctuations must not be confused with some excessive
liquidity. If the banks were unable to grant sufficient credits,
the nonbank investors would take care of this owing to the tremendously growing savings and, of course, always within the framework
of funds available at a given moment. The credit range of the
banks is not changed by this, and for the total situation it makes
no difference who invests more in credits and less in securities,
or vice versa. (29)

---

27. *G. Garvy [74] remarks concerning the distinction between active and idle balances (distinguished frequently in academic literature as M_1 and M_2): "What is meant by reference to
idle balances is the excess over amounts normally required to meet
smoothly an anticipated flow of payments. It is frequently said
that balances created through loan extention are particularly active. This may or may not be so. The process which is frequently
referred to as the activation of idle balances is best looked upon
as a reshuffling in the ownership distribution of checkbook money
and, more generally, in liquid-asset holdings as interest rates
rise. The activation of balances is thus a complex process."*
28. *It is often emphasized that a major element of
strength in our economy consists in the high quality of commercial
bank assets (cf., J. Bogen [20], <u>Journal of Commerce</u>, January 13,
1958).*
29. *T. G. Gaines [68] remarks: "Still another illus-*

The term "plenty" has no meaning at all in the above con-
notation. The problem of a permanent inflationary liquidity does
not pose itself. It cannot be correct that "the phenomenon of inflation is connected with the predominance of the liquidity of the
total economy as compared with the volume of goods of the total
economy." The volume of money is only a result of the volume of
goods. (30) We must always remember that money supply merely represents a means of exchange. (31)

---

*tration of old attitudes that are unrelated to today's reality is
the impression that commercial bank credit differs in some important way from other types of credit. One finds constant references
to changes in bank credit outstanding, but only seldom are references made to total credit.... A similar rapid expansion of credit
through other financial intermediaries in recent years has not
created the same alarm.... All that is required is a shift of em-
phasis away from commercial bank credit, money supply, and other
such partial objectives.... "*

*30. J. C. R. Dow [48] comments: "Money was a stock, and
yet we were trying to use it to control flow; and it was very hard
to get an explanation of how and why changes in a stock effected
expenditures flows."*

*G. Haberler [87]: "Money may conceivably play a role of
minor importance. It is possible that in some, or even in all
circumstances it adjusts itself to changes in production without
exerting an active influence."*

*D. H. Robertson [171]: "The amount of this circulating
capital in existence depends partly on the size of the annual flow
of goods and services which we call the 'real national income,'
and partly on the speed with which, on the average, goods are made
ready for the consumers use, or in other words on the length of
what we have just called the average period of production of
goods."*

*V. F. Wagner [213]: "There is a thesis that sensible uti-
lization of cash reserves and surpluses through credit may render
possible a more vigorous and rational employment of real capital.
This assertion cannot be offhand rejected, but it lacks the necessary theoretical foundation."*

*F. T. Juster [114] remarks in a review of G. Katona's The
Powerful Consumer [118]: "Economists will also be unhappy with
what seems to be some evident confusion.... The discussion of liquid assets and spending in Chapter VIII seems to suppose that consumers, rather than the monetary authorities, determine how much
liquid assets will be in existence."*

*31. W. H. Hutt [106] asks: "May it not be that Marshall
was shrewdly correct in his continuous preaching that the 'only*

It is to be considered, furthermore, that any credit originates on the basis of production, since people generally incur
debts in order to enlarge the existing production or to acquire
consumers' or producers' goods and services. This connection does
not disturb an orderly functioning of the economy in the course of
time, if the increment in debts do not exceed a reasonable limit.
In the postwar years, credit was never "unsustainably large," as
is sometimes held.

It can therefore be maintained, from the point of view of
the total picture, that credit is linked intimately with production and turnover, similarly to money supply as a means of exchange. (32)

Section 8
The neutrality of money is defined in various ways in economic literature. It is convenient to distinguish the following
types of definitions:

a) The money supply is neutral only if all events in the
money economy correspond to an ideal type of a pure exchange economy, according to the laws of the equilibrium theories; if it does
not impair or falsify the legitimacy of the market economy, respectively the competition rules, derived from the theory out of
the monetary economy under consideration; if the monetary system
and nonmonetary intermediaries hold only private domestic debt
(and money) behind their issues of money and nonmomentary indirect
debt...and the government has no control over the portfolio of the
monetary system; if it has a pure mediating role. (33)

b) The neutrality of money, as a general principle, requires that the monetary authorities be out of the business of
dealing in debt altogether...and the inability of changes in the
nominal stock of money to affect the rate of interest, real output
and wealth, and other real variables. (34)

c) According to the so-called neutral money theory, it is
assumed in general that a constant money supply would result in a

---

thing to be said about currency is that it is not nearly as important as it looks'?"

32. W. Egle [50] notes: "The additional amounts appear-
ing on the market for consumers' goods must have, similarly to the
old money, quality of income, i.e., they must be recompense for
productive work (of labor, capital, or entrepreneurs)."

A. Gambino [72] remarks that every kind of credit is backed
by savings even in monetary form.

33. J. G. Koopmans [124], H. Braeutigam [21], J. G. Gurley and E. S. Shaw [86], W. R. Peade [158].

34. J. G. Gurley and E. S. Shaw [86].

constant money income, with increasing productivity forcing a decline in prices. (35)

As long as it is assumed that the monetary authorities influence the level of the money stock, and thereby the economic activity, neutral money is impossible; any governmental influence,
conscious or unconscious, must deviate from the genuine development. From this standpoint, it is correct to say that a neutrally
functioning money and credit economy is already precluded ex definitione (with these two categories, a tendency to derangement is
given which is imposed, on the whole, through the existence of the
monetary economy); furthermore, that money is, of course, never
"neutral" in the sense of being merely an instrument or servant:
it always exercises some positive influence on the course of
events; that on more general assumptions money is not neutral, because the rate of output depends on the money supply; that neutrality of money is virtually a utopia and theoretically inappre-
hensible. (36)

In line with this argumentation, it is maintained that the
presupposition for a neutrality is a constant relation between the
actual availability of cash and the demand for money for current
payments; a combination of inside and outside money (outside money

---

35. *A. H. Hansen [90].*

*W. P. Egle [52] writes: "'Neutral money' is only a rela-
tive concept referring to a state of affairs in which money would
be deprived of certain 'undesirable' (essentially de-stabilizing)
features of potentialities, without interference with those of its
properties believed to be responsible for the superiority of a
money-using economy over a barter system. In brief, the legiti-
mate problem is that of seeking a monetary arrangement which is
optimally devoid of monetary influences which are detrimental to
the 'ideal' of macro - as well as micro - economic balance of the
economy."*

*J. G. Koopmans [124] discerns, besides, between the neu-
trality of abstract money, the unity of counting, and the neutrality of concrete money as a means of exchange.*

*D. H. Robertson [172]: "The implications of the policy of
neutral money have been explored in terms of behavior of prices,
of the rate of interest and of various types of income. A supple-
mentary criterion of neutrality has been sought in the degree to
which the banking system succeeds in acting as a true intermediary,
that is in giving effect to the thrifty intentions of the public,
without either outrunning them on the one hand or allowing them to
go to waste on the other."*

36. *V. F. Wagner [213], F. A. von Hayek [212], W. J. Fellner [60], O. Veit [208, 209].*

is money that is backed by foreign or government securities or
gold; or fiat money issued by the government)...breaks the neutrality of money; the policy of neutral money is possible only in
an elastic monetary system, but not in one left to the free play
of economic factors; the volume of money would have to be adjusted
in order not to affect the demand for goods. (37)

All these impediments to neutral money are nonexistent in
the light of our presentation. Neutral money is, therefore, conceivable according to the definitions cited above, though with
some reservations. The main qualification is that a strict price
stability is impossible. Since the problem of inflation can be
broached only at a later point, we can merely rely here on the
record showing that in the United States the rise in prices took
place in small degrees, whereas the improvement in the quality of
products must also be taken into account. The rise in prices is,
in any case, smaller than the increase in capital invested on interest rates. Due to the imperfections of the market prices tend
to increase gradually, and the money supply will expand correspondingly, because the economy needs it for its larger turnover.
Against this development probably not much can be undertaken under
the present circumstances. While money is thus formally not constant in value, it can be claimed that it is reasonably neutral,
at least in the short run. This can best be seen from the fact
that, in practice, the circuit in "values in production," that is,
in real capital, develops independently, disregarding an eventual
instability in the value of money as a means of exchange.

----

37. O. Veit [208], J. G. Gurley and E. S. Shaw [86], W.
Egle [50].

W. Egle [50] remarks furthermore: "All forms of growth ne-
cessitate an enlargement of money circulation...a change in the
volume of production which F. A. von Hayek denotes as 'real' con-
ditioned changes in demand for money. One of the tasks set up by
the policy of neutral money is to avoid disarrangements. It can
be mastered only in the frame of an elastic currency system."

H. Irmler [107]: "Some hold that precise statements concerning neutrality respectively nonneutrality of money is impossible in the actual state of knowledge, others hold that price stability is a decisive criterion. It would be a discovery of the
philosopher's stone, if one succeeded in fathoming the character-
istics of neutral money, and, moreover, in finding out a monetary
order which could adjust continuously and automatically the money
supply to this ideal goal."

L. W. Mints [149] maintains that stabilizing the quantity
of money provides no real stability, since it leaves room for
fluctuations in the velocity of circulation.

Concerning other definitions of neutrality quoted under b) and c), the government is bound to manage its debt somehow, and should be regarded as a normal - although the biggest - partner in the market. Its transactions do not impede the value of the currency; the renewal of its debts does not change the total availability of credit, and its new indebtedness increases slowly and can be relatively easily absorbed by the market. In our system, the government is normally unable to affect noticeably real output, wealth, or other variables; it can, however, influence the level of interest rates, but this has only a negligible effect on prices. Finally, the condition that with increasing productivity neutral money should force a decline in prices is unrealistic, because in the first place usually producers and labor take advantage of rising productivity.

In this connection, it seems that the question of "monetary illusion" should not represent a difficult problem. (38) If in any calculation the possible instability of prices can roughly be taken into account, as discussed above, such an illusion ought to disappear and cause no disturbance. The problem presents a theoretical nicety rather than a real issue.

Section 9
In the second half of 1966 an unusual situation developed in the United States monetary market. The uncommon conditions brought about strange enunciations on the part of monetary authorities and some economists. It is instructive to mention those declarations and commentaries, because they are particularly characteristic of misjudgments in monetary and economic events and eventual prospects when the total picture of the economy is not taken into account. Since the situation became more complicated,

---

38. D. Patinkin [159] defines "monetary illusion" as follows: "An individual will be said to be suffering from such an illusion if his excess-demand functions for commodities...do not depend solely on relative prices and real wealth, inclusive of initial real balances."

A. Gambino [73] remarks: "Operators can now be regarded as being completely immune from 'monetary illusion' (as defined by D. Patinkin)."

W. P. Egle [51]: "In most cases the attempt at neutralizing aims simply at a reform of monetary policy in the direction of creating a reliably stable currency, whereby not only the question of cumulative fluctuations in the quantity of money as such, but also the problem of 'monetary illusion' as a further cause of monetary disorder, would find satisfactory solution in an indirect manner."

the expressed opinions - not founded on systematic considerations - were all the more unjustifiable.

In this period, interest rates reached exceptionally high
levels and "monetary policy was tightest in the last forty years,"
allegedly because no restraint through fiscal policy had been applied. In evaluation of this state of affairs, the following comments were made:

Unquestionably, more monetary restraint would be a serious
risk. There is some risk of a financial crisis if monetary tightness is pushed much further. Tight money can cause certain financial crises, but the government should choose to take care of
them. (39)

The real danger is some kind of financial panic in which
borrowed money could not be had at any price, and in which both
stocks and bonds found no buyers. Although no one in government
was saying so openly, it was this kind of danger that was worrying
the President, even if it was not imminent. There is danger of
genuine financial chaos or even panic, in which people will hoard
money in anticipation of higher interest rates and higher prices.
(40)

Sterner restraining measures could trigger a recession.
The monetary brakes can be slammed on so hard as to help turn a
boom into a recession. (41)

In a letter from the presidents of the twelve regional
Federal Reserve Banks to all member banks of the system, it was
emphasized concerning their loans to business: "While such credit
requests often appear justifiable when looked at individually, the
aggregate total of credit-financing business spending has tended
toward unsustainable levels." (42)

---

39. *Wall Street Journal*, November 14, 1966, W. F. Butler
[30] and P. A. Samuelson [185].

40. New York *Times*, September 4, 1966 (editorial), and
November 27, 1966; E. Janeway [110].

41. R. B. Williamson [219], and *Wall Street Journal*, August 31, 1966.

42. New York *Times*, September 2, 1966.

A. Hayes [98] pointed out: "If monetary policy is relied
on too heavily and is pressed too far, there is always a real danger that it may lead to financial crisis or a serious reversal of
the economy, or both...founded in the fear that interest rates
would rise still further or that credit might actually become un-
available. Interest rates had already reached such extreme levels
(by historical standards) that they were contributing to a real
fear of financial crisis. We are doing our best to walk a knife-
edge; we were seeking to restrain excessive credit expansion while

All these comments are easily refuted on the basis of the
presented theory of monetary turnover. No money can be hoarded
and withdrawn from the total economy. All money is put through
the channels of the monetary circuit, so that commercial banks and
other financial intermediaries will always strive to grant credit
to the full degree of the given possibilities. This tendency is,
besides, admitted in the quoted commentaries. Somewhat higher,
and even still higher, interest rates would not change this situation. A financial panic, let alone a recession, cannot result
from these conditions. Since the Federal Reserve by itself does
not tighten credit, it cannot precipitate financial crises (unless
it aims at them intentionally by means of entirely unreasonable
measures in its operations). The increment in domestic availability and absorption of credit in 1966 evolved as smoothly as in
the preceding years (cf., Tables 1 and 3). Credit cannot tend
toward unsustainable levels because its volume is limited by genuine savings.

Section 10
In the course of the discussion in this chapter, we have
shown that, as far as possible, our investigation takes into account the overall situation in relation to any question under consideration. This standpoint was also maintained in both proofs
based on Flow of Funds Accounts and the bank credit range (Chapters 3 and 4). Indeed, any calculation which comprises credit
ranges of different sectors in connection with other sectors, must
embrace the whole economy. We will refer henceforth to this rule
of conduct in all our investigations as the principle of the total
picture.
In setting up this principle, we proceed from the point of
view that in any microeconomic or partial analysis a cursory
glance embracing the whole economy is at all times necessary (as
already frequently indicated). All problems in the economy are
closely interrelated, and one must not pick out some questions and
examine them in isolation. A dissection is inadmissible. In med-
icine, for instance, one might study the single branches only with
certain qualification; economic life, however, constitutes so much
more of a unity, and changes in one field will usually produce
changes in other fields (see footnote 43 for a pertinent comparison with psychology). One cannot, for instance, elaborate the

---

*avoiding such heavy pressure or the development of such sharp or
extreme market movements as to foster an atmosphere of panic."*
    *W. F. Treiber [205] remarked that in 1966 "by late summer
the upward ratcheting of rates and heavy prospective credit demands led to fears that financial markets would break under the
strain."*

question of wages without taking into consideration, say, credit conditions, although these areas are seemingly far apart.

In any economic study one ought to keep in mind that at the end the situation must be evaluated in relation to the total picture. If this is not done, one will usually arrive at a wrong conclusion. If the interconnection with all relevant factors is not contemplated, the estimation will frequently be a guess, and sometimes one might contend everything and the reverse with seemingly equal justification. (43)

Accounting is the most powerful tool of the principle of the total picture. It exactly registers any performance and its offset, and brings all events into a meaningful, perspicuous relationship. It enables us to conjure up abstracts of accounts of any economic units and groups, so as to obtain a total picture for successive, convenient periods; only in this way does the analysis become coordinate and systematic. Through this procedure, one is in the position to examine the circuit of money and values in their incessant flow. It is thus possible to realize, for instance, that it is essential to incorporate statements of the condition of the Federal Reserve into the total turnover, as its constituent part, or, to give another example, to imagine that all

---

43. *G. Schmölders, R. Schröder, and H. St. Seidenfus [186] indicate: "In the field of psychology, a form of thinking must, therefore, be applied, which had overcome the contrariety between the mode of examination in physical and moral sciences. 'An onset to such a form of thinking lies in a thinking decided everywhere by ingenious whole-part-connections, and in a way of consideration which, with actual activated functions, also grasp the contents on which the functions act' (O. Kroh, Psychologie, Berlin, 1954 [125])."*

W. Röpke [178]: "Economic science requires the constant application of supreme attentiveness and a large dose of that intuitive power which enables us to keep our eyes on all the complicated threads at once, and to emulate the juggler who never loses sight of a single one of the balls he is keeping aloft. As one scholar of my generation somewhat exaggerately puts it, 'such thinking in terms of relationships...undoubtedly' is one of 'the most difficult problems the human intellect can encounter' (O. Morgenstern, Die Grenzen der Wirtschaftspolitik, 1934 [150])." In our opinion, this assertion of O. Morgenstern is not exaggerated.

S. Schoeffler [188]: "...various kinds of commentary and ...the studies that analyze the influence of a given factor X or another given factor Y...usually are guilty of artificial isolation, at least."

commercial banks represent a simple, united bank and to ask from what such a bank could create and grant additional credit.

If one loses sight of the total picture, the question remains open as to where funds in the economy originate, and how and when money and credit come into being. (44) Since no record is maintained about these funds and money, they may appear and disappear according to intuitive and, therefore, random conjectures. In these considerations, such "unknown" funds are added and subtracted under various conditions. Since money and credit creation is a rather complicated procedure, it is not necessary to know what exactly happens; important is that additional funds can be available. In any discussion about future development one refers to the part which these unknown funds could play. Besides, because of these unknown funds, the threat of inflation looms in the background as something indefinite.

Some examples follow:

Many economists hold that if only spending is encouraged, production and GNP will grow to ever higher grounds. However - apart from other considerations - investment out of given savings must decrease by the same amount, by which consumption increases (Keynesian theories on this subject cannot be discussed at this point).

On the proposal that the twelve Federal Reserve Banks should transfer to the Secretary of the Treasury interest-bearing obligations of the United States in the aggregate principle amount of thirty billion dollars, and that the transferred obligations should be canceled and retired, W. McC. Martin, Jr. [142] answered: "Deficit must be financed by market borrowing, in which the credit of the United States government in the eyes of our own citizens is

----

44. S. Kuznets [127] writes: "Insofar as credit creation or financing through new money issues takes place, voluntary and forced savings are intermixed.... The difficulty is that our observable records of savings and capital formation do not permit us to make that distinction.... The existence and development of the power of credit creation represent an important complex.... Available data give us no inkling of the extent to which the savings proportion in this country has been affected by the credit-creating power of the banks or by the money policy followed by the government.... Forced saving through credit creation by financial institutions and government is subjected to limits of its own, in its possible effect on voluntary saving."

W. Röpke [177]: "Capital can be built by savings, self-financing, savings through government coercion (investment of tax money), and bank credit (whereas consumption is compulsorily reduced in consequence of rising prices)."

continuously put to the test, so that any deterioration in that credit is immediately evident for all to see." This answer is quite beside the point and does not mention the essential fact that this transfer could not change the overall situation and would affect only the internal reckoning between the government and the Federal Reserve Banks.

G. Ackley [2] warned in July 1965 that if the potential revenue growth were not used up by government spending or by tax cuts, it would not materialize because the economy's growth would be slowed down, and added: "Unless we make the right disposition of the potential revenue growth, and at the right time, a large part of it could be aborted." But if money is not spent by the government, it will be used for investment, and this switch would not slow the economy's growth; nothing can be lost here.

As it appears from the quotation in footnote 44, S. Kuznets is of the opinion that money and credit creation must somehow be covered by savings. However, it is not known how this process develops. It seems as though a fourth dimension exists and the resulting gaps are subsequently counterbalanced.

Section 11
The understanding of the development in the monetary turnover constitutes the whole difference between a correct and incorrect evaluation of almost all economic processes and events. We claim that for this understanding systematic empirical investigations, examining the whole economy in proper perspective, are urgent. Unfortunately, a kind of axiom of noncalculability in the money circuit has been seemingly set up. This total lack of computing renders any progress impossible. In particular, idle balances and granted credit remain independent and erratic factors. If, then, some occurrences in the economy cannot be understood, a deus ex machina explanation is offered to make them plausible, as G. Katona [117] observes. (45)

---

45. *G. Katona [117] notes also: "In the United States, the large increase in money supply from 1942 to 1944 was accompanied by a moderate increase in prices, while prices rose substantially shortly after the end of the war when the money supply did not increase.... (These irregularities) have been identified under the terms 'velocity of money turnover' and 'willingness to spend.'"*

J. Viner [210] stresses "the usefulness and indeed the essentiality of empirical research, including systematic statistical research. It is only by means of such research that we determine the external validity, the relevance to reality, of abstract theories of economic mechanism." Incidentally, K. Brunner

---

[23] *remarks in a review that "Viner seems to contend that we pos-*
sess no systematic knowledge of monetary process, and therefore
skillful, experienced judgment of monetary authorities is the best
guide for policy."

C. R. Whittlesey [217] comments: "It is simply not possi-
ble to demonstrate conclusively whether a given change in the vol-
ume of credit is the cause of a change in business activity or the
change in business activity is the cause of the change in the vol-
ume of credit. It is entirely conceivable that at one time cau-
sality may run in one direction and at another time in the oppo-
site direction.... But on one point all must agree: the only
course that eliminates risk of disillusionment is to accept the
view that the actual effectiveness of monetary policy is uncer-
tain."

[1]   Ackley, G., according to the New York *Times*, "Inflation Threat Called 'Remote,'" June 17, 1965.

[2]   Ackley, G., according to the New York *Times*, July 21, 1965.

[3]   Adams, E. S., "Monetary Management's Impact Upon Commercial Banks," *Commercial and Financial Chronicle*, November 14, 1957.

[4]   Adams, E. S., "Low Pegged Interest Rates Threaten Public Welfare," *Commercial and Financial Chronicle*, March 20, 1958.

[5]   Allen, C. E., "Defending the Independence of the Federal Reserve System," *Commercial and Financial Chronicle*, June 13, 1957.

[6]   American Bankers Association, Resolution Committee, *American Banker*, October 28, 1966.

[7]   Anderson, C. J., "Monetary Policy – A 1914 Model in the Space Age?" *Commercial and Financial Chronicle*, February 4, 1960.

[8]   Anderson, R. B., "A Number of Elements in Current Economic Situation," *Commercial and Financial Chronicle*, April 24, 1958.

[9]   Balderson, C. C., "Current Credit Developments," *Commercial and Financial Chronicle*, May 9, 1957.

[10] Balogh, T., Committee on the Working of the Monetary System, *Principal Memoranda of Evidence*, London, 1960, vol. 3, pp. 31-47.

[11] The Bank for International Settlements, *Annual Reports*.

[12] Barton, H. C., Jr., "Adjustment for Seasonal Variation," Federal Reserve *Bulletin*, June 1941, pp. 518-28.

[13] Bell, E. V., "America Cannot Afford to Gamble with Recession or Depression," *Commercial and Financial Chronicle*, February 13, 1958.

[14] Bell, E. V., according to P. Heffernan, "Hard Debt Moves Facing Treasury," New York *Times*, May 25, 1958.

[15] Bellemore, D. H., "Is the Business Cycle a Relic of the Past?" *Commercial and Financial Chronicle*, May 1, 1958.

[16] Bernstein, E. M., "The Role of Monetary Policy," *Commercial and Financial Chronicle*, January 30, 1958.

[17] Bernstein, P. L., "Inflation, Growth and Employment," Commission on Money and Credit's *Research Studies*, 1963-64, review article, *Journal of Finance*, September 1964, pp. 530-33.

[18] Board of Governors of the Federal Reserve System, *Annual Reports*.

[19] Bogen, J., "The Bond Market Puzzle," *Commercial and Financial Chronicle*, October 17, 1957.

[20] Bogen, J. "Easy Money to Play Key Role in Spurring Business Snapback," *Journal of Commerce*, January 13, 1958.

[21] Braeutigam, H., "Konjunkturpolitik und neutrales Geld," *Schmoller's Jahrbücher*, 1958, H.5, pp. 47-86.

[22] Breckner, N. V., review of *Monetary Studies* 1-6, American Bankers Association, 1955, *American Economic Review*, Supplement, May 1957, pp. 443-44.

[23] Brunner, K., review of *In Search of a Monetary Constitution*,
       E. L. Yearger, ed., 1962, *Journal of Political Economy*, De-
       cember 1963, pp. 616-18.
[24] Brunner, K., "Institutions, Policy and Monetary Analysis,"
       Journal of Political Economy, June 1965, pp. 197-218.
[25] Burgess, W. R., *The Reserve Banks and the Monetary Market*,
       New York, Harper & Brothers, 1946.
[26] Burgess, W. R., according to R. Phalon, "Burgess Sees Need to
       Lift Debt Ceiling," New York *Herald Tribune*, April 23, 1957.
[27] Burgess, W. R., "Federal Debt and Budget in Past Four and a
       Half Years," *Commercial and Financial Chronicle*, June 27,
       1957.
[28] Burgess, W. R. (letter to the editor), *Wall Street Journal*,
       July 12, 1957.
[29] Burns, A. F., *Prosperity Without Inflation*, New York, Fordham
       University Press, 1957.
[30] Butler, W. F., according to E. L. Dale, Jr., "No Major Setback
       for Economy Predicted in Survey of Experts, New York *Times*,
       September 8, 1966.
[31] Cassel, G., *The Theory of Social Economy*, vol. 2, London, T.
       F. Unwin, 1923.
[32] Chandler, L. V., "Recent Trends in U. S. Monetary Policy,"
       Economie Appliquée, October-December 1956, pp. 431-49.
[33] Chandler, L. V., "Impact of Monetary Policy," Commission on
       Money and Credit's *Research Studies*, review article, *Journal
       of Finance*, September 1964, pp. 497-500.
[34] Chippendale, J. T., Jr., "Our Reporter on Governments," *Com-
       mercial and Financial Chronicle*, December 26, 1957.
[35] Chippendale, J. T., Jr., "Our Reporter on Governments," *Com-
       mercial and Financial Chronicle*, June 13, 1957, May 8, 1958.
[36] The Commission on Money and Credit, *Money and Credit*, Engle-
       wood Cliffs, N. J., Prentice-Hall, 1961.
[37] Commission on Money and Credit's *Research Studies*, 1963-1964,
       (9 volumes), Englewood Cliffs, N. J., Prentice-Hall, 1963-64.
[38] Copeland, M. A., "Social Accounting for Moneyflows," *Account-
       ing Review*, July 1949.
[39] Copeland, M. A., *A Study of Money Flows in the United States*,
       National Bureau of Economic Research, 1952.
[40] Copeland, M. A., "Some Illustrative Analytical Uses of Flow-
       of-Funds Data," in *The Flow-of-Funds Approach to Social Ac-
       counting, Appraisal, Analysis, and Applications*. A Report of
       the National Bureau of Economic Research, Princeton, Prince-
       ton University Press, 1962, pp. 195-222.
[41] Culbertson, J. M., "Timing Changes in Monetary Policy," *Jour-
       nal of Finance*, May 1959, pp. 145-60.
[42] Culbertson, J. M., *Full Employment or Stagnation*, New York,
       McGraw-Hill, 1964.
[43] Daane, J. D., according to the New York *Times*, October 25,
       1966.

[44] Dacey, W. M., "Treasury Bills and the Money Supply," *Lloyds Bank Review*, January 1960, pp. 1-16.

[45] Dawson, J. C., Comment in *The Flow-of-Funds Approach to Social Accounting, Appraisal, Analysis, and Applications*. A Report of the National Bureau of Economic Research, 1962, Princeton University Press, 1962, pp. 465-67.

[46] Dillon, D., according to A. J. Large, "The 'Need' for Debt," *Wall Street Journal*, November 8, 1962.

[47] Dow, J. C. R., Committee on the Working of the Monetary System. *Principal Memoranda of Evidence*, London, 1960, vol. 3, pp. 76-105.

[48] Dow, J. C. R., "International Factors Causing and Propagating Inflation," II, pp. 37-53, in D. C. Hague, ed., *Inflation*. Proceedings of a Conference held by the International Economic Association, London, Macmillan, 1962.

[49] Duesenberry, J. S., "Discussion of Friedman's *The Demand of Money*," Papers and Proceedings of the *American Economic Review*, May 1959, pp. 528-29.

[50] Egle, W., *Das Neutrale Geld*, Jena, Verlag Gustaw Fischer, 1933.

[51] Egle, W. P., review of H. H. Lerner, *Marktwirtschaftliche Theorie des neutralen Geldes*, 1959, *Zeitschrift für Nationalökonomie*, Band XXI, H. 1, pp. 147-48.

[52] Egle, W. P., "The Four Approaches to Monetary Reform: A Critique," *Zeitschrift für Nationalökonomie*, Band XXII, H. 1-2, pp. 4-19.

[53] Eucken, W., *Grundsätze der Wirtschaftspolitik*, Bern, A. Francke AG. Verlag, 1952.

[54] Federal Reserve Bank of New York, *Bank Reserves, Some Major Factors Affecting Them*, November 1953.

[55] Federal Reserve Bank of New York, *Annual Reports*.

[56] Federal Reserve Bank of Richmond, *Monthly Review*, April 1957.

[57] Federal Reserve *Bulletin*, "Seasonal Adjustment Factors for Demand Deposits Adjusted and Currency Outside Banks," March 1955, pp. 252-55.

[58] Federal Reserve *Bulletin*, "Flow of Funds Seasonally Adjusted," November 1962, pp. 1393-1407.

[59] Feifel, H., *Die Anwendbarkeit der modernen Kreditschöpfungslehre auf die besondere Art des Sparkassengeschäftes*, Berlin, Duncker & Humblot, 1959.

[60] Fellner, W. J., *Emergence and Content of Modern Economic Analysis*, McGraw-Hill, 1960.

[61] Fertig, L., "Inflation: Cause and Prospect," *Commercial and Financial Chronicle*, December 19, 1957.

[62] Forstmann, A., *Neue Wirtschaftslehren*, Berlin, Duncker & Humblot, 1954.

[63] Forstmann, A., *Volkswirtschaftliche Theorie des Geldes*, II. Bd., Berlin, Duncker & Humblot, 1955.

[64] Friedman, M., *Studies in the Quantity Theory of Money*, University Chicago Press, 1956.

[65] Friedman, M., *A Program for Monetary Stability*, New York, Fordham University Press, 1960.

[66] Friedman, M. and Meiselman, D., Reply in D. D. Hester, "Keynes and the Quantity Theory," A Comment on the Friedman-Meiselman CMC Paper, *Review of Economics and Statistics*, November 1964, pp. 364-77.

[67] Friedman, M., and A. Jacobson Schwartz, *A Monetary History of the United States, 1876-1960*, National Bureau of Economic Research, 1963.

[68] Gaines, T. C., in "Is the Money Supply the Economy's Thermostat?" *Banking*, January 1968, pp. 52-5.

[69] Gaines, T. C., "Financial Innovations and the Efficiency of Federal Reserve Policy," pp. 99-118, in *Monetary Process and Policy: A Symposium*, George Horwich, ed., R. D. Irwin, 1967.

[70] Gaines, T. C., in H. Bratter, "Congress and Monetary Policy: A Perennial Issue," *Banking*, July 1968, p. 115.

[71] Galbraith, J. K., "The Public Sector Is Still Starved," *Challenge*, January/February 1967, pp. 18-21.

[72] Gambino, A., "Die Leistung des Kredits für das wirtschaftliche Wachstum," *Weltwirtschaftliches Archiv*, March 1963, pp. 47-56.

[73] Gambino, A., "The Influence of the Public's Behavior on Liquidity Creation," Banca Nationale del Lavoro, *Quarterly Review*, December 1964, pp. 397-410.

[74] Garvy, G., *Deposit Velocity and Its Significance*, Federal Reserve Bank of New York, November 1959.

[75] Gaskin, A., "Liquidity and the Monetary Mechanism," *Oxford Economic Papers*, October 1960, pp. 274-93.

[76] Gestrich, H., *Neue Kreditpolitik*, Wien, Julius Springer, 1936.

[77] Gestrich, H., *Kredit und Sparen*, Jena, G. Fischer, 1944.

[78] Gilbert, M., Jaszi, G., Denison, E. F., and Schwartz, C. F., "Objectives of National Income Measurement: A Reply to Kuznets," *Review of Economics and Statistics*, August 1948, pp. 181-82.

[79] Goldenweiser, E. A., *Monetary Management*, New York, McGraw-Hill, 1949.

[80] Goldenweiser, E. A., *American Monetary Policy*, New York, McGraw-Hill, 1951.

[81] Goldsmith, R. W., according to A. C. Littleton and V. K. Zimmerman, *Accounting Theory: Continuity and Change*, 1962.

[82] *Great Britain Committee on the Working of the Monetary System*, Report, August 1959, London, H. M. Stationary Office, 1959.

[83] *The Guaranty Survey*, July 1957.

[84] *The Guaranty Survey*, March 1958.

[85]   Gurley, J. G., "The Radcliffe Report and Evidence," *American Economic Review*, September 1960, pp. 672-700.

[86]   Gurley, J. G. and Shaw, E. S., *Money in a Theory of Finance* (with a mathematical Appendix by A. C. Enthoven), Washington, D. C., The Brookings Institution, 1960.

[87]   Haberler, G., *Prosperity and Depression*, Geneva, League of Nations, 1941.

[88]   Hahn, L. A., in Weber, A., ed., *Bankkredit und langfristige Investitionen*, Berlin, Duncker & Humblot, 1954.

[89]   Hall, J. C., "The Spectre of Inflation and Mortgage Market Crisis," *Commercial and Financial Chronicle*, October 23, 1958.

[90]   Hansen, A. H., *Monetary Theory and Fiscal Policy*, New York, McGraw-Hill, 1949.

[91]   Hansen, A. H., "Monetary Policy," *Review of Economics and Statistics*, May 1955, pp. 110-19.

[92]   Hansen, A. H., *The American Economy*, New York, McGraw-Hill, 1957.

[93]   Harrod, R. F., "Radcliffe Report. Is the Money Supply Important?" *Westminster Bank Review*, November 1959, pp. 3-7.

[94]   Hauge, G., "Problem of Prosperity," *Commercial and Financial Chronicle*, March 21, 1957.

[95]   Hauge, G., "Plain Truth about Money in Current Political Campaign," *Commercial and Financial Chronicle*, September 29, 1960.

[96]   Hayes, A., "Insight into the Money Market and the New York Federal Reserve," *Commercial and Financial Chronicle*, December 20, 1956.

[97]   Hayes, A., according to the New York *Times*, October 16, 1957.

[98]   Hayes, A., "Monetary Policy in an Overheated Economy," Federal Reserve Bank of New York, *Monthly Review*, November 1966, pp. 235-40.

[99]   Heffernan, P. "Bond Prices Fall to Long-Time Low," New York *Times*, June 5, 1957.

[100] Hellwig, H., *Kreditschöpfung und Kreditvermittlung*, Stuttgart, Curt E. Schwab, 1958.

[101] Hellwig, H., "Kredittheorie des Bankiers," *Zeitschrift für das gesamte Kreditwesen*, 1960, Heft 17, pp. 807-10.

[102] Henderson, R. F., "Money in Practice," in P. Thorneycroft and Others: *Not Unanimous, A Rival Verdict to Radcliffe's on Money*, A. Seldon, ed., Institute of Economic Affairs, 1960, pp. 36-52.

[103] Hester, D. D., "Keynes and the Quantity Theory: A Comment on the Friedman-Meiselman CMC Paper," *Review of Economics and Statistics*, November 1964, pp. 364-77.

[104] Humphrey, G. M., "Statement Defending the Administration's Economic Record," New York *Times*, June 19, 1957.

[105] Humphrey, G. M., according to the New York *Times*, July 29, 1957.

[106] Hutt, W. H., *The Theory of Idle Resources*, London, Jonathan
       Cape, 1939.
[107] Irmler, H., "Natürliches Geld - Neutrales Geld," *Ordo*, 1950,
       pp. 322-32.
[108] Ittensohn, J., "Gibt es eine amerikanische Währungspolitik?"
       Zeitschrift für das gesamte Kreditwesen ("Die Zukunft des
       Dollars"), 1964, Heft 1, pp. 32-34.
[109] Jacoby, N. J., "A Program to Speed the Return of Prosperi-
       ty," *Commercial and Financial Chronicle*, April 17, 1958.
[110] Janeway, Elliot, according to the *Wall Street Journal*, Au-
       gust 18, 1966.
[111] Johnson, H. G., "Some Implications of Secular Changes in
       Bank Assets and Liabilities in Great Britain," *Economic
       Journal*, September 1951.
[112] Johnson, H. G., "Quantity Theorist's Monetary History of the
       United States," *Economic Journal*, June 1965, pp. 388-96.
[113] Johnson, M. O., "Interest Rate Trend and the Bond Market,"
       Commercial and Financial Chronicle, February 27, 1958.
[114] Juster, F. T., "Review of G. Katona's *The Powerful Consumer,
       1960*," *Journal of Political Economy*, October 1961, pp. 503-4.
[115] Kaldor, N. "The Radcliffe Report," *Review of Economics and
       Statistics*, February 1960, pp. 14-19.
[116] Kareken, J., review of *The Flow-of-Fund Approach to Social
       Accounting, Appraisal, Analysis, and Applications*. A Report
       of the National Bureau of Economic Research, 1962, *American
       Economic Review*, June 1963, pp. 504-6.
[117] Katona, G., *Psychological Analysis of Economic Behavior*, New
       York, McGraw-Hill, 1951.
[118] Katona, G., *The Powerful Consumer*, New York, McGraw-Hill,
       1960.
[119] Katona, G., A. Lauterbach, S. W. Steinkamp, *Business Looks at
       Banks*, Ann Arbor, University of Michigan Press, 1957.
[120] Kellenberger, E., "Kreditschöpfung und Geldschöpfung," in
       Wirtschaftstheorie und Wirtschaftspolitik, Festschrift für
       A. Amonn, Bern, Francke-Verlag, 1953, pp. 89-104.
[121] Kerschagl, R., a review of H. J. Lierow, *Der Geldschöpfungs-
       koeffizient der Kreditbanken in der Bundesrepublik*, Volks-
       wirtschaftliche Schriften, H. 30, 1957, *Schmoller's Jahr-
       bücher*, 1958, Heft 6, p. 114.
[122] Keyserling, L., a review of M. Friedman, *Capitalism and Free-
       dom*, 1962, *Annals* of the American Academy of Social and Po-
       litical Science, November 1963, pp. 195-96.
[123] Köhler, H. J., *Der Begriff "Geldmenge" und seine Problema-
       tik, Finanzwissenschaftliche Forschungsarbeiten*, Heft 21,
       Berlin, Duncker & Humblot, 1960.
[124] Koopmans, J. G., "Zum Problem des 'neutralen' Geldes,"
       Beiträge zur Geldtheorie, hrsg. v. Hayek, Wien, J. Springer,
       1933.

[125] Kroh, O., *Psychologie*, in *Universitas Litterarum*, Berlin, 4. Lieferung, 1954.

[126] Kuznets, S., "Discussion of the New Department of Commerce Income Series - National Income: A New Version," *Review of Economics and Statistics*, August 1948, pp. 151-79.

[127] Kuznets, S., *Capital in the American Economy, Its Formation and Financing*, National Bureau of Economic Research, Princeton, Princeton University Press, 1961.

[128] Leutner, H., *Geldstrom - und Liquiditätstheorie*, Frankfurt a.M., Fritz Knapp Verlag, 1962.

[129] Lindahl, E., *Studies in the Theory of Money and Capital*, New York, Farrar & Rinehart, 1939.

[130] Little, I. M. D., Neild, R. R. and Ross, C. R., Committee on the Working of the Monetary System, *Principal Memoranda of Evidence*, London, 1960, vol. 3, pp. 159-67.

[131] Littleton, A. C., *Structure of Accounting Theory*, American Accounting Association, Monograph no. 5, Chicago, 1953.

[132] Littleton, A. C., and V. K. Zimmerman, *Accounting Theory: Continuity and Change*, Englewood Cliffs, N. J., Prentice-Hall, 1962.

[133] Lutz, H. L., "The Case for a Limitation of the Federal Debt," *Commercial and Financial Chronicle*, February 19, 1959.

[134] Martin, W. McC., Jr., "Role of the Credit and Monetary Policy in the Economy," *Commercial and Financial Chronicle*, December 23, 1954.

[135] Martin, W. McC., Jr., Hearings before the Subcommittee on Economic Stabilization, June 12, 1956, in *Conflicting Official Views on Monetary Policy*, Washington, D. C., Government Printing Office, 1956.

[136] Martin, W. McC., Jr., "Reserve Policy During Inflation and Deflation," *Commercial and Financial Chronicle*, December 13, 1956.

[137] Martin, W. McC., Jr., "No Magic in Monetary Policy," *Commercial and Financial Chronicle*, May 2, 1957.

[138] Martin, W. McC., Jr., "Interest Rates and Inflation," *Bankers Monthly*, September 1957.

[139] Martin, W. McC., Jr., "Exerting Enough Pressure But Not Too Much," *Commercial and Financial Chronicle*, February 13, 1958.

[140] Martin, W. McC., Jr., a letter to Senator Robertson, according to the *Wall Street Journal*, May 1, 1958.

[141] Martin, W. McC., Jr., according to an article "Martin Sees 'Hopeful Indicators,'" *Wall Street Journal*, July 15, 1958.

[142] Martin, W. McC., Jr., "Statements to Congress," Federal Reserve *Bulletin*, July 1965, pp. 947-49.

[143] Martin, W. McC., Jr., "Basic Considerations Governing Federal Reserve's Economic Role," *Commercial and Financial Chronicle*, December 16, 1965.

[144] Martin, W. McC., Jr., and Hayes, A., according to the New York *Times*, August 17, 1962.

[145] Matterssich, R., "The Constellation of Accountancy and Eco-
       nomics," *Accounting Review*, October 1956, pp. 551-64.
[146] Meade, J. E., "Is the National Debt a Burden?" *Oxford Eco-
       nomic Papers*, June 1958, pp. 163-83.
[147] Meltzer, A. H., "Improvement in the Balance of Payments: A
       Response to Monetary Policy or to Ad Hoc Fiscal Policy,"
       Journal of Business, July 1965, pp. 267-76.
[148] Mills, A. L., Jr., "The Not Too Well Known Nature and Scope
       of Monetary Policy," *Commercial and Financial Chronicle*,
       May 15, 1958.
[149] Mints, L. W., *Monetary Policy for a Competitive Society*,
       New York, McGraw-Hill, 1950.
[150] Morgenstern, O., *Die Grenzen der Wirtschaftspolitik*, Wien,
       Julius Springer, 1934.
[151] Morgenstern, O., *On the Accuracy of Economic Observations*,
       Princeton, Princeton University Press, 1950, 1963.
[152] Moulton, H. G., *Can Inflation Be Controlled*, Washington,
       D. C., Anderson Kramer Associates, 1958.
[153] Murad, A., "The Ineffectiveness of Monetary Policy," *South-
       ern American Journal*, January 1956, pp. 339-51.
[154] Nadler, M., *The Credit Situation, Hanover Bank*, 1957.
[155] Nadler, M., *Recession and Recovery, Hanover Bank*, 1958.
[156] Nadler, M., *Expansion of Bank Credit, Hanover Bank*, May 1960.
[157] O'Leary, J. J., "Near- and Long-Term Outlook for Business
       and Capital Market," *Commercial and Financial Chronicle*, Oc-
       tober 17, 1957.
[158] Paede, W. R., *Das neutrale Geld - "Schleier" oder "ökono-
       misches Kraftfeld," Volkswirtschaftliche Schriften*, H. 32,
       Berlin, Duncker & Humblot.
[159] Patinkin, D., *Money, Interest, Prices*, Evanston, Ill., Row,
       Peterson, 1956.
[160] Patman, W., according to the *Journal of Commerce*, November
       21, 1957.
[161] Popper, K. P., *The Open Society and Its Enemies*, Princeton,
       Princeton University Press, 1950.
[162] Popper, K. P., *Logic of Scientific Discovery*, New York, Bas-
       ic Books, 1959.
[163] Popper, K. P., *The Poverty of Historicism*, New York, Basic
       Books, 1960.
[164] Popper, K. P., *Conjectures and Refutations*, London, Reutledge
       and Kegan Paul, 1963.
[165] Reierson, L., "Business Recession and Economic Growth,"
       Commercial and Financial Chronicle, May 15, 1958.
[166] Riefler, W. W., "The Price of Stability," *Commercial and Fi-
       nancial Chronicle*, January 24, 1957.
[167] Ritter, L. S., "Analyzing the Effectiveness of Monetary Pol-
       icy," *Commercial and Financial Chronicle*, June 22, 1961.
[168] Ritter, L. S., "The FOF Accounts: A New Approach to Financial
       Market Analysis," *Journal of Finance*, May 1963, pp. 219-30.

[169] Ritterhausen, H., *Bankpolitik*, Frankfurt a.M., Fritz Knapp Verlag, 1956.

[170] Robbins, L., *An Essay on the Nature and Significance of Economic Science*, London, Macmillan, 1935.

[171] Robertson, D. H., *Essays in Monetary Theory*, London, P. S. King & Son, Ltd., 1940.

[172] Robertson, D. H., *Money*, The Cambridge Economic Handbooks, Cambridge At The University Press, 1944.

[173] Robinson, Joan, "Radcliffe under Scrutiny. General Liquidity," *The Banker* (London), December 1960, pp. 790-95.

[174] Robinson, Joan, *Economic Philosophy*, London, A. Watts & Co., 1962.

[175] Rodgers, R., "Corporate Financing Trends and Outlook," *Bankers Monthly*, December 1957.

[176] Rodgers, R., "Impact of Monetary Policy Change on Savings and Loans Associations," *Commercial and Financial Chronicle*, April 3, 1958.

[177] Röpke, W., *Explication Economique du Monde Modern*, Paris, Librairie Médicis.

[178] Röpke, W., "The Place of Economics among the Sciences," in M. Sendholz (ed.) *On Freedom and Free Enterprise*, Princeton, N. J., D. Van Nostrand, Inc., 1956.

[179] Roosa, R. V., *Federal Reserve Operations in the Money and Government Security Markets*, Federal Reserve Bank of New York, June 1956.

[180] Roosa, R. V., "The Radcliffe Report," *Lloyds Bank Review*, October 1959, pp. 1-13.

[181] Roosa, R. V., "The Changes in Money and Credit, 1957-59," pp. 261-63 in "Controversial Issues of Recent Monetary Policy," *Review of Economics and Statistics*, August 1960, pp. 245-82.

[182] Rothman, A., Office of Statistical Standards, Bureau of Labor Statistics, "Seasonal Factor Method," June 21, 1962, pp. 223-26, in Proceedings of 20th Interstate Conference on Labor Statistics (June 19-22, 1962, Atlantic City, N. J.).

[183] Samuelson, P. A., in "The Economics of Eisenhower: A Symposium," *Review of Economics and Statistics*, November 1956, pp. 357-85.

[184] Samuelson, P. A., "Reflections on Monetary Policy," pp. 263-69 in "Controversial Issues of Recent Monetary Policy," *Review of Economics and Statistics*, August 1960, pp. 245-82.

[185] Samuelson, P. A., according to E. L. Dale, Jr., "No Major Setback for Economy Predicted in Survey of Experts," New York *Times*, September 8, 1966.

[186] Schmölders, G., R. Schröder, H. St. Seidenfus, *John Maynard Keynes als "Psychologe,"* Berlin, Duncker & Humblot, 1956.

[187] Schneider, E., *Einführung in die Wirtschaftstheorie, III Teil, Geld, Kredit, Volkseinkommen und Beschäftigung*, Tübingen, J. C. B. Mohr (Paul Siebeck), 1953.

[188] Schoeffler, S., *The Failures of Economics, A Diagnostic Study*, Cambridge, Harvard University Press, 1955.

[189] Seldon, A., "Radcliffe in Perspective," in P. Thorneycroft and Others: *Not Unanimous. A Rival Verdict to Radcliffe's on Money*, A. Seldon, ed., Institute of Economic Affairs, 1960, pp. 101-13.

[190] Seltzer, L. R., "Control of Bank Portfolios as an Instrument of Monetary Control," Papers and Proceedings of the *American Economic Review*, May 1952.

[191] Shea, G., "The Outlook," *Wall Street Journal*, January 6, 1958.

[192] Shea, G., "The Outlook," *Wall Street Journal*, January 20, 1958.

[193] Shea, G., "The Outlook," *Wall Street Journal*, March 21, 1960

[194] Shea, G., "The Outlook," *Wall Street Journal*, December 2, 1963.

[195] Shepardson, C. N., "What Can Monetary Policy Do in our Economic Climate," *Commercial and Financial Chronicle*, December 5, 1957.

[196] Solow, R. M., "Friedman on America's Money," *The Banker*, November 1964, pp. 710-17.

[197] Sproul, A., "Money and Banking and Our Economic Well Being," *Commercial and Financial Chronicle*, September 11, 1958.

[198] Stucken, R., *Geld und Kredit*, Tübingen, J. C. B. Mohr (Paul Siebeck), 1957.

[199] Stucken, R., *Die Krisis der Geld- und Kreditpolitik*, Institut "Finanzen und Steuern," nr. 40, July 1961.

[200] Stutzel, W., according to H. Hellwig, "Kredittheorie des Bankiers," *Zeitschrift für das gesamte Kreditwesen*, 1960, Heft 17, pp. 807-10.

[201] Suchestow, M., *The Changed Structure. A Different Picture of the Monetary Economy*, Winterthur (Switzerland), P. G. Keller, 1960.

[202] Szymczak, M. S., "Review of Monetary Policy Actions," *Commercial and Financial Chronicle*, July 3, 1958.

[203] Thomas, W., "Trends in the Money Market," *Commercial and Financial Chronicle*, July 11, 1957.

[204] Tobin, J., "The Monetary Interpretation of History," *American Economic Review*, June 1965, pp. 464-85.

[205] Treiber, W. F., "Making Discount Window Welcome to Member Banks," *Commercial and Financial Chronicle*, August 31, 1967.

[206] United States Department of Commerce, "Meaning of Seasonal Adjustment," *Business Statistics*, 1963.

[207] *United States Monetary Policy: Recent Thinking and Experience*, Hearings before the Subcommittee on Economic Stabilization, December 6 and 7, 1954, Washington, D. C., Government Printing Office, 1954.

[209] Veit, O., review of H. H. Lechner, *Marktwirtschaftliche Theorie des neutralen Geldes*, 1959, *Ordo*, 1962, pp. 381-83.

[210] Viner, J., "International Trade and Its Present Day Relevance," in *Economics and Public Policy*, Washington, D. C., Brookings Institution, 1955, pp. 100-30.

[211] Voertman, R. F., review of E. O. Edward (ed.) *The Nation's Objectives*, 1964, *Journal of Finance*, December 1964, pp. 704-7.

[212] Von Hayek, F. A., *The Pure Theory of Capital*, London, Macmillan, 1941.

[213] Wagner, V. F., *Geschichte der Kredittheorien*, Wien, Julius Springer, 1937.

[214] Warbuton, C., "How Much Variation in the Quantity of Money Is Needed?" *Southern Economic Journal*, April 1952, pp. 495-509.

[215] Weiler, E. T., "The Impact of Severe Monetary Restraint on Monetary Flows," in *The Flow-of-Funds Approach to Social Accounting, Appraisal, Analysis, and Applications*. A Report of the National Bureau of Economic Research, Princeton, Princeton University Press, 1962, pp. 239-56.

[216] Wheeler, J. T., "Economics and Accountancy," in M. Backer (ed.) *Handbook of Modern Accounting*, Englewood Cliffs, N. J., Prentice-Hall, 1955, pp. 43-76.

[217] Whittlesey, C. R., "Central Bank Policy in the Light of Recent American Experience," *Weltwirtschaftliches Archiv*, Band 78, Heft 1, 1957, pp. 17-46.

[218] Wijnholds, H. W. J., "Die heutige Lage der Geldtheorie," *Zeitschrift für die gesamte Staatswissenschaft*, 1956, Heft 3, pp. 464-86.

[219] Williamson, R. B., according to the *Wall Street Journal*, August 18, 1966.

[220] Wilson, J. S. G., "Radcliffe Report," *Westminster Bank Review*, November 1959, pp. 7-15.

[221] Wilson, T., "The Rate of Interest and Monetary Policy," *Oxford Economic Papers*, October 1957, pp. 235-60.

[222] Wood, E., *Monetary Control*, University of Missouri Press, 1963.